101 Tips From The Marketing Masters

Ways To Supercharge Your Marketing & Exponentially Grow Your Business

Brendan M. Egan & John S. Shegerian

This book can be made available at a discount when purchased in quantity for education, sales promotions, or corporate use. Please contact us by visiting www.TheMarketingMasters.com for more information.

Names: Brendan M. Egan, John S. Shegerian, authors

Title: 101 Tips From The Marketing Masters

Subject: Marketing, Digital Marketing, Business Growth

ISBN: 9781658179515

Written & Printed in The United States of America

Special considerations and thanks to Lauren Sangalis and Dean Sangalis for helping make this book possible.

Thank you for purchasing our book.

We wrote this resource to help business owners begin to understand what goes into successful marketing campaigns, and be able to jump start their marketing and grow their business.

If at any time before, during, or after reading you would like to talk with Brendan or John further, or setup a free one-on-one consultation, their direct contact information is included below.

Brendan Egan
888-788-6880
Brendan@TheMarketingMasters.com

John Shegerian
888-788-6880
John@TheMarketingMasters.com

To our families, friends, employees, business partners, and clients.

Without you, none of this would ever be possible.

For all who have helped me get to where I am today, I cannot thank you enough. There are too many names to list. Growing a business takes an army. Thank you to those who impact my life daily – Allison, my parents, siblings, family, friends, and clients – without you, none of this would be possible.

-Brendan

For Tammy, Cortney, and Tyler. The three of you are my home and my universe.

-John

Our clients mean the world to us. And we strive to provide the highest level of service and best results humanly possible. Thank you to all our clients for their continued support and trust in letting us market them. It is a responsibility we don't take lightly.

-Brendan & John

Brendan and John's marketing strategies were the key to our growth. Without their expertise, Engage never would have made it off the ground, much less grown into the company it is today. This book is a great read full of useful marketing tips from two of the best in the business. Highly recommend reading it.

-Daniel Hennes, Co-Founder & CEO, Engage

I've worked with Brendan for over 8 years and no one comes even close to his expertise as a digital marketer. If you want things done correctly, I recommend studying and implementing all the tips in this book.

-Mike Munter, Digital Marketing & Reputation Expert

Brendan and John can market just about anything. Marketing yourself as a speaker is not easy, but they immediately had a plan for me, and grew my booking volume immensely. This book is a must read if you are interested in learning how to grow your business.

-Jake Olson, First Blind NCAA Football Player & Professional Speaker

I've worked with John for over twenty years and with Brendan for over ten. They both have some of the most innovative and unique marketing ideas which I have seen firsthand grow numerous businesses including ERI. This book puts their marketing knowledge and experience in the hands of business owners all around the world.

-Kevin Dillon, Co-Founder & CMO, ERI

"For us athletes and celebrities, marketing is critical to maintaining your brand. This book teaches specific strategies to stand out among your peers and help get yourself and your brand added exposure and visibility."

-Jeremy Roenick, NHL Legend & Olympian

Brendan and his team are agile problem solvers who hold the highest regard for professionalism. Since 2014, they have helped us develop a strong online presence which has resulted in increased rankings and consistent high volume of traffic being driven to our site. We can barely keep up with the increased leads!

-Reinaldo Piloto, Marketing Brand Manager

We are thrilled with the work that Brendan and his team did on our website. Their professional suggestions significantly enhanced every element on our site. The average time spent on our website has doubled and the bounce rate has been cut in half. Donations keep our not-for-profit alive, and this new design and marketing work has substantially increased our listener donations. They were a pleasure to work with on this very important project.

-Bill Hardekopf, Director, AllWorship.com

Foreword – By Brendan M. Egan

I grew up in a mid-sized suburb on the north shore of Chicago. I was fortunate to be born into a comfortable upper class family.

But while my friends were sitting around playing video games, I was always looking for ways to innovate and push the envelope.

I recall my first computer, a Packard Bell desktop that was larger and heavier than most desks today. The computer worked great, but one night at the age of 7, I decided to take the entire computer apart. And put it back together.

I knew nothing about the internals of a computer, but I quickly became self-taught. Hard drive. Memory. Processor. Pretty soon, I found myself not just taking apart and upgrading my computer, but writing simple code and programs on it as well, and trying to automate simple tasks that in 1995 were all done manually.

Fast forward a few years, and I found myself looking for ways to make money. At age 9, I went door to door and started a leaf blowing business, raking in a few thousand dollars, which to a 9 year old may as well made me a millionaire.

The next winter, which was a very snowy one in Chicago, I was braving the cold and lugging our family's snow blower door to door, bring in more money.

I realized very early on in life that while my family could afford me luxuries many people merely dream of, I wanted to make a name for myself and find a way to make my own money.

Fast forward a few years, and I would do exactly that.

Sell, sell, sell! I recall seeing the panic-stricken stock traders running across the screen on my tube television on the evening news. It was 2007, I had just started my first year of college, and I was looking for a challenge.

Having worked the usual assortment of jobs in high school—ranging from boat yard boy to retail clerk—I was ready to try something new. Armed with information that the stock market was potentially ready to plummet, I took to the Internet and began searching for everything I could find on stock trading. Day trading, swing trading, investing—indicators, technical vs. fundamental based trading, price action trading—I was absorbing as much information as I possibly could. I skipped on ordering books for my first semester of college and used that money to order trading books from Amazon to learn more. I joined several online forums, asked questions, e-mailed gurus; I was obsessed with learning all I could about trading.

I opened my first trading account, funded it with some money I had saved from working throughout high school, and dove into the markets. Night after night I would watch the evening news and see traders quitting, losing money, literally jumping out of windows as the market began to crash, and it motivated me more and more to want to succeed in trading.

My first few trades were total duds. Fortunately, I didn't lose much, but by now the market was starting to fall pretty hard and I barely knew how to place a trade, let alone how to short a company to make money when the market was moving downward. I found a few mentors who were willing to chat with me online during the trading day and show me the ropes, and before long, I was placing trade after trade and starting to find success even in a down market.

Fast-forward to late 2008, and I was not only doing better than the traders I saw every night on TV, but I was thriving. With the success I found, I wanted to give back and help others interested in starting to trade, and especially those taking trading into their own hands after their advisors lost them nearly everything. I started as an unpaid intern for a couple different trading websites, helping them with miscellaneous tasks like moderating forums, producing content, improving SEO, and general marketing.

I was then ready to embark on a new challenge—writing a 100-page trading course and self-producing it into a series of over 50 videos. This was a massive undertaking on its own, but I then continued to teach myself HTML, build a website called *Learn To Trade*, form a corporation, and eventually launch it into what would be one of the highest rated trading courses online. It was in forming this first business that I got my first taste at marketing, and it was straight up drinking from a fire hose.

I sold thousands of copies of the trading course, offered one-on-one consulting to new and experienced traders from six continents, and this was all before I was even able to legally buy a beer and celebrate. We ranked on the first page when you Googled nearly any term related to us—price action trading courses, learn to trade, trading tips—and, I didn't realize it at the time, but in building the company, my skills for development, business growth, and digital marketing had surpassed my skills for trading.

It was around that time, as I progressed through college, that a few friends of mine wanted to take to the Internet and try their luck at businesses. Naturally, they asked me to help them get their website set up, put together a marketing plan, and execute on a digital strategy. Before long, I found I was having less and less time for trading (and quite frankly less interest) and was spending more and more time on marketing. The one facet of marketing that especially interested me was search engine optimization (SEO), the process of ranking higher on Google searches. This was as much an art as it was a science, and before I graduated college, I had started my second business—Simple SEO Group.

I quickly learned that the world of selling services to other businesses was very different from selling courses to those looking to make money in the stock market. Longer sales cycles, in-person meetings, multiple decision makers, competitive bids—these all were commonplace in the marketing services world. While I dreaded this side of the business, I found a true passion in executing the actual marketing campaigns.

Not too long after starting the company, I set a goal for myself to make $50,000 in my first 12 months after college or go out and find a "normal" job. Needless to say, I crushed that goal, and have been growing year after year, every year since, into a 7-figure agency.

Along the way, I've made a few enemies and even more friends, made some big mistakes and even bigger successes, and even committed to a work-life balance, even though just last week I found myself at my desk until 2am.

Month after month, new client after new client, things were going great. While a workaholic at heart, those who know me well know there are fourteen weeks of the year that most Chicagoans hold sacred—that short time between Memorial Day and Labor Day when the weather is nothing short of phenomenal—and during that short window of opportunity, I'm known to slip away from my desk a little early on Fridays.

It was a gorgeous Friday afternoon in July, and I was plowing through e-mails at record speed so I could get away from my desk and out into some sunshine. Just as I was wrapping things up, with one foot quite literally out the door, my phone rang. I glanced over to see the caller ID and didn't recognize who was calling, so I quickly answered it.

On the other side of the call, I recall hearing a businessman explaining business after business, success after success, and talking for what seemed like enough time for the sun to set and rise all over again. All I was interested in was soaking up some Vitamin D, so I rudely interrupted him and said, "Look, I'm not really sure who you are, or what you are looking for, but could we schedule a call to talk more about this on Monday?"

Understandably angry, the gentleman exclaimed, "What's your name? Let me talk to your manager." To which I hastily exclaimed back, "I'm the owner of the company!"

It was at that point that there was a brief moment of silence, and the gentleman on the other side of the phone, in a mellow voice said, "Wait. You're Brendan?" As if I was someone worth knowing, or could do something to help this guy in some way no one else could. He then went on to say, "I read all about you on IdeaMensch. Let's start this call over.

Hi Brendan, I'm John." I recall a flood of emotions. First, I was astonished someone actually read my interview on IdeaMensch (which is an amazing interview site that interviews entrepreneurs and business owners, but I didn't think anyone would read an interview about a kid running an SEO company).

Second, as I Googled "John Shegerian" and read through his Wikipedia page, I was impressed at how much he had accomplished in his life and in the business world. And third and most importantly, I was still interested in getting some sun!

"I'm going to be in Chicago on Monday on some business, how does lunch at noon sound?" With a clear way for me to now get outside, I responded, "Perfect. See you then."

John and I met for a one-hour scheduled lunch that Monday, and almost three hours later, we were finishing up talking about all the different ways we could work together.

Fast forward yet again a few years, and after working together on a half dozen projects, and finding massive marketing success on each one, we partnered up to form The Marketing Masters, a sister company to the company I founded years prior, offering marketing services to high-end clientele.

With both businesses thriving and continuing to expand, we now serve over 300 clients from a wide array of industries. Our clients are diverse, ranging from large e-commerce websites to serving multiple trial lawyers of the year award winners, from fortune 500 companies to small startups, manufacturing companies to medical professionals and everything in between.

And much like I found great enjoyment and success in teaching others how to trade over ten years ago, I'm looking forward to finding even more joy, success, and new relationships through writing this book and continuing to help businesses grow beyond what they ever dreamed possible. Any business can shoot for the stars, and with a solid marketing plan, the right marketing tactics, knowledge, and experience, I truly believe any company can grow to be as large as their wildest dreams.

Brendan M. Egan
Entrepreneur. Marketer. Leader.

Foreword – By John S. Shegerian

When you look back and try to deconstruct how someone gets to a certain point in their life—or why they do what they do, or became who they became—some journeys are very obvious. Others are more opaque. Luckily, mine is the former.

My dad, also John Shegerian, owned a color separations and printing company in the New Jersey and New York City Metropolitan area. It was called Litho Masters. And yes, my partner Brendan was kind enough to allow me to pay homage to my nascent and joyful beginnings by naming our company The Marketing Masters.

Anyway, my dad owned one important business that served all the original Mad Men in the booming advertising world on Madison Avenue. Since I'd worked for my dad since my early teens, I was raised with a bird's eye view inside the best ad agencies in NYC with some of the most exciting and iconic personalities in the creative advertising world.

Let me share a few of the backgrounds of some of the key people I was exposed to so that you can better understand who inspired me to do what I do today.

David Deutsch, the founder of David Deutsch and Associates. He was a kind ad leader who was always encouraging me whenever I ran into him while delivering artwork to his agency. His son Donny, also famous, later took over his agency and grew it tremendously—he actually had me on his late TV show, The Big Idea. Off air I told him of my fond memories of his legendary dad and Donny was very touched and thanked me for sharing my memories.

Jerry Della Femina, the founder of Della, Femina, Travisano & Partners, who was referred to as the "Madman" of Madison Avenue. He's probably known as one of the biggest inspirations for the television series Mad Men. From creating the iconic Joe Isuzu to the Meow Mix theme, his creative genius was always inspiring to me. Jerry showed me that good and creative work could be a fun and exciting process as well.

George Lois was simply larger than life, and brilliant if I might add. He created "The Big Idea" on Madison Avenue and helped create so many memorable advertising campaigns including "I Want My MTV", VH1, "I Want My Maypo" and "Think Small" for Volkswagen. I was lucky to be in his presence not only because of my dad's company and our work with his agency, but because I also went to high school (The McBurney School) with his son Luke. George truly left an indelible mark on all whom he touched and I was thankful to be included in that group.

Last, but not the least, of my youthful iconic inspirational and creative legendary teachers was Phil Dusenberry. He was the genius behind BBD&O when I got to meet him and I was honored to work on many of his famous ad campaigns.

These campaigns included Pepsi and so many others. One of fondest memories was when I was up in his offices at 383 Madison Avenue. I would see his director's chair sitting outside his office and it almost had a mysterious halo of invincibility around it. Embroidered on the back of the chair was his "referred to" name—it just said GOD. This truly summed up the magnitude of the impression of my formative years around these guys—I was just a kid from Queens who grew up with very humble beginnings.

I came to love the marketing, advertising, and brand building business side of the industry because of my dad exposing me to the world of creative artists, makers, and some of the titans of the industry. During this time, I realized that the possibilities are limitless and the joy is in the process.

This is why I do what I do. Today, I get to enjoy the journey with my wonderful partner Brendan and the best clients we could have ever imagined.

A New Generation Meets An Old Problem

Hopefully our book of tips that you are about to read will bring you a huge bucket of fresh new sales leads. We technically call them PNC's, possible new clients.

So, after reading this book, your next challenge will be to determine what will give you the best chance of closing these sales leads.

I will now share my personal secret superpower with you.

Always Be Closing . . . Glengarry Glen Ross

A-B-C. A-always, B-be, C-closing. Always be closing. Always be closing.

My Secret Superpower

I have been very lucky to have participated in the technological revolution. First starting with Financialaid.com in 1998. Then with ERI www.eridirect.com in 2005, which I co-founded and where I am still the Executive Chairman. Today, it's with The Marketing Masters.

There is no doubt that technology has made the world a better and more connected place in so many ways.

But there is dark side to technology; loneliness, social isolation, and all the negative things that attach to these growing trends.

These trends have created new challenges in the business of sales and marketing.

It has been somewhat incredible and fascinating to see a new generation of young salespeople who are both afraid and adverse to picking up the phone to speak with a sales lead and, maybe even more importantly, they don't like meeting clients or potential sales leads in person. As a business owner whose lifeblood is new sales and revenue growth, this new trend is both terrifying and potentially fatal to every business owner and entrepreneur. Therefore I am constantly telling our sales team at ERI that nobody I know has ever closed a new client over Facebook, Instagram, Snapchat, text message, or even email.

The technological revolution has deeply depersonalized all of us and changed how we interrelate with one another—and that realization can be the death of anyone's sales program.

Therefore at ERI, and any brand I am involved with, I have created the Facebook rule for our sales and client services teams. It is simple.

Get your face out of Facebook and go get into someone's face in person. Sales are closed nose-to-nose, plain and simple.

To encourage this, I always try to lead by example. It truly doesn't matter if you have to go by train, plane, car, or even walk—just go and meet with all your sales prospects and current clients in person.

Here is the punch line as to why this is my secret superpower.

When I was 22 years old, *everyone* had business meetings in person. It was normal. It was polite business. It worked! But since the advent and acceleration of the technological revolution, we have depersonalized the personal connection that true business partnerships and relationships are supposed to have.

Therefore, in 2020 and beyond, it is in my experience that if you personalize your business relationships, it will be extremely appreciated by all whom you touch and will set you way apart from most of your competition. Why? Because most people don't do it anymore!

For example, last year I spent over 200 nights and travelled 150k miles on the road for ERI, meeting clients, potential new clients, and speaking at trade events. We've since had our best year ever and have the biggest sales pipeline in our history.

Unfortunately, there are no easy ways around this superpower. No tricks or shortcuts. It is a discipline and lonely grind much of time.

But in truth, it really works. Nothing I have ever done works as well as this method. I hope you try it and make it part of your business practice.

And Now A Word On My Partner

Brendan has already recounted how we met and our history together, so no need to repeat ourselves here.

I'm very lucky to be part of the first wave of newly minted dot.com millionaires with my previous company, FinancialAid.com, but it has its upsides and downsides (as do most success stories).

For me, it is important to note, once you become an Internet entrepreneur with a good origination story and big liquidity event, everyone wants to befriend you—especially every alleged or self-proclaimed Internet marketing guru. I found the vast majority of these people to be frauds, charlatans and just plain con men. Some were mediocre and others were clueless.

Brendan is so vastly different. He is loaded with intelligence, boundless energy, and an impeccable character. He is also grounded and humble for all the massive financial success his talents have brought him over the last 15 years.

He is a family favorite of my wife Tammy, who is the CEO of ERI, and my children Cortney and Tyler. Cortney and Tyler are entrepreneurs as well who have adopted him into the Shegerian family and enjoy working with him on their own business ventures.

I could not be more honored and proud to partner with Brendan.

One Final note—without Brendan, Marketing Masters would not be one of the leading marketing companies in the US. Also, without Brendan, ERI would not be the leading brand in our industry.*

Thank you for reading our first book. We have numerous other books planned on subjects that truly matter to us. All knowledge is power when properly applied and we hope you use our tips as some great tools in your marketing and sales arsenals.

John S. Shegerian
Innovator. Maker. Leader.

* The Marketing Masters has never been compensated for any work with ERI or any of its affiliates. Brendan manages ERI's online marketing business needs and requests through his own independent company, Simple SEO, which is owned only by him, and has no legal or financial association with me.

Table of Contents

Part 1: The Marketing Basics

Part 2: Search Engine Optimization (SEO)

Part 3: Digital Advertising

Part 4: Social Media

Part 5: Rich Media

Part 6: Web Design / Development

Part 7: E-mail Marketing

Part 8: Public Relations (PR)

Part 9: Offline and Traditional Marketing Mediums

Part 10: Lead Nurturing and Handling

Part 11: Tying it All Together

Part 1 – The Marketing Basics

This book is broken up into ten parts, each consisting of multiple chapters (101 chapters in total). Each chapter is designed to provide at least one actionable tip to help you with your marketing.

Before we start diving into specific marketing tactics, there is a little bit of housekeeping to be done.

The focus of part one of this book is to provide an introduction to marketing, set the groundwork for marketing your business, and provide some general tips and information on how to get the most out of the marketing tactics that will follow throughout the book.

This book is loaded with information, and designed for both business owners who may be novices at marketing, as well as established marketing veterans looking to gain an outside perspective.

We have three favorite mantras that we try to live life by:

1. *Learn something new every day. No matter how big or small.*
2. *Even if you read 400 pages and learn one new tip, it was all worthwhile.*
3. *Marketing is a marathon not a sprint.*

We truly believe these all hold true to this book. Depending on your level of marketing experience, you may learn thousands of new tips, or if you are a seasoned pro maybe just a few, but regardless, as long as you learn something new and actionable, it was all worthwhile.

When it comes to marketing, the reality is everyone wants to jump on the latest short-lived, hot fad, but the truth that few discover is that putting in hard work and grinding with time-tested strategies is, in our opinion, the only way to succeed. This book provides some insider tips and tricks that we have learned over the years, but it is still going to require you put in the time and effort to see results.

Marketing isn't magic. Marketing isn't fast. Marketing isn't easy. But if you have a sound strategy and put in the time, you *will* see positive results.

Chapter 1: What Marketing Is and Is Not

To truly master marketing, it's important to take the time to understand exactly what it is and what it is not. Without this understanding, everything you learn will be difficult, if not impossible, to apply strategically to your day-to-day operations.

Think about it… how are you supposed to master any marketing tips if you don't understand what marketing is? You're not. We've seen businesses try and it's definitely not pretty.

While there are many substantial definitions, we believe *The American Marketing Association* says it best: "Marketing is the activity, set of institutions, and processes for creating, communicating, delivering, and exchanging offerings that have value for customers, clients, partners, and society at large."[i]

The "activity, set of institutions, and processes" involve the actions that you'll need to take to create and develop your product and/or service, and to advertise in a way that reaches your target audience. This activity involves research, analysis, trial and error, and more than a few restless nights. The important thing to remember is that marketing is ongoing. It's not something that you can simply check off your to-do list. It will be with you from ground zero and stay with you until the end. Marketing is what connects you to the world; it's how you establish the value of your product—your offerings—and ultimately your brand.

Let's consider the development of Apple's products. Their marketing began when Steve Jobs and Steve Wozniak decided to show the world the first *Apple I* computer instead of leaving it in the garage, where its value couldn't be appreciated. From that initial revelation, direct advertisement, uniform branding, personalized messaging, product development, and accessories have all been part of their marketing strategy. If they never morphed their product into a company and marketed it to the world, they likely would have continued their lives building processors in their parents' garage. Effective marketing can be the difference between a hobby and a successful company.

Now let's consider the Microsoft *Zune*. A lot of people are probably asking themselves, "What's a Microsoft *Zune?*" and that's understandable. The *Zune* was an MP3 player similar to the iPod, but Microsoft didn't effectively market it to their target audience, so it failed. They weren't aggressive enough with their strategy. In fact, even though they had a massive budget and loyal Microsoft followers, the *Zune* never got more than a single digit market penetration.[ii] Why? They didn't commit to an ongoing marketing strategy. The release was followed by years of silence. Only after all that time had passed did they realize they needed to show the world how the *Zune* out-valued the iPod. Unfortunately for them, it was too little, too late.

Marketing is a process, not something that you implement once and put in your "done" pile. It encompasses the continual development of your company, inside and out. "Marketing covers all aspects of a business, including product development, distribution methods, sales, and advertising."[iii] You need marketing every step of the way if you want to see any growth. Marketing is not simply advertising. Marketing is how you make you and your business known. It's how you establish value and generate interest in your product or service day after day, month after month, year after year.

Once you understand this, you can move on and start using our proven marketing methods to take your business to the next level.

Chapter 2: Is My Product, Service, or Business Marketable?

After you have a basic understanding of what marketing is and is not, it's important to understand that marketing efforts aren't the sole reason a company succeeds or fails. You can have the greatest marketing strategy in the world, the best team, and the most innovative campaigns, but if your business isn't marketable to being with, it won't make a difference.

People come up with business ideas every day, and there's a reason that we only see roughly 2 out of every 10 succeed. It all boils down to whether your business is *a good idea.* Is it filling a current void in the marketplace? Are there a large number of people who would immediately benefit from it? Are there other businesses with the same or eerily similar products/services already operating successfully?

You need to look at your idea in terms of the value it offers to the public. If you can easily identify a target audience and build a plan to out-sell your competitors, you're off to a good start.

Initially, you're going to need to spend a good amount of time doing market research. Market research is "a way of collecting information you can use to solve or avoid marketing problems."[iv] Doing this prior to launching your product and business will save you time, stress, and money perhaps even some embarrassment.

Think about who will benefit from your product or service and consider the advice from The Staff at Entrepreneur Media, Inc.:

1. **"Who are your customers?"[v]**

   Define the demographics, occupation, lifestyle, education, and income of your target customers. Take some time to thoughtfully brainstorm as much detail as possible about them. The more time you spend researching, the more likely you'll be successful when you transform your idea into a business.

2. **"What do they currently buy?"[vi]**

   Think about an average day in the life of your customer. Write down their current spending habits that relate to your field of interest. Put some thought into how much they buy at once, how often they buy something, and what price they tend to find justifiable.

3. **"Why do they buy what they do?"[vii]**

   If you've developed an idea based on a current need that you have in your life, try and extend that outward to the world. Try and put yourself in the minds of your future customers as best as you can and consider why they would buy the product you're developing.

4. **What will make them buy from you?"[viii]**

   Finally, assuming you will have competitors in the market, you need to consider why someone might switch from buying from a trusted brand to buying from you. This will help you understand whether it's possible to rise above the competition. Are you filling a need that's already saturated with solutions? If so, how can you make your product or service stand out from the crowd? Think about the competitive edges and how you'll establish your own unique selling perspective.

Don't expect to take a few hours and answer these questions right away. Look at sales figures, annual reports, buying habits, customer motivation trends, and anything you can get your hands on with detailed, reliable, and up to date information. We'll be the first ones to tell you that market research is tough. But if you're serious about your business, it's worth it. There are also tons of online tools and programs available for you to use to help you gather information. If you want to take it one step further, you can buy information about your market from reputable companies.

This might be a little expensive, but it's a great investment if you want your business to see success.

After you've done an extensive amount of market research you should know whether your business is marketable. If you can definitively answer the above questions and are able to put a plan in place to get you to the top, you've probably got a pretty good idea stirring. If not, see how you could make changes to your business plan before launching. Remember, even the greatest marketing can't save a bad business idea.

Chapter 3: Marketing as an Art and a Science

Chances are, you're a firm believer in at least one of these sayings: "Marketing is an Art" or "Marketing is a Science." Those that argue the former frequently reference the countless hours of creativity that go into every marketing strategy. Those that argue the latter defend their answers with justifiable evidence, research analysis, and measurable results. So, who is right? Is marketing an art or a science?

What if we told you that neither person is right, but neither person is wrong? Well, it's true. Instead of viewing marketing as an either-or situation, marketing should be viewed as both an art and a science.

Let's begin by looking at the definition of art. The Oxford Dictionary defines it as, "The expression or application of human creative skill and imagination, typically in a visual form such as painting or sculpture, producing works to be appreciated primarily for their beauty or emotional power."[ix]

There are professionals on marketing teams who are 100% dedicated to creating a specific demand for the product or service, a specific beauty, that appeals to their target audience. Marketing is centered on expressing your brand and should inspire people to want to use your product.

To do this they need to create a prototype of a person inside their head and predict if their designs will draw them in. A strong marketing campaign allows potential customers to easily imagine having and using your product/service in their lives.

When the campaign launches, marketing involves creative copywriting, unique branding, and CTAs that incorporate many more artistic aspects.

On the other hand, marketing is undeniably also a science. Science is defined as, "The intellectual and practical activity encompassing the systematic study of the structure and behavior of the physical and natural world through observation and experiment."[x]

You continually measure, analyze, and record results, then change whatever isn't working and try again. Your scientific goal is to influence your target audience's behaviors, and to do so you need to make predictions every step of the way. After you act, the results are recorded and studied. Did your marketing efforts work? Did you have a high conversion rate? What's the average amount of money that a new customer spent? Do you have any repeat customers? Results are analyzed through scientific calculations and mathematical equations.

If you want to be successful, consider each action and decision of your marketing campaign from both the artistic and scientific perspective. Remember, "the science should lead and measure; the art should inspire and create."[xi]

As much as you may want to continue arguing that marketing is more one over the other, success will come only when you treat it as both.

Chapter 4: Marketing Is Essential

Nearly every successful company views marketing as a necessary and serious investment. Think about the cliché, "If a tree falls in the forest, and no one is there to hear it, did it really fall?" If you start a company, and no one knows anything about it, did you really start a company? It's debatable.

We understand that working on a new or struggling business brings about a slew of complex problems paired with an often-hectic environment. These problems take precedent, and non-essential investments and action items are pushed off to the side. Well, marketing needs to stop being viewed as non-essential. Time and time again we see companies push off marketing for "tomorrow" and "tomorrow" never comes, or when it does come, it is too late.

According to Wagner (*Forbes*, 2013), one of the five reasons that 80% of startups "crash and burn" is because they lacked a niche in the market.[xii] Unfortunately, we are often approached by businesses that want to market themselves but don't truly understand their market or how they fit into it.

What does this mean exactly? The businesses that failed didn't specialize in a niche, didn't define their target audience, and didn't invest in marketing. They didn't reach the people they needed to in order to see any profit.

Marketing is the heart of your business. It's an investment of time, money, and creativity accompanied by an invaluable return on investment (ROI). Through marketing, you'll foster growth, generate leads, and provide an essential foundation for your company by establishing your brand. Over time, your company's brand has the potential to increase influence and foster an unbeatable loyalty with your customers. Don't believe us? Consider the companies you're loyal to and their brand image.

So, what's the problem? It's usually money.

Most companies don't have bottomless wells of funds, and fear of the unknown creates cautious investors. While no one can be 100% sure that investments will yield a profit, strategic marketing is going to give you a much better opportunity for success. Just be smart about it. If you need to start small and work your way up, that's okay. Create a plan and trust that your investments will generate leads and sales over time. The *Harvard Business Review* says: "The key is to remember that while marketing expenditures hit immediately, every dollar you spend today is building your brand as an asset for the future."[xiii]

If you want to have a future for your company, and a profitable one at that, invest in a strategic, multi-tiered marketing plan.

Case Study: A 100-Year-Old Company Fighting to Stay Alive

Just because you've done your research, defined your market, and have executed for 100 years doesn't mean you'll necessarily still be in business tomorrow. All too often companies forget to future-proof their businesses, especially their marketing.

We started working with a small manufacturing business—around 30 employees—that has been around for over 100 years. Everyone told them to jump into e-commerce, so they did, and with a mixed bag of results. They had just fired their relationship with their prior marketing company before hiring us, and the first thing we noticed was they simply weren't marketing their products properly.

As a primarily business-to-business (B2B) company for the last 100 years, they failed to connect the dots and become a hybrid business-to-business (B2B) / business-to-consumer (B2C) company in the online world. Rather than optimizing for phrases and buying ads for complex product names, they needed to dummy things down and go after the phrases and terms consumers were targeting. They also needed to improve their buying process with consumer-friendly attributes like a more lenient refund policy, free shipping, and other perks.

In just a few months, we turned their online sales from anemic to booming, tripled their conversion rate, and helped them reach profitability in their new digital presence. Know your market. Know your consumers. Know your products. And most importantly, know your niches and what the people in those niches value most.

Chapter 5: What is ROI and How Is it Calculated?

As we discussed in Chapter 4, marketing is an investment worth making. However, to ensure you're investing in a marketing strategy that brings results, you need to consistently monitor your return on investment (ROI).

If you're unsure how to accurately measure and monitor your ROI, don't worry. It's easier than you might think. Check out the formula below.

$$ROI = \frac{(\text{Gain from Investment} - \text{Cost of Investment})}{\text{Cost of Investment}} \times 100$$

To truly understand your ROI, it's important to monitor all platforms—all your social media, any print or televised ads, digital campaigns, and the company's website. This allows you to stop throwing money away at unsuccessful tactics. If you're paying thousands of dollars for a 20 second TV commercial and no one is acting on it, we recommend making some changes. Instead of continuing to waste away your precious marketing budget, you should be regrouping, pinpointing flaws, and developing new strategies based off the success of your other marketing methods.

While we don't advise putting all your eggs in one basket, analyzing your allocated funds and making the appropriate changes will give you a stronger plan on how to increase your ROI. Monitoring your successes and failures is a surefire way to ensure your marketing money is invested wisely. Scale what works, cut back on what doesn't.

Now, let's walk through this together. You need to focus on **one** of your marketing efforts at a time to accurately calculate and compare them.

All you need to do is take the profits you've earned through one of your marketing efforts and subtract your initial cost of investment thus far. Divide that number by your initial cost of investment and multiply it by 100 to view your ROI as a percentage. Let's look at the math using a real-world example.

Say you spent $5,000 on a social media marketing campaign. Through careful tracking and analysis, you find that you've earned $5,832 through this specific campaign. Therefore,

$$ROI = \frac{(\$5,832 - \$5,000)}{\$5,000} \times 100$$

$$ROI = 16.64\%$$

While you haven't had a very strong ROI yet, you're still earning more than you spend. This is a great example for businesses just starting out. As you monitor and evaluate the success rate of each individual metric you're using, and make changes depending on what's working and what isn't, you'll start to see your ROI get larger and larger. Campaigns often have negative, short- to medium-term ROIs, but as long as you don't have a negative ROI in the long run, we consider it a win.

If you find that your ROI is consistently low and you're not seeing any profit growth, consider reevaluating and revamping your marketing strategy. Unfortunately, with very minimal profits, business longevity is unrealistic. Be honest with yourself, make necessary changes, and continue to monitor your ROI for success.

ROI – Where Should I Invest?

One of the most common questions we are asked is, "Where can I get the largest ROI?" Unfortunately, the answer to this varies by business and by niche.

In our experience, digital delivers a higher overall ROI than traditional offline marketing mediums, but it all depends on where your potential customers are located. We have countless case studies to the contrary of businesses in more traditional markets doing much better with print ads in a magazine than with online ads. We also have seen some industries do better with advertising on Bing than Google, especially when targeting an older demographic.

The best way to know what will yield the strongest ROI is to dedicate an experimental budget to new marketing mediums when they are available and see for yourself. Remember, marketing is as much an art as it is a science.

Chapter 6: Tracking and Measuring ROI

Knowing what ROI is and how it's calculated is great knowledge to have, but learning how to actually track and measure ROI is what's going to help you with your marketing efforts. The problem is that this can be difficult. In fact, "76% of marketers are still struggling to track the ROI of their campaigns."[xiv] This is because there are a ton of different factors that play into this process and it can be hard to pinpoint exactly where your results are coming from.

Let's start with how to track ROI.

To successfully track your ROI, start by clearly identifying what your marketing goals are. This allows you to differentiate useful, relevant data from everything else. Then, use one of the methods below to track your ROI.

1. **Call Tracking**

   The first method is through using a tracking phone number. You can create a different tracking phone number for each one of your campaigns, and therefore quickly and easily see which ones are successful and by how much. This allows you to objectively see what's working and what's not—both online and offline. Or, if you don't want to use a different number, you can still use your main number or a vanity number. Just give people an offer code in your marketing campaigns for them to redeem and you can easily pin that offer back to a marketing campaign. Make sure that if you do use call tracking the number stays valid well beyond the duration of the marketing campaign.

2. **Google Analytics**

   The next method of tracking your ROI is through Google Analytics. It's fairly easy to use, compatible with tons of other programs, and completely free. Once you connect your website to Google Analytics, it will start automatically tracking all your basic website traffic. Take a second to configure your site correctly to ensure accurate tracking.

Start out by setting up all of your different goals or conversions in the application. This will help track your website's traffic and show you whether or not any action comes from that traffic. Next, create a specific URL for each campaign using Google's URL Builder so you can separate and identify the results with ease. If you have any e-commerce sites, follow the detailed instructions on the Google Analytics Tracking Guide to set everything up. You can also head over to these guides for a more detailed look at any of the above set-up. After set-up, log in to Google Analytics daily, weekly, and monthly to see your tracking results.

3. **Leads and Sales**

In order to track your leads and sales, create a CTA that directs your potential customers to a specific landing page. Use one for each of your different campaigns so you can differentiate the results. Keep track of how many people visit each page and how many sales you get from each.

4. **Putting it All Together**

After you've begun to track your ROI efforts, you'll want to use a 3rd party tool to marry everything together. This allows you to see everything as a whole and move on to successful measurements. On the most basic level, you can do this in Excel by exporting data from steps 1-3 above and combining it in Excel. There are also countless third parties that will help the number crunching phase to be a little bit easier.

After you've successfully tracked your ROI, take a few minutes to determine how much money you've invested on each different method. This will help you accurately measure and calculate your final ROI. It's important to note that measuring ROI at different times will yield different results and often your efforts today won't show results until months, even years, down the road.

Here are a few of our favorite ways to measure ROI.[xv] They get increasingly more confusing, so if you're trying to calculate it and have difficulties, consider bringing in the professionals.

1. **Single Attribution**

    This is the easiest and most common way to measure ROI. It's done by "assigning all of the value to the first (or last) program/person that touched the deal."[xvi] It's relatively straightforward, but can cause data to be skewed in long sales cycles. For example, if someone first saw a TV ad for your company, but then saw 5 additional marketing pieces, that TV ad would receive credit, as it was the first touch point.

2. **Single Attribution with Revenue Cycle Projections**

    This method takes single attribution and adds revenue cycle projections to combat long-term sales cycles. Rather than waiting for results, look at the current impact and use it to estimate the long-term results. It's a calculated estimate based on past performance.

3. **Multi-Touch Attribution**

    While it'd be great to use single attribution methods for each of our campaigns, it's unrealistic. Throughout the course of a marketing campaign there are many different touches from an increasing amount of people. To measure multi-touch attribution, "start with whatever action you're analyzing and work backwards to identify each significant touch that affected all of the contacts with that particular deal."[xvii] After these are identified, it's time to allocate revenue. You can equally divide the revenue by number of touches or go into more detail based on time, role, and program type. If you're just starting out, we recommend dividing by touches.

4. Test and Control Groups

Another method of measuring ROI is done through science. Identify a test group and a control group and apply the marketing campaign to a portion of each group. Since the control group will have stable factors, you can identify any differences in your test group and get a clear view of the results. This can get expensive, but it's able to test just about anything.

5. Full Market Mix Modeling

This is a fairly unused model of measurement, with "only 3% of B2B marketers using it."[xviii] Due to the complications and time commitments it takes to use this method, we figured we'd only touch briefly on it. If you want to learn more about how to use this model, contact a marketing professional.

After you've tracked and measured your ROI for each campaign, you can go back and input your numbers (gain from investment and cost from investment) into the ROI formula to determine what your ROI is.

If reading the above has your head spinning, keep it simple at first and stick to a single attribution ROI model. For most small to medium sized businesses, it will still give you a fairly clear picture of your ROI.

ROI Measurements – Perfecting the Imperfect

ROI measurements aren't always perfect. In fact, most of the time they are simply a calculated guess. In the real world, one-to-one tracking isn't always that easy.

However, over time and with volume, a clear ROI picture is painted. While it isn't always critical to know if your campaign is running at 203% or 206% ROI, what is important is to have a general idea of whether you are seeing a 1x, 2x, 2.5x, or 10x ROI.

If a marketing person (or agency) can't at least give you a pretty close estimate to what your ROI looks like, you should run, not walk, in the other direction.

Every marketing and sales action must be driven by ROI.

The beauty of digital marketing is that ROI is much easier calculated and tracked than in offline mediums. SEO, Google Ads, website traffic—they all can be tracked fairly easily once the initial setup work is performed. This makes it much easier to scale what is working and cut what isn't.

The bottom line is that while ROI tracking isn't always perfect, you need to do it in some semi-accurate form to succeed as a business and know where you should invest more or cut back.

Chapter 7: Marketing Assets Mean Nothing Without Building a Brand

Before we delve any deeper into the aspects of marketing, we want to make sure that you have a strong understanding of branding and what it means to your company. It's great to build up marketing assets, but they'll serve no purpose if you're not building a brand.

David Ogilvy, commonly known as "The Father of Advertising," explained branding as "the intangible sum of a product's attributes: its name, packaging, and price, its history, its reputation, and the way it's advertised."[xix] Branding is a foundational element of your company that is integral to your success. It might not happen overnight, but if you develop a brand that speaks to your target audience, and stay patient, you'll see an exponential rise in recognition, loyalty, success, and trust. It will simmer and circulate through word of mouth before you know it.

Consider some of the most famous brands in the world: Apple, Facebook, Amazon, Coca-Cola, Disney, Microsoft, McDonald's, IBM, Nike, and Honda. You likely pictured their company logo the minute you read their name. This isn't necessarily because they have a great logo, it's because they have a great brand. You can have the best logo in the world, but without a strong supporting brand, it means nothing.

All the most famous brands know exactly who their target audience is and how to resonate with them. They work on conveying a company philosophy in a way that evokes feelings of connection between their audience's values, mindsets, and expectations. They evoke a sense of loyalty in their customers that's hard to compete with.

Think about it this way: stronger brand recognition = better marketing ROI = more profit.

If you're still skeptical, consider the study *Significant Objects*.[xx] In this study, researchers purchased items at yard sales and flea markets that were essentially garbage. Their goal was to inflate the item's value by creating a brand, telling each object's "story." They succeeded, with the items selling at auction for a 2,700%

markup.[xxi] The authors summed up the significance of branding: "Stories are such a powerful driver of emotional value that their effect on any given object's subjective value can actually be measured objectively."[xxii] Your brand should tell a meaningful and impactful story of your product and company, thus creating an emotional connection with your target audience.

We understand that investing in the careful cultivation and implementation of your brand through marketing is invaluable. Take the time to think about what type of story you want your brand to tell and how it will connect you with your target audience.

From here, market through every platform you have available. Utilize social media, website affiliations, commercials, advertisements, pay per click, and so on. Which brings us to our next point.

Chapter 8: The Difference Between Branding and Lead Generation

When most people start developing a business or committing to their marketing strategy, they're introduced to a plethora of new terms. These terms are essential to a deeper understanding of the world you're entering, but can start to blur together. Consider branding and lead generation. They're both strong parts of a good marketing plan, but have inherent differences that you need to understand. In Chapter 7, we learned about the importance of building a brand. Now let's compare brand building to lead generation.

Remember, branding is what people think of when they hear the name of your company, or a product/service that you provide. It's the image that comes to their mind, the jingle that rings in their ears, and the values that are instilled in their hearts.

On the other hand, lead generation, which involves various forms of marketing, both digital and offline, is used to attract customers. The goal is simple. You want to generate leads so you can convert them into sales. There are a number of different ways to do this, and each business will have their own preferred method—the one that gives them the best results. Some examples of lead generation are direct response mailing campaigns (physical mailing), television advertisements, newspaper or magazine advertisements, billboards, contests, company offers or giveaways, digital campaigns including SEO, PPC, e-mail marketing, and more.

Lead generation and branding go hand in hand, and both are necessary to see success in your marketing activities. For example, you set up a simple Google Ads campaign to run some digital ads with a focus on generating leads. A consumer searches, sees some ads on Google, but has never had any prior exposure to your brand so clicks on a competitor ad and makes a purchase.

In this scenario, had that consumer been exposed to your brand in the past through some sort of branding, they may have clicked on your ad instead. You can run reports, measure your ad share lost to competitors, and analyze all day long—without balancing your branding and lead generation efforts, your ROI will suffer.

Many companies go after lead generation because they feel it will lead to a more direct ROI. And while this is true, your brand needs to be built and supported to get the strongest and most consistent ROI possible.

An engaged company gets way more attention—and business—than a disconnected one. Don't believe us? GNC discovered that "by actively engaging on social media, they were able to increase inbound sales from social media by 25%."[xxiii] This extra touch—extra branding—can make a dramatic difference in your bottom line. Take the time to do it yourself or hire a marketing manager to help. Either way, it'll be well worth it in the end.

Chapter 9: Bridging the Gap Between Branding and Lead Generation

There are a ton of moving parts to both branding and lead generation, but a basic understanding can go a long way. Instead of focusing on their differences, we wanted to take a minute and explain the connection between the two and how neither one can exist without the other. In fact, the best, and most successful, marketing practices are a fusion of these two strategies.

Consider branding, the foundation of your company that tells a story to your target audience. It's often incredibly overt and works to illicit a sense of recognition and loyalty into your customer's minds. Then, lead generation comes in. It's the aggressive actions taken in order to convert your target audience into customers. It's what gets people to take action.

But don't underestimate the amount of strategic alignment required to perfectly blend your brand's culture and value with your lead generation techniques. "Brand building and lead generation are inexorably linked—but they also involve subtly different objectives, which require slightly different approaches."[xxiv] In other words, you can't lump them into one action since they require separate tactical planning and management.

Once you've outlined your business goals, and how your brand fits into your strategy to achieve them, you can start focusing on lead generation. This will come much more naturally than trying to work on them simultaneously. Essentially, branding is plowing the field and lead generation is planting the seeds.

You should be mindful of your core values when dealing with all of your content. This includes advertisements, blog posts, downloadable content, photos, infographics, and even your color scheme and fonts. Everything produced by your company should fit together in a seemingly effortless manner.

When you've infused your core values into your brand, with a natural flow into all your marketing content and strategy, you've truly optimized how you generate leads to maximize your marketing ROI. This is what it means to bridge the gap between branding and lead generation.

Case Study – A Tale of Two Businesses

One of our clients is involved in two similar businesses in two different states under two completely different brand names. In one state, they are a borderline household name in their respective niche. In the other state, they are somewhat lost in a sea of similar competitors and savvy marketers.

They came to us with a focus on lead generation. And by focus, we mean that is the only metric they wanted to measure our success or failure by. We explained that there is more to it than just measuring the success of lead generation—we needed to build up their brand to truly improve their lead generation. But like many businesses, they weren't willing to take a risk in investing in something with an uncertain outcome.

We engaged in two campaigns side by side, doing the exact same activities for each business in each state. After nearly two years, we stepped back to look at the results.

The company that has strong brand recognition saw over a 650% increase in their inbound leads during the campaign. The company which did not have a strong brand only saw a 150% increase. Same lead generation tactics, same marketing plan, same niche, and yet very different results.

Your brand is worth more than you may think, even when it comes to lead generation.

Chapter 10: Creating a Business Model

If you want to develop a legitimate, sustainable business venture, you will need both a business model and a business plan. A business model focuses on how your company will bring in revenue. A business plan goes into more detail about what's needed to implement your model. It's therefore no surprise that it's better to start with a business model. This will be very cerebral and creative, including a lot of introspection about your values and what you're going to offer in terms of both product and services. Simply put, "a business model is how a company creates value for itself while delivering products and services for its customers."[xxv]

This will include using a lot of the information from Chapter 2, when you determined if your business was marketable, so take a second to go back and review. A successful business model considers your target audience, potential future partnerships, and the value you're bringing to the market. You'll be comparing these with your current resources, any anticipated costs, and ways moving forward to generate revenue.

Alexander Osterwalder, co-founder of the Business Model Canvas, determined that there are nine key building blocks for any sustainable business model to function:[xxvi]

1. **Value** - How are you filling the needs of your customers?

2. **Customer Segments** – Who are you targeting or delivering your value to?

3. **Channels** – How are you delivering this value to your customers?

4. **Customer Relationships** – How will you engage and establish a relationship with your customers?

5. **Revenue Streams** – How will you generate revenue from your customers?

6. **Key Activities** – What do you need to do to execute your value proposition?

7. **Key Resources** – How are you creating value for your company; what assets do you contribute?

8. **Key Partners** – Are there other organizations or partners who could support your value proposition? Will they help you deliver it?

9. **Cost Structure** – What will it cost to deliver this model?

If you find it difficult to answer these questions, or if you've previously determined that your business isn't marketable, take some time to reassess your ideas. If you can't accurately describe your infrastructure and revenue plan, you're not going to have a sustainable business. If everything looks good, you can put everything together in a nice, cohesive document and label it "Business Model."

Then it's time to move on to goal setting.

Chapter 11: Effective Goal Setting: Measuring Short-, Medium-, and Long-Term Success

Before you can develop a sustainable business plan, it's important to take a look at your goals. We've seen numerous businesses fail because they only set short-term goals and didn't have a concise way of combining them into their long-term efforts. Or they set only long-term goals and became discouraged when they didn't reach them fast enough.

The way to combat this is by effectively setting short-term, medium-term, and long-term goals during your planning cycles. When you do this, and measure them for success along the way, you'll gain the momentum you need to tackle your big goals while still making progress on smaller goals. Start by thinking of your big, long-term goals and work backwards.

Make sure every one of your goals is SMART, a.k.a., Specific, Measurable, Attainable, Relevant, and Time-based. Let's start with your long-term goals.

Long-Term Goals (18+ months and often years)

These goals aren't going to be easy to measure right from the start, but they're a good starting point if you're going to be working backward. You'll be combining your long-term goals with short-term efforts in order to keep sight of the bigger picture. Matthew Baker, of FreshBooks, best describes this as "business planning through the lenses of a microscope and a telescope."[xxvii] As long as you don't let the day-to-day operations distract you too much from what really matters, you'll be well on your way to success.

Consider a few of these great examples of long-term goals.[xxviii]

- ✓ Name recognition (believe us, this takes time)
- ✓ Brand awareness (when your company has reached celebrity status)
- ✓ Brand reputation
- ✓ Becoming an influencer or leader in your market
- ✓ Strong SEO rankings

✓ A large, engaged social media following

Keep these goals in the back of your mind with every decision you make and try not to lose sight of them. Every now and then, put down your microscope so you can gaze out from your telescope.

Medium-Term Goals (6-18 months)

Now that you've defined your long-term goals, you can use them to work backwards and formulate some meaningful medium-term goals. These are goals that are achievable within the next 6, 9, or 18 months, and the cycle can continually repeat until you've hit the long-term planning phase. We need these goals to move through our business development, just like we need adolescence to move from infancy to adulthood. This phase is usually a turning point for your company. It's a period of acceleration and momentum. It's when you fine-tune based on the lessons learned and your achievements so to propel your business further toward success.

Simply put, this is the time to focus on analysis, growth, financial stability and responsibility, improved brand, expanded reach, a loyal customer base, and a plan to surpass your competition. You might have to make some investments in market research, product development, and marketing strategies, but sometimes you need to spend money to make money.

Here are a few examples of well planned, medium-term goals:

✓ Reanalyze your business and create a sustainable financial strategy to promote longevity and success
✓ Increase the efficiency of internal operations
✓ Increase sales by X% each month (this number will depend on your realistic growth opportunities)
✓ Have a fully developed content and social media team in place
✓ Find influencers in your industry to endorse your product or service
✓ Set up a pay per click (PPC) campaign and fine tune it to find a strong ROI

Often times, medium-term goals will be more tactical than long-term goals. At the end of the day, always remember to keep your eye on the prize. "Medium-term goals in your business plan, and its companion marketing plan, are those required to reach your long-term goals. You might consider developing a medium-term marketing plan around a meaningful goal along the way."[xxix]

Short-Term Goals

Finally, it's time to take a look at your short-term goals. These will be more focused on internal and external operations, infrastructure, employee wellness, increasing sales, and marketing. The most important of these goals are improving website traffic and conversion rates (sales). Short-term goals are action-oriented tasks, so the timelines will be much shorter—within a day, a few weeks, a couple of months, and up to one year.

Some examples of common short-term business goals include:

- ✓ Define your core values and establish your company culture
- ✓ Give performance-based reviews in order to increase productivity and keep operations running smoothly
- ✓ Create a hiring plan with interview questions, ideal qualities, and experience wanted
- ✓ Have bi-monthly executive meetings to review progress
- ✓ Create buzz-pieces or freebies to generate product interest
- ✓ Increase web traffic by X% each week
- ✓ Increase conversion rates by X% each month
- ✓ Grow social media followers by X% each month and be consistently engaged
- ✓ Track leads generated from each marketing campaign
- ✓ Create 5 new blog posts per month for your website
- ✓ Craft 3 new television ads to split test their effectiveness

Short-term goals are highly tactical and highly task orientated. They drive the action, which leads to medium- and even long-term success.

When these goals are set consistently and accurately measured, you can clearly and concisely identify any early indicators of failure. This allows you to make necessary changes, realign your strategy, and try something else. Plus, clearly defined goals are essential when creating your business plan.

Case Study – Patience Is a Virtue

*It seems like almost every week we get the same phone call. "Hi, my name is ___ and I'm looking for someone to **quickly** improve my online marketing and SEO." **Quickly.** In the day of Amazon same day shipping, everyone wants everything fast. But fast isn't always what's best. And when you tell them that, coming from a place with little trust established, they often call up the next company, which will gladly accept their money for a short time at the expense and failure of the business.*

The reality in marketing is that there truly are short-, medium-, and long-term marketing objectives. And that doesn't mean you should blindly embark on a 2-year SEO campaign without results—monitor your results in ALL your campaigns in real time, and over the course of a 2-year SEO campaign, for example, you will see a trend established in as soon as a few months.

The chart below shows a typical journal over a long-term SEO campaign. Notice that while results can be seen early on, true measurable success doesn't come until nearly two years in.

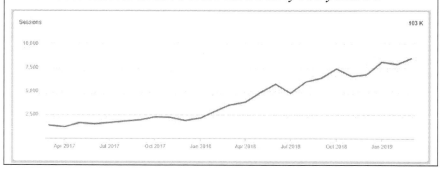

Chapter 12: Creating a Business Plan

If you have a good business model in place, creating a business plan can be exciting. It's a way to analyze your future business from an objective and pragmatic view that will show you the endless possibilities that are yet to come. In addition, your business plan will help you determine whether or not something will be a waste of money or time, saving you tons of stress and frustration. Even if you have an existing business or have been around for years, it's important to have a clear and updated business plan to act as your road map to success.

It's about analyzing possibilities and setting yourself up for success through swift, effective execution.

You'll start by developing an organized conceptual framework of your business. For people that love to-do lists, you're in for a treat. A business plan is basically a comprehensive to-do list that will get your company from point A to point Z and beyond. It will incorporate your branding and lead generation strategies, your business model, and all of your short-, medium-, and long-term goals.

If you've come this far, we think it's safe to assume that you've already got the basic idea for your business in mind and you've worked through the steps in our previous chapters.

So, what's next?

Think past the short-, medium-, and long-term goals you laid out in Chapter 11 and consider the overall goals of your company. What do you want to accomplish? Where do you see yourself and your business in the future? What's your visionary goal? According to Maria Marshall, professor at Purdue University, "visionary goals usually fall within four general areas: service, social, profit, or growth."[xxx]

The next step in creating a sustainable business plan is to create a vision and mission statement. Your vision statement encompasses who you want to become, your core values, your dream, and your desired future. It can be an internal statement that helps fuel your passion and productivity. Your mission statement is what you'll share with the public. It clearly defines who you are, what you do, who you do it for, and how you do it. Your mission statement articulates your purpose and fosters connection with your target audience. It shares how you'll impact your market and the world through your business.

Start with a rough draft and fine-tune it over time. Everything can be amended prior to your debut. Keep in mind that a business plan is never short-tracked. It takes a lot of time and effort and there's a good chance you'll need to make changes.

Now, let's take a look at the 10 most important parts of any business plan.

1. Executive Summary

The first part of your business plan is an executive summary. This is an overview of your entire business and strategy, essentially a preview of what's to come. We recommend writing this last so you can create a more succinct summary, keeping it between 2-3 paragraphs at most. Talk about what your company does, how you stand apart from the competition, your expenditure, profit and revenue projections, and your allocation of funds.

2. Company Analysis

This is pretty straightforward. Talk about how your company was formed, what achievements, if any, has it accomplished so far and the different executives involved. If you have yet to make any achievements—which is completely fine as a new business—talk about those you expect.

3. Industry Analysis

When you analyze your industry, you're simply doing research on the current standards in sales, trends, and revenue. This means taking an in-depth look at your competitors and how they're holding up. Use the SWOT analysis (strengths, weaknesses, opportunities, and threat analysis) and PESTLE analysis (political, economic, social, technological, legal, and environmental) to cover both your internal factors and the macro-environmental hurdles that will impact your company.

Additionally, make sure you consider the overall market size of your products or services so you can move on to in-depth customer analysis.

4. Customer Analysis

This is where you'll take your target customer audience and do a thorough analysis. You'll want to break them into sub-groups and individuals based on similar interests and purchasing habits. Remember the market research you did back in Chapter 2? Use that data to identify your target base, their habits, preferences, needs, and how your product offers them value or fills a void in the marketplace.

If you don't have any data compiled, or if you want a more accurate representation of your specific target audience, consider creating a survey. If you do, know that people are more inclined to fill them out if you offer something. Use a multiple-choice survey to ask about their demographics, location, income, interests, need for the product, different packages and purchasing options, and at least one open-ended question for detailed analysis. You can use programs like MailChimp or SurveyMonkey.

Remember, this part of your business plan is for determining how your product will best serve the need of your customers, and getting feedback from real people is a great way to ensure you're on the right track.

5. Competitive Analysis

This analysis is doing exactly what you just did with your customers, but with your competition. Objectively analyze what your product offers that theirs doesn't and what they may be offering that you aren't (or can't). This strategy helps you work through any missing pieces and strengthens your business before your competition has a chance to wreak havoc.

Look at the competition's products, brand, public recognition, financial standings, staff/employees, customer cost, customer base, location and availability of products, marketing strategy, and business operations. To find the best information, check out their annual purchase reports, internal (if you can) and external presentations. Your goal is to "stalk your competitors"[xxxi] and find their weaknesses so you can do better.

6. Marketing Plan

Your marketing plan is a major part of your business plan, but it's also a core piece of this book. After you've read all of our *101 Tips*, we have no doubt that you'll have this mastered, but for now let's go over a basic overview to be included in your business plan. Remember what we said in Chapter 4? Your marketing plan is essential and it is the difference between seeing success and failure.

Your marketing plan should be broken down into specific sections:[xxxii]

- ✓ Executive Summary
- ✓ Target Audience Analysis
- ✓ Unique Selling Proposition (USP)
- ✓ Pricing and Positioning Strategy
- ✓ Distribution
- ✓ Offers/Promotions
- ✓ Materials
- ✓ Strategy

- ✓ Online Marketing
- ✓ Conversion Strategy
- ✓ Partnerships and Joint Ventures
- ✓ Referral Strategy
- ✓ Price Increase Strategy[xxxiii]
- ✓ Customer Retention
- ✓ Projected Financial Gains

Throughout the rest of this book, we'll touch on these things in more detail, so don't worry too much about them for now.

7. Operations Plan

This part of your business plan focuses on maximum profitability and offering the best customer service while keeping operational costs down and your team members happy. Address all the moving parts, including location-related details, day-to-day operations, legal requirements, personnel requirements, any inventory projections, and information on your suppliers.

8. Management Team

Here you'll provide the background, educational history, experience, and information related to the all-star team that you've put together. Think of this as a place to really sell your team to any investors and work out why they're the perfect fit for your company. Identify key leaders, executive members, and anyone else who is committed to making your business successful. Always highlight any previous successes this these team members have had in their past careers and businesses.

9. Financial Plan

And here comes the fun part. Your financial plan is a numbers game. You need to include your income analysis, a balance sheet, and a cash flow statement to provide an accurate view of your current standings and prospective future. Don't forget about your start-up feeds, inventory, utilities, salaries, any revenue, distribution costs, loans, or office supplies. Be as detailed as you possibly can to get the most accurate results. Remember these are only best guess forecasts, and don't lose sleep over them not being 100% accurate.

10. Summary/Conclusion

All you need now is a summary to tie everything together and drive home any final points. This doesn't need to be too long, especially if you have an executive summary, but it's a nice way to wrap up your business plan.

That's about it! We understand that it's a lot to digest, but it's worth the effort in the end. If you need help formulating your business plan, check out the available resources online or consider getting in contact with a professional. It's money well spent and will help set up your business for success well beyond your marketing.

Chapter 13: Budget Friendly Marketing

After cracking the surface of the wonderful world of marketing, you're probably ready to get started. We understand that with all the costs of running a business, new or existing, it can be difficult to scrape together the funds for a proper marketing budget. But recall the information in Chapter 4. Marketing is an essential investment. We believe you should eventually invest in a multi-faceted, strategic marketing plan, but until then there are some options for smaller budgets.

Many of these budget-friendly marketing tools will be discussed in more detail later, so feel free to use this book as a reference and jump around as needed. As an overview, some of the most effective, yet inexpensive, marketing tactics are as follows:

- ✓ Maintain a strong, up-to-date website
- ✓ Utilize search engine optimization (SEO) best practices
- ✓ Register your business with Google My Business
- ✓ Build an opt-in e-mail list and utilize e-mail marketing
- ✓ Write guest posts, give testimonials, and build back-links to your website
- ✓ Post strong, engaging content on your blog
- ✓ Attend local events and hand out unique business cards
- ✓ Create partnerships and affiliate programs
- ✓ Engage on blog posts, social media, and other industry leader's pages
- ✓ Host webinars or free giveaways
- ✓ Create a Yelp listing and any niche specific listings for your business
- ✓ Utilize social media's free advertising
- ✓ Create, share, and distribute infographics
- ✓ Share case studies and testimonials
- ✓ Create a free LinkedIn profile

Small business marketing doesn't have to break the bank. With a little effort, you can promote yourself and your company through proven strategies. The only thing to keep in mind is that for some of these tactics, you'll need to invest the time and patience it takes to research, learn, and understand how to implement them on your own. Don't try and utilize too many of these at once. Instead, pick a few items that interest you and work on doing them well.

If you'd rather focus your time and energy on other parts of your business, it's worth it to bring in the professionals.

Marketing Masters Pro Tip: Know Your Limits

Late in 2019 we started working with a large business that was handling their social media marketing in-house. Specifically, one division was using LinkedIn to generate leads for their sales team. Their average cost per lead was $65.

They thought they were doing a great job in-house, and were talking to us about a totally separate project when they asked if we could help connect LinkedIn with their CRM for them.

While in there, we noticed a few glaring issues, and asked them if we could take on managing their campaign. They said they didn't have the budget, and we quickly explained how affordable just managing their LinkedIn campaign could be.

They agreed, and after just 45 days, we had their cost per lead down to $32. The same quality leads, at half the cost.

When accounting for the management fee they paid to us, their actual cost per lead goes up from $32 to $37, but we still saw a dramatic improvement.

Budget friendly marketing can mean doing things on a budget, but it can also mean being smarter with your money. Sometimes having a specialist help you out can make your budget go even further than you imagined. Don't ever be penny wise and dollar foolish when it comes to your marketing.

Chapter 14: Bringing in the Professionals

Maybe you've implemented the aforementioned budget-friendly marketing strategies and they're not making the impact you'd hoped. Maybe you want to see stronger results in less time. Maybe you simply don't have the time to do the research it takes to handle your own marketing. You're not alone. In fact, 63% of company's say that their top marketing challenge is generating the traffic and leads needed to convert people into customers.[xxxiv] If you want to see stronger results in less time, it's time to bring in the professionals.

The benefits of hiring a professional marketing agency far outweigh the costs. It's much more effective than trying to handle everything yourself. Not only will you save time by outsourcing this integral part of your business plan, you'll ensure that the job is done right the first time around. We've had tons of frustrated businesses owners approach us for marketing help after wasting weeks, months, even years, on attempted self-marketing.

You see, marketing experts have a level of experience that's hard to match. Malcolm Gladwell, an esteemed writer and reporter, claims that it takes 10,000 hours to become an expert in a specific field.[xxxv] Marketing professionals have put in these hours, know what works and what doesn't, and will get you the results you need to propel your business forward. They have a specific set of core competencies that will help you maximize revenue.[xxxvi]

In addition to the level of expertise that comes with a professional marketing company, it also helps to get an outside perspective on your company. It can be hard to evaluate your business from an objective view, especially when you're just starting out, so if you want to truly succeed, look at marketing as an investment worth making.

However, if you're going to bring in a professional marketing agency, you want to make sure that you find the right one. With so many different agencies to choose from, this process can be overwhelming. The most important thing is finding someone who fits well with your company, meshes with your personality, and has the skills and experience you're looking for. Consider the following questions:

- ✓ What are your areas of expertise (e.g. digital or offline) and even within those areas what is your focus (e.g. SEO, PPC, e-mail)
- ✓ What is your marketing process when working with a client?
- ✓ How will you improve our SEO?
- ✓ How do you approach different aspects of digital marketing?
- ✓ What kind of technology do you use?
- ✓ How do you combine the different parts of digital marketing to formulate an overall plan?
- ✓ Who will we be working with on your team?
- ✓ How do you communicate with your clients? How often?
- ✓ How do you measure success? What analytics do prioritize?
- ✓ What does your fee include? How/what do you charge?
- ✓ What makes you different from other companies? Why should we choose you?
- ✓ Do you have a portfolio of previous work? Can you show me successful campaign analytics from previous clients?
- ✓ What makes you a good fit for us?

Don't be afraid to ask these types of questions to each marketing agency that you're interested in working with. This is your business and you want to ensure that if you pay for marketing help, you get the right marketing help. Find someone you trust and who has the experience needed to help bring you success.

For the next several parts of the book, we are going to jump into specific marketing tactics and strategies your business can utilize for both branding as well as lead generation. Whether you plan on doing these marketing activities yourself or hiring the professionals, it's important to have an understanding of what is going on and some of the tips and tricks to get the most out of each strategy.

Case Study: You Get What You Pay For

It's easy for us to sit back as marketing professionals and say, "You get what you pay for when it comes to marketing." But this couldn't be further from the truth.

As experts who have been in this industry for almost two decades, we've seen proposals for marketing campaigns range from $200 to $2 million each month, and literally everything in between.

This is not a public service announcement saying to spend more. But rather a reminder to spend smart.

If you opt to hire an outside marketing firm, hire one whose experience matches your expectations. If you are a small, local flower shop, you don't need a marketing agency that requires a 6-figure retainer. A local, smaller shop may give you the best bang for your buck. And likewise, if you are a large and growing law firm, spend the money to hire an agency with the experience to handle your needs and help you grow to the next level.

Don't be afraid to strategically invest in marketing help. It pays dividends when done properly.

Part 2 – Search Engine Optimization

Search engine optimization. SEO. The process of pulling out your hair in frustration, yelling at the computer screen, questioning your sanity, but then running all the way to the bank when it works.

SEO is the process of optimizing your website to rank well on search engines such as Google, Bing, and others. And it can be the bane of some marketer's existence.

Fortunately for you, we'll spare you as many gray hairs as possible as we've already developed a time-tested and proven strategy for consistently ranking well in search results. And that's what this section of the book is all about.

SEO is one of our agency's specialties. And we truly believe it is just as much an art as a science. While art can't be taught, this section will go deeper into the science of SEO and provide tips from agency insiders on how to execute a successful SEO campaign.

Chapter 15: What's Involved in SEO, Anyway?

Search engine optimization (SEO) is one of the most perplexing and frustrating parts of digital marketing. It can be difficult to understand, it's ever changing, and it can cause a lot of headaches for those who try to implement it without a basic understanding.

However, SEO can also be the most rewarding part of a digital marketing plan to those who master it.

As SEO experts, we've put together several chapters that delve into the most important aspects of SEO, showing how to use both on-site and off-site factors to increase your search engine results page (SERP) rankings and generate more traffic. SEO involves very strategic methods that work in favor of the algorithms put in place by the most popular search engines, such as Google, Bing, and Yahoo. In the following part of this book, we will walk through everything you need to know about SEO, starting with Black Hat and White Hat SEO tactics and the importance of playing by the rules. While everything we teach applies to all the major search engines, our primary focus will be on Google since it accounts for about 85+% of search traffic. Worth noting is that Bing can be a fantastic search tool for businesses in the B2B space or for those targeting an older demographic.

As an overview, we'll tackle the following topics involved in SEO and how to use them to your advantage.

Keywords are the essence of SEO. In order for any SEO efforts to actually work, you'll need to utilize specific keywords throughout your static content and any blog posts or web pages. However, all keywords are not created equal. It's important to understand how to find the right keywords for your industry, niche, and business, and how to use them in an ethical way that yields results. We'll delve into the differences between competitive keywords and long-tail keywords, how to find which ones to use, and when to use them.

After you've mastered keyword research, you'll learn how to use them with on-site factors such as title tags, headlines, meta-tags, internal links, and static content. When you do this correctly, your efforts can pay off almost immediately. As a side note worth mentioning early on, whenever we discuss linking or "getting links," we're referring to backlinks or external links. For all intents and purposes, when talking about linking your pages to each other within your website, we will explicitly say, "internal linking."

Once you've optimized your site internally, we'll focus on how to gain links naturally, how to generate them manually, and how to reach out to your contacts to get easy links—all of which help raise your ranking in SERPs.

Finally, we'll end with an overview of how to create content that Google, and your readers, will love. We'll mainly focus on the frequency and structure of these posts and how to tie in your keywords naturally.

By the end of this section, you'll have a stronger understanding of SEO that you can immediately use to your advantage. Don't worry if some of these things don't make sense to you now, by the end of this section, you'll be on your way to being an SEO pro.

Chapter 16: A Word on Black Hat SEO

While it's great to have an underlying idea of what SEO is and what's involved, there's a lot more to it than you may think. The algorithms that search engines use to rank content, websites, and businesses have changed since they first began, and they continue to do so day after day and year after year. However, when SEO was first introduced, it was a whole different ballgame.

A rather shameful type of SEO is "Black Hat" SEO. Black Hat SEO is a combination of techniques that are used to *supposedly* boost your Google search ranking without much genuine effort. In the professional marketing world, we consider this the easy way out and the sure-fire way to failure. It might originally appeal to over-worked executives, swamped content managers, and those who may not have a firm grip on SEO best practices, but it should at all cost be avoided.

What exactly is the problem with Black Hat SEO, you ask? Put simply, it doesn't work. Or if it does work, the results will be very short lived at best.

Ever since the introduction of the first search engine, people have been looking for ways to circumvent or "trick" search engine algorithms. Back in the day, when search engines were completely rudimentary, it was easy to slip past their algorithms, which look for low quality, spammy, black-hat SEO, mainly because they didn't exist. Additionally, Google really was not dominating the search engine game until 2007-08. There were a number of search engines vying for position including Yahoo, Webcrawler, Excite, Lycos, and a number of others. Most of these search engines had fairly game-able algorithms, ripe for the pickings.[xxxvii] This is when Black Hat SEO first gained traction.

Black Hat SEO is essentially cheating to attempt to increase your standing in a Search Engine Results Page (SERP). It involves unethical keyword stuffing, content spinning, content duplicating, paid and automated link building, repeatedly typing keywords into backgrounds using invisible text, stuffing meta-tags and descriptions, non-relevant link building, spam comments, cloaking, sketchy site re-directs, and essentially everything you need to avoid.

There was a time when this worked. It drove traffic to sites and boosted a business' standings in a SERP. It was an easy solution to get to that coveted #1 spot on the results page, placing a misleading business at the top of your industry. Unfortunately, if these businesses were willing to cut corners and rely on conceit for optimized SEO, they generally failed to be reputable, high-quality companies worthy of a consumer's money.

It's easy to understand how companies that employed these tactics weren't very trustworthy, and search engines eventually caught on. Now algorithms are continually evolving, with hundreds of updates a year, to outsmart Black Hat SEO and other unethical efforts.

As a general rule of thumb, if you're doing something that feels "wrong" or doesn't bring much value to your business or to your website visitors, chances are it is considered "Black Hat" or at the very least falls into a grey area. All of the strategies we're about to discuss will not only benefit your organic results, but will also provide increased marketing value to your business. This is known as White Hat SEO.

Chapter 17: You Can't Outsmart Search Engines

For those of you who think you can still use Black Hat SEO or other "cheat-worthy" tactics, we want to drive home this point: you can't outsmart search engines. It is literally impossible to do long term, and attempting to do so will harm your position on a SERP.

The people at Google and other reputable search engines are smart. They know when you're utilizing Black Hat SEO tactics, building up more links than you should with the same anchor text, shamelessly increasing your keyword density above a normal amount, and when you're just being downright ignorant. Once search engines realize you're doing this—and they will—you'll find yourself on page 87 of Google results, or worse, your site may be de-indexed from Google all together. We promise that absolutely none of your target customers are going to find you if you cannot be found on Google. Not to mention in the most server cases, your site may no longer even appear if someone searches for your brand!

Search engines are downright militant. What seems like a shortcut will likely be a shortcut to the end of your reputation or worse… your business.

If you found a tiny sliver of hope in surpassing the esteemed search engines, it won't last long. Google changes its search engine's algorithm around 500-600 times per year![xxxviii] That's a lot to keep up with, which is why using proper SEO methods is so important. It's easier to just implement SEO best practices instead of trying to outsmart the geniuses that write the algorithms.

Even if you're in a rush and want quick results, it is still more beneficial to take the time and implement one successful SEO tactic from start to finish, rather than attempt to push the envelope. There are short-term wins in the SEO world that we'll show you in the upcoming chapters. Don't try and overnight your way to page #1 for the most competitive terms in your industry, as you'll end up potentially blacklisted from the major search engines.

Some examples of Black Hat SEO (or even being in the gray area) and trying to game search engines include:

- ✓ Using any sort of automated tool for link building. There are hundreds of pieces of software that will build links for you, and none of them will work.
- ✓ Stuffing keywords or making any sort of change that doesn't benefit your website visitors.
- ✓ Trying to build links from a bunch of different websites you own to your main website.

Search engines are smart, and they penalize you for trying to outsmart them. Instead, focus on ways to make them happy and get your business to the top of a SERP in a way that's sustainable and legitimate.

Chapter 18: A Word on White Hat SEO

Hopefully we've effectively steered you away from attempting to trick search engines by using Black Hat SEO techniques. This has likely left you wondering how you're supposed to boost your company's ranking in a SERP. That's where White Hat SEO comes in.

White Hat SEO involves "SEO tactics that are in line with the terms and conditions of the major search engines, including Google."[xxxix] We need to focus on SEO that doesn't work on outsmarting the search engine's highly effective algorithms. It should be noted, however, that technically *all* SEO is against Google's policy. White Hat SEO is just less risky and is proven to be a good way to get ahead in search results. It is something every major business does, and we can personally guarantee 99+% of websites on the first page of Google for any keyword have engaged in some form of SEO.

White hat SEO takes into consideration the fact that real human beings will be reading your content and that quality is a huge determinant of whether readers will trust your company. This is the complete opposite of Black Hat SEO, which is only concerned about search engine results. The two are opposing techniques and if you want to be successful, you should only focus on White Hat SEO. In fact, White Hat SEO will come to have a major influence over everything you do online.

Some examples of White Hat SEO tactics include:

- ✓ Optimizing your meta-tags and title tags to match your keywords without overly "keyword stuffing"
- ✓ Creating unique, compelling content for your website that focuses on specific keywords but doesn't overly use the same terms over and over
- ✓ Building links to your website through quality business directories, content sharing, and creating value on the internet

In the first chapter of this section, we briefly went over the things that are integral for your business' success in SEO strategies. All are included in White Hat SEO. Utilization of these practices may take your site a bit longer to climb in the rankings (compared to dodgy SEO practices), but the payout will be much greater than taking the lazy way out, and inevitably failing.

The rest of this section will discuss all the steps you can take, and the processes you can implement, if you want to grow in the rankings of a SERP. It's a combination of everything from the aesthetics of your site, keywords, content, internal links, backlinks, meta-tags, titles, consistency, and persistency.

With that being said, we want to take the time and break everything down for you in a way that's easy to understand. Let's get started.

A Word on Ethical SEO

In the eyes of search engines, technically all SEO is against guidelines. Search engines want to show content that is best for their users, and they believe their algorithms are strong enough to show the best results without any sort of SEO work.

The reality is that search engines are imperfect. They evaluate a website based on specific metrics, and don't necessarily always know the best result to show a searcher. For example, let's say you are looking for an electrician. Google will serve up to you the electrician in your area that maybe has the most reviews but not necessarily the best, or the one that has the most backlinks, but not necessarily the fastest response time. Metrics that matter in the real world are somewhat ignored by search engine algorithms. Things like customer service, price, response times, quality of work, and other important factors aren't directly part of what search engines evaluate.

This, in part, is why even though all SEO is technically against search engine guidelines, it is required if you want to reap the massive benefits of search engine traffic. And it is why doing "ethical" or "White Hat" SEO is a fairly safe practice when done right, and is something that can greatly benefit your business.

Chapter 19: How to Work with Search Algorithm Changes Instead of Against Them

Before we jump into implementing strong White-Hat SEO tactics and how to do so, we want to take a moment to talk about algorithm changes.

Like we mentioned in Chapter 17, Google changes it's algorithms frequently. "Each year, Google changes its search algorithm around 500–600 times. While most of these changes are minor, Google occasionally rolls out a "major" algorithmic update (such as Google Panda and Google Penguin) that affects search results in significant ways."[xl]

The main take-away from this is that most of these changes are minor. Rather than attempting to read and update all your tactics each time Google rolls out with an algorithm change (a.k.a., roughly twice a day), it's better to just keep implementing strong, White Hat SEO. Aside from a few major updates, not terribly much has changed in the SEO world over the last 5 years. Yes, there are always new things to consider like mobile usability, page load times, whether your site uses SSL, and other factors that now impact SEO, but the core principals of SEO have remained fairly consistent. Those doing White Hat SEO continue to succeed, and those trying to cheat the system are finding it is harder and harder.

If you're doing things the right way and not trying to outsmart search engines, these minor algorithm changes aren't going to greatly affect your results. If you try and change your strategy each time something changes, you're not going to get anything else done—if you can even keep up with them in the first place. Rather than starting fresh after each algorithm update, make minor tweaks in your strategy when large algorithm changes occur.

Most of the algorithm changes are automated, and Google is faster and smarter than any of us, so focus on doing the right thing, and you'll be fine.

Remember how we mentioned that Google makes about 500-600 algorithm changes a year? It'd be near impossible to go through and effectively change your entire strategy for each of these updates. Luckily only a few of these updates are major and should require action.

When a major algorithm change occurs, that's when you should take the time to make sure all your content, pages, and websites are updated to reflect that change. To keep up with these changes, keep an eye on Moz.com. They have a real-time Google Algorithm timeline that lets you see all of the major updates, how they will affect you, and how you should change your strategies to reflect them.

They highlight all the major updates sorted by year, which can be helpful to see any patterns in updates. Focus on what affects you, so unless you're genuinely curious, stick to your current year and onward. In each year, the updates are broken down per incident and include a list of helpful articles that explain what the change means for website owners and how to take the necessary steps to optimize your site for the change.

To make sure you're able to easily adapt, focus on creating "intelligent content that aligns with the customer journey to deliver a successful and memorable experience."[xli] Focus on building links on sites that actually seem like they are legitimate and will help people find you.

To stay as up-to-date as possible, check this site often. If you keep it bookmarked, it won't take long to visit and see if there have been any major changes. This keeps you at the top of your SEO game and helps you stay in line with Google's automated AI programs that continue to evolve every day.

Rules change and Google's AI continues to get smarter with their algorithms. If you want to continue to grow, you have to work with the changes instead of against them.

Chapter 20: Pick Your Competitive Keywords Wisely

Keyword research is the foundation of any SEO campaign. If you don't pick the right keywords, everything else you do will be a waste of time at worst, and at best not as efficient as it could be.

When starting out, most business owners aim to bolster their marketing plan by finding and using the most competitive, highest trending keywords. Why wouldn't they? It seems like the most logical approach.

But for long-term success, it's usually not.

The reason behind this is because the top-trending, most competitive keywords are exactly that—everyone, everywhere uses them and wants to rank for them. This is especially true if a major company or corporation holds those top-ranking positions for a specific keyword. They have an unbelievable amount of influence, reputability, and customer loyalty. And with that comes a tremendous amount of links and domain strength. It will be hard, if not impossible, to outrank them. And it likely took them years upon years to achieve that.

Competitive, short-tail keywords can be difficult to maneuver. They carry lots of different meanings and are used by thousands of different industries interchangeably. Let's consider a website designer trying to rank on a SERP. They do some research and see that "design" is a top-trending word. That's great, except when you look in a broad context, completely different industries are also using this keyword—graphic designers, web designers, fashion designers, and interior designers.

This is an example of a short-tail competitive keyword, one that only contains one or two words. They are hard to compete with because they lack detail. You essentially drown in a sea of generalities. In addition, the time and effort needed to rank for a keyword this competitive is massive, and the chances of success are slim.

Instead, focus on less competitive keywords or long-tail keywords.

Rather than trying to cram everything that your business represents into one word, create less competitive keywords or even long-tail keywords and use them to compete for rankings. This allows you to better reflect the aspects of your company that you're trying to highlight. It also gives you a fighting chance to get to the #1 position on a SERP.

Case Study: Dealing with Egos Vs. What Is Best for Web Traffic

One of the most frustrating parts of running an SEO campaign for a client can be dealing with their egos as it relates to SEO. When we perform keyword research, we identify a mixture of competitive and long-tail keywords that will help drive success for the client.

Success, to us, is increasing their traffic exponentially, increasing their number of sales or leads, and ultimately driving strong ROI.

Oftentimes, however, business owners don't understand this basic fact. They pick the most competitive keyword in their industry (or worse yet, some random keyword that they think describes their business), Google it, and if they aren't on page 1 then we must not be doing our job, regardless of their traffic increases and ROI.

Check your ego at the door when it comes to keywords. Rather than investing money into terms just to pad your ego, focus on the terms that you can realistically rank for and that will deliver traffic and an ROI. Select keywords that have good search volume but are also realistic for you to rank for, given your SEO budget. And as things progress, don't be afraid to add new or more keywords to the mix and eventually add in those highly competitive terms.

Chapter 21: What Are Long-Tail Keywords and Why Are They Important?

If you want both short- and long-term success with your SEO efforts, long-tail keywords are the way to go. Specific, descriptive keyword phrases containing a minimum of three words, often more, long-tail keywords target smaller, more distinct groups of people that are searching for things in your niche or business. This is contrary to short-tail keywords, which address the entire population and can be difficult to rank for.

Long-tail keywords are therefore more likely to rank higher on a SERP simply because they are less competitive and will require far less work to optimize. Since they're so descriptive, the competition for the exact phrase is smaller than a one- or two-word phrase used by large numbers of people. It may seem odd to target a 5-word keyword phrase, but if you know how to do it—which we'll discuss in the next chapter—you'll succeed.

The reason that these types keywords are so important is because while they might not draw as much traffic to your website, they'll draw the *right kind* of traffic. We're talking about high-quality traffic that will lead to conversion, turning visitors into customers. Long-tail keywords are highly effective as you move to the point-of-purchase. Plus, people often use them more frequently to avoid having to weed through irrelevant search engine results. In fact, "roughly 75% of page views are the direct result of long-tail keywords."[xlii]

Let's look at an example. You want to find an ecommerce graphic designer in Chicago. Rather than searching for "designer" you search "ecommerce graphic designer in Chicago." The comparative results are undeniable. The former search will likely give you graphic designers from all over the world, specializing in thousands of different areas. From a business standpoint, the competition for the word "designer" is just too difficult to compete with.

The latter will give you results specific to your request, therefore making it easier to find someone that fits your needs exactly. This is ideal in the business world because securing that #1 spot in the SERP will propel your business forward. "Managing long-tail keywords is simply a matter of establishing better lines of communication between your business and the customers who are already out there, actively shopping for what you provide."[xliii]

The point of long-tail keywords is to yield the most customized results that match what your visitors are looking for. The more specific you are, the more likely you'll get found.

Another advantage of using long-tail keywords is that it takes more of them to accumulate a large amount of traffic. You may be thinking that is a disadvantage, and it would be easier to just rank for a few competitive keywords. However, one of the biggest advantages to long-tail keywords that most people forget is that it is far less risky to rank for dozens or hundreds of long-tail phrases compared to ranking for a few competitive phrases.

We've seen time and time again with our clients who insist we cover a few competitive keywords that if just one of those terms drops slightly in rankings, it has a tremendous impact on their traffic and bottom line. Long-tail keywords are less risky and more diverse, just like if you were investing, and hence provides protection to your web traffic to minimize the impacts of algorithm updates and competitors, and provide a more stable and steady flow of traffic to your site.

Case Study: Long-Tail Simply Works

One of our long-term SEO clients insisted we only focus on competitive terms. After we discouraged them until our voice was hoarse, we obliged and only went after competitive terms.

Fast forward a few years, and several of their largest competitors were either acquired by larger companies or raised millions of dollars to expedite their growth. They invested literally millions into SEO, where we were spending 5 figures a year. While we're good at SEO, even we couldn't keep up with the scales that tilted. Slowly but surely, we went from having over 50 competitive keywords in the 1-3 slot to having all those keywords on the bottom of page 1 or on page 2. And their traffic went from around 100,000 unique organic visitors a month to just 20,000.

Soon thereafter, the phone call from a furious client came in, and after we met with them to show them what happened, they quickly wanted to adopt a long-tail strategy.

After about 15 months of long-tail work, we were able to rank several hundred long-tail keywords, and their traffic is currently almost back to where we started. And what was even better than the traffic returning was the conversions. The long-tail keywords, since they were highly relevant to what the searcher was looking for, converted almost 2x better than the competitive terms!

Had they let us adopt this strategy from day 1, they would have originally seen even more traffic from the mix of keywords, and certainly would have an insurance policy on the future as their long-tail terms would still be driving traffic even when new competition comes in to knock down some of the competitive terms.

Go long-tail for long-term results!

Chapter 22: How to Find (Research) Competitive & Long-Tail Keywords

After understanding what competitive and long-tail keywords are and why they're important, you're ready to jump into optimizing your content with them. There's still a bit of work that needs to be done, however—work that will allow you to start seeing results fast.

This work is primarily research.

While you could just pick a few keywords and implement them throughout your site, you'd be wasting time. You need to know what keywords will work in your niche, what the competition looks like, how much content you can develop with them, and which word combinations will get you the most search traffic. That's why we've dedicated an entire chapter on finding the best competitive and long-tail keywords for your business.

The primary tools that you'll be using are keyword tools. They're still as important as ever, and even marketing professionals continue to use them because of the success they generate. Our favorite keyword tools are actually the free ones, like Google Keyword Planner. This tool can be found within any Google Ads account, and will give you exact search traffic for specific keywords as well as recommendations for other similar terms.

Combine this powerful tool with Google Webmaster Tools where you can see all the keywords people have used to find your website historically, and you've got a recipe for success.

Now, let's walk through this process together.

The first step in finding keywords is starting with an anchor word or general theme. Choose a short-term keyword applicable to your business that you'd like to use. According to Yoast, a company that engineers of the most popular WordPress SEO tools, "The main topic or theme of your blog [website] is the number one keyword (or key phrase) you want people to use to find you."[xliv] Fo r example, if you're in the marketing business and your niche focuses on graphic design, you'd start with "graphic design"—easy enough. From here, open Google Keyword Planner and type "graphic design" into the text box labeled "searching for new keyword and ad group ideas."

One of the greatest things about this free tool is that it self-generates. Click on the next tab over, labeled "keyword ideas," and you'll see hundreds of different opportunities involving the phrase "graphic design," along with the number of monthly searches, the competition level, and the different groups that use them already. Your goal is to find relevant keywords that have high monthly searches. The important part here is *relevance*. To identify which keywords are relevant and which aren't, go back and look at how you defined your target audience. Think about what their search intent is by asking yourself, what will they be searching for? Are they looking for "how to" articles? Are they trying to learn a new skill? Do you want to inform them on what your product does or how they'll benefit from your services? You can look at your competitor's keywords to see how they've been doing using specific words and phrases and try and mirror them.

If it's not relevant, it will be hard to expand into a long-tail keyword that resonates with your audience. When you focus your efforts on words that are relevant and have good search intent behind them, you will be able to develop legitimate, high-quality content that your audience actually wants to read. The more specific you are to your target audience, the more conversions you'll see.

Once you've narrowed down your options, copy one of your relevant long-tail keywords into the search box on Google Keyword Planner to produce a list of different long-tail variations.

Various options involving "graphic design" will populate, and again, look at the statistics and choose something relevant with a high search volume and low-medium competition. You can choose something with high competition, as well, just know that it will take more work to move your site up in a SERP—but it is possible.

Take as many of the long-tail keywords from these suggestions as you'd like and focus different pages on your website—or different blog posts—on these keywords. Again, since these are so specific in nature, long-tail keywords tend to lead to more conversions than short-tail keywords, so they're worth spending the extra effort to develop.

Use a mix of commercial (ready to buy) and informational (ready to learn) keywords for visitors in different stages of the funnel—i.e., those who are browsing and those who are ready to make the jump and purchase a product/service. You need to think of user intent search engine optimization like a funnel. There is a ton of website traffic on the Internet. Your goal is to get people at the right spot in the funnel to take action.

Use Google Analytics to measure the click-through rate and conversion percentage of each of your long-tail keywords and then make changes as needed.

Another way that you can find long-tail keywords is by simply using the Google search bar. Start typing in short-tail keywords that are relevant to your industry and take notice of the search suggestions that pop up. Google puts these there for a reason—they're the most commonly searched for keywords—so you can quickly and easily see what people are looking for prior to using any Keyword tools. From there, ask yourself, "How can I make this more specific to what I do?" You can also compare anything that appears in the "searches related to..." section at the bottom of the Google search results page to boost your brainstorming efforts.

If you want to take a more proactive approach, see what people are saying about products/services related to your industry. Head to forums, discussion boards, reviews, and comment sections and see if you can find any questions, comments, or concerns that continue to pop up. When you do, use your customer's feedback, questions, or comments to formulate a long-tail keyword and you'll be targeting something that people are already talking about. This is a great addition to your long-tail keyword strategy.

When implementing these long-tail keywords into your content, make sure to follow White Hat SEO rules and not to overdo it. Keep the percentage of use on the lower end—3-4% is the absolute maximum—to avoid any potential penalties, and keep the content reading naturally. Include keywords in your content, headings, indexing, sitemap, and meta-tags/descriptions. If you have old content, go through and try and jazz it up with some new long-tail keywords. Our biggest piece of advice here is don't get hung up on quantity with long-tail keywords. Instead, focus on quality and you'll get the results you're looking for.

Marketing Masters Pro Tip: Use Feedback for Long-Tail!

Do your customers often ask the same question over and over? We know ours do. And we use that to our advantage.

Train all your employees every time a customer asks a question to enter it into an Excel file or database. Each month, take those questions and research them or share them with your marketing company. These questions often make some of the best long-tail keyword topics that otherwise you may never have stumbled upon!

This system is easy to set up and forces you to not only answer your customer's questions in a helpful way, but will also drive a huge amount of additional traffic to your website and blog. Just think, if your customers have these questions, so do the customers of your competitors, and it's a fantastic way for them to find you!

Chapter 23: The Top 4 On-Site SEO Factors You *Must* Optimize

Now that you've chosen your long-tail keywords to implement throughout your website, it's time to get to work on your SEO. In this chapter, we'll focus on the Top 4 on-site SEO factors that are absolutely non-negotiable when optimizing your site. If you don't optimize them, you won't see results—it's as simple as that.

In fact, we've had numerous businesses approach us saying that they've been doing everything they could to optimize their site for SEO, but they weren't seeing any results. After taking a deeper look, almost every company wasn't hitting all four of these on-site factors. We cannot stress the importance of these enough, so if you want to see results, read on.

1. Title Tags and Headlines

The most important on-page SEO factor is your title tag and headlines. A title tag is a backend HTML element that identifies the title of your web page. They are the clickable links displayed on SERPs, which clearly inform the reader what that page will be about. To differentiate this tag, you use HTML coding as follows:

<title>Top 4 On-Site SEO Factors</title>

Whatever is included between the angle brackets appears as the title of your page. While there is no set character limit, we recommend something less than 60 characters so that the entire title is easily displayed, and this is also the guidance that comes from most search engines. When creating these title-page tags, you need to use your competitive or long-tail keywords. They entice people to click on your page, are used in Google's ranking algorithms, show up at the top of web browsers, and are displayed across social media networks. If you don't optimize your title tags, you'll lose a ton of potential traffic and thus, sales.

Create a unique title for each page and avoid over stuffing them with keywords.

A headline is similar to a title tag, but uses <h1>, <h2>, and so on, and works to address numerous different audiences. "The key difference between these tags [title and header] is where their content appears. That difference impacts how search engines and web surfers analyze your page."[xlv] Title tags show up in search engines, while headlines are displayed on your website. Regardless, they still need to be optimized with your long-tail keywords to help you get the results you need. The most important is the "H1" tag. You should ensure every page on your website has one and only one H1 tag. H2 and H3 are also important, can be used multiple times on a page, and should complement your H1 tag. Stick to one major keyword per headline to get the best results.

2. **Meta-tags**

The second most important on-site SEO factors you need to optimize are meta-tags. There are many different types of meta-tags, but one of the most important in terms of SEO optimization is a meta-description tag.

These are the tags that will appear as a brief summary underneath your title tag on a SERP. They're longer than title tags—between 50 and 300 characters—and help give readers insight as to whether they'll find what they're looking for on your page. These descriptions are where you'll need to persuade visitors to click on your link.

These tags won't directly help boost your rankings, but they will increase the number of people who visit your website, helping to move you higher in SERPs. According to Yoast, if you want to write a good meta description tag, you need to include the following elements: "make it actionable with a clear call-to-action, include structured content that matches that of the page, incorporate focused keywords, and make it unique."[xlvi] Give your readers a sneak peak of your page that will make them want to read more. When you do this, your click through rate increases and so does your ranking on a SERP. Plus, the more people that click on your link, the more likely they are to convert into customers.

There are also several other key meta-tags worth looking at. The meta-robots tag and index tag tell Google whether they should or should not index your site. Having this set to "noindex," which accidently happens more than you would think, would result in your entire site never appearing on search engines no matter how hard you work!

3. Static Content

When we refer to static content, we're talking about all the content that is on your website and doesn't change over time. These things include your home page, navigation menus, "about" page, headers, footers, permanent product and service pages, and other static sections. Think of this content as the skeleton for your website.

It's important to optimize these for SEO. For this reason, you should focus more on long-tail keywords that revolve around the theme of your site and your business' brand. Neil Patel, a popular SEO influencer, recommends that, "The goal of your homepage should be to let Google know what the underlying theme of your site is and what type of product you're offering."[xlvii] Rather than trying to rank for a competitive keyword, focus on ranking for a few different long-chain keywords that let people know what your company does or what you offer.

Business 2 Community gives us a great example: "Make use of the natural opportunities to insert your keywords. For example, a home builder's website could swap out the term 'new communities' for a more powerful term that shows up in more search results, like 'new home development communities in Toronto,' and so on."[xlviii]

Pair this with an easy to navigate, visually centered, and informative homepage, and you've got a recipe for success. However, remember to clearly explain what it is that your company does. If you don't, your visitors might end up confused and leave to find one of your competitor's sites.

Your content should also be unique. Don't ever show the same content on multiple pages on your website, and similarly don't ever take content from other sites and post it on yours.

Follow this formula across all your static content pages to see the best results.

4. Internal Links

The last major on-site SEO factor that you should be optimizing is internal link building. Many people get confused because there are two types of link building: external and internal. From here on out, whenever we mention "link building," we will be referring to external link building—anytime we discuss internal link building, we will call it "internal linking."

Internal link building is simply linking one page of your content to another page of your content that spans across one website—basically linking your pages together. Internally linking all your pages will give you a massive ROI in terms of SEO. In addition to better SEO, this helps improve your website's navigation, hierarchy, conversions, and visitor flow.

For example, if you write an article about the "Ten Best Places to Go Hiking this Summer," you might link to a prior article you wrote on the best lightweight hiking boots, or how to stay cool on long hikes. This proven method is another reason why quality content that is organically rich with keywords is so important. Internal links help people fall down that "Open Link in a New Tab" rabbit hole on your website.

To accomplish this, there are seven commandments of internal linking[xlix] for top-notch SEO:

1. Create tons of content – which creates more linkable content
2. Use anchor text links instead of images
3. Link deep within the structure of your site and avoid using links from your homepage and contact us page
4. Use natural links – link content that is valuable to the reader and comes naturally in a sentence
5. Use relevant links – ones that complement the content on each page
6. Use follow links (as opposed to no-follow)
7. Use a reasonable number of internal links – focus on being helpful rather than overbearing – we recommend less than 5 internal links per 500 words of copy

If you follow these commandments for each of your posts, you will see success with minimal effort. The hard part about link building is getting backlinks—which we'll talk about in Chapter 25, 26, and 27.

As you'll see, there are many other on-site SEO factors that you can also optimize for better results, but the above are the Top 4 that should never be ignored. The companies that we mentioned before saw almost immediate success after implementing these best practices, and we're sure you will too. If you want to take it a step further, you can take the time to implement some of the rest of the on-site SEO factors, which we'll explore in the next chapter.

Chapter 24: The Not-as-Important On-Site SEO Factors

If you practice optimizing the previous Top 4 on-site SEO factors for your website, you should be in good standings. However, we'd be remiss if we didn't at least mention some of the other, not-as-important on-site SEO factors. These factors do make a difference when you start to compile them, but at the end of the day they don't even come close to the previous Top 4.

Gaining an edge over your competition in highly competitive industries means digging deep and doing things that other websites simply aren't.

These on-site factors have been proven to boost your sites SEO, however, so if you've got the time and the bodies to implement them, we won't hold you back.

Brian Dean, an SEO expert, comes out with a different list of "Google's 200 Ranking Factors" each year. This list includes, hypothetically, nearly everything involved in Google's algorithm, and we definitely implement a few of them from time to time. However, as he states in his blog, "Some are proven. Some are controversial. Others are SEO nerd speculation."[1] We recommend taking a look at some of them and implementing the ones that you want to give a try. If they work for you, great! If not, you can move on to other factors. Just keep in mind that these factors are not nearly as critical as the ones mentioned in the previous chapter. We're big believers in being efficient and maximizing ROI, and as such, trying to ensure your site is compliant with all 200+ factors that Google looks at will not only make you pull your hair out, but it will kill any potential ROI you would get from SEO due to the time commitment.

The categories that Brian Dean sorted these 200 factors into include different aspects of domain name, page-level, site-level, backlink, user interaction, special algorithm rules, brand signals, on-site webspam and off-site webspam factors. Instead of listing all 200 factors, we wanted to give you a few of the most relevant ones.

1. Keyword use in your domain name – this means having your keywords in your URL. It's nice to have, but by no means required.
2. Keywords in subdomain – if you use a sub-domain, using a keyword-rich sub-domain can help, but again is not required.
3. Keyword density – this is fairly important. You don't want to have your keywords appear too frequently (or too infrequently). While we don't measure it page by page, shoot for 3-4% keyword density.
4. Page loading speed – this is critical, especially as mobile continues to dominate web traffic. Ensure everything possible is done to make your website load as fast as possible for all devices.
5. Entity matching
6. Site architecture – this is basically your website site map and URL structure. Ensure it is easy and logical and your most competitive pages are "close" to your domain name (not buried deep in your website)
7. Image optimization – this is important for keywords, which show image results (or if you want to rank your images well). Include a caption, alt tag, and title tag for all your images and ensure they are keyword rich.
8. Keyword prominence
9. Mobile-friendly update
10. Helpful "supplementary content"
11. Multimedia
12. Broken links – this is very important, and you should regularly audit your website both for SEO purposes as well as general usability to ensure you don't have any broken or dead links on your site.
13. Reading level – as Google becomes smarter and smarter, this becomes more and more important. Gone are the days of computer generated "spun" content. Ensure your content has a high readability/reading level to maximize success.
14. Affiliate links

15. Domain authority – this is important and will be covered as we dive deeper into link building.
16. WordPress tags
17. Keyword in URL
18. Bullets and numbered lists
19. User friendly layouts
20. Presence of sitemap
21. Terms of service and privacy pages
22. Breadcrumb navigation
23. YouTube
24. Repeat traffic
25. Direct traffic
26. Number of comments
27. Geo targeting
28. Branded searches
29. Attached social media pages
30. Known authorship
31. Affiliate sites
32. And more

The list goes on and on, and some of these are things that you'll likely be implementing without even thinking, while others will take a lot of research and work for little return. Instead, focus on the major on-site factors we discussed earlier and a few off-site factors—link building and content—which we'll cover in the rest of this section.

Chapter 25: How to Build Links to Your Website Manually

Link building in general is one of the most important parts of off-page SEO, and arguably one of the most important parts of SEO altogether. When we run SEO campaigns for our clients, over 70% of our time is usually spent on link building.

As mentioned previously, your site will be ranked higher on Google if you have a higher volume of links to your site from high quality pages. There are several ways to practice link building, but we'll start with an overview of how to build links manually.

Manual link building takes the practice into your own hands. It is a proactive approach to foster more links back to your website, but it is not a process of unnatural link building. Let's talk about that for a second.

Unnatural link building is the process of paying, or trading, for links back to your website. For instance, it's not smart to sign up for an un-godly number of paid directories, where you need to pay for your website to be listed. Sure, a few relevant paid directories here and there are fine and will help your SEO efforts, but if you start to sign up for more than necessary, Google will catch on and penalize you. Signing up for an abundance of paid directories could land you in the Google doghouse.

Similarly, you should never offer money to another website to link back to yours. Link buying is extremely dangerous and unethical and you should avoid anyone that approaches you with an offer.

It can also be dangerous to link swap with another site. If you are both in a similar niche and find a few articles that will mutually benefit your readers, you can make a few link requests. You do not, however, want this to become a habit. If it does, and you're caught, you will be in a much worse position than when you started.

And lastly, you want to avoid what are called link networks, link farms, blog networks, and similar sites. These are basically sites that are built for the sole purpose of link building. Some are free, but more often than not they are paid, and can land your site in some pretty hot water with Google.

If you want to stay in line with Google's algorithm guidelines, you need to take a different approach. First and foremost, be genuine in your online activity. It's easy for people to tell when someone is acting only because they want something in return.

✓ **Leave Relevant Comments on Blog Posts**

Find people in your industry that are influencers or have a lot of traffic flowing through their blog. Take the time to read their posts, and if you have something *relevant* to say, say it. Link your Gravitar with your picture and website information, so if anyone wants to check out the person behind the words, they can follow back to your site. Don't just randomly comment on a blog and leave a link to one of your pages. This is a bit sketchy and can get you reported and penalized.

When you start to foster a genuine discussion and leave relevant insight, people will get curious about what you have to say and will start to check out your personal website. This will both help your SEO efforts while also adding referral traffic to your site.

✓ **Write Guest Blog Posts**

Guest blogging has become one of the greatest ways to manually build links back to your site—if it's done properly. Don't abuse this practice. Instead, seek out blog owners in your niche, where you have something worth saying that people want to read. When writing guest blog posts, write them as if they were being published on your site—with high quality. Be smart about this and use it to increase awareness about your expertise in your niche. Propose a few different ideas to some of the bloggers you'd like to write for, contact them genuinely, and make sure that you use a voice that's consistent with the writing style on your own site. If they like it, they'll publish it to their website or blog with a link back to your site. Again, don't over-do this and only write guest blog posts that are legitimate and relevant to your industry.

✓ Directories

Directory backlinks are links built through sites like Yelp, Yellow Pages, and more. There are different directories based on location, niche, business type, and even general directories. Pick a few of your favorite, maybe one in each category, and submit your URL to be added to the directory. This will create an immediate backlink. Just avoid over-doing this, as Google's algorithm will eventually catch on, especially if you submit hundreds of paid directory links.

✓ Broken-Link Building

One way to manually build links is through fixing broken-links. It's a great way to create seamless backlinks quickly and, quite frankly, easily. All you need to do is find a website that has broken-links on certain pages and report them to the owner of the site. It works best to suggest a few alternatives to fix the link and include yours in the list. As always, make sure that the websites you're looking for are relevant to your niche. Since you've gone out of your way to help the owner of the site, chances are high that they'll backlink back to your page. To make this process easier, download Google's Check my Links. Be aware though, that this isn't a guaranteed way to get a backlink.

✓ Infographics

Everyone loves infographics. They're easy to read and communicate the point in a straightforward way. With the popularity of visual data on the rise, use it to your advantage. Create an infographic, but make sure it's compelling and relevant. Include your website and start sharing. If it's good, you'll get a ton of backlinks from this method. If it's bad, try analyzing what went wrong and make a new one.

✓ **Watch Your Competitors**

Make sure you know what happens when your competition publishes new content. Do they get a lot of attention? If so, what are they doing to get that attention? Watching your competitors can give you valuable insight as to how to appeal to your target audience. It will also show you the best ways to get and build backlinks in your niche. Try downloading Monitor Backlinks for an easy way to watch your competitors *and* get in-depth reports on their actions.

✓ **Promote Content**

If you produce great content, you need to take the time to promote it. The initial outreach will be tedious, but if it gets global attention then you'll find yourself with hundreds, maybe thousands, of backlinks. Promote your content to other websites, on social media, and influential bloggers in your niche.

✓ **Donate**

Finally, consider donating to a nonprofit that you value. When you donate, most organizations will link back to your website and list you as a contributor. If you're going to donate for the sake of backlinks, make sure that you find a company that will give you one by doing a little research on Google.

You may also want to consider press releases for major events in your company. They may not get you much in terms of SEO value anymore, but informing the public of any newsworthy changes or milestones is a great way to bolster recognition. The main thing to understand when manually building links is that you want to show your target audience that you have something to offer. Work on becoming part of a community, fostering relationships, and increasing your reach in the online world. There are other manual ways of link building, but as Google continues to evolve, many have been pushed to the Black Hat column, and are punishable if used. Instead of putting all your effort into manually building links, it's time to start fostering natural link building, which is what we'll discuss in the next chapter.

Chapter 26: How to Take Advantage of Natural Link Building

After you've gone through and built some links manually, you'll see why you still need to put in some extra work. Manually building links will help get you where you need to be, but you also need to encourage natural link building.

Natural link building is when someone else—bloggers, influencers, website owners—link back to your content, information, or products because they find value in what you're saying or offering. They want to offer your webpage or products/services as a source or tool to their readers, and do so because your information is credible, reliable, and unique. Natural link building is when people do this without you having to ask them. It's widely considered one of the best, and safest, off-site SEO techniques to increase your rankings on SERPs.

So, let's take a deeper look at how to take advantage of natural link building. There are a few overarching things that you need to focus on to build natural links.

✓ **Produce High Quality Content**

The first step in building more natural links is creating quality content. Throughout this book, you'll notice that this is a common theme, because at the end of the day, *content is king*.

If your content is good, people will want to link back to it. If your content is poor, they won't.

Regardless of what stage of growth you're in, write for large audiences with confidence and authority. Find your voice and use it. You need to produce unique content to attract the attention you need to get natural links. We'll delve into all you need to know about content in Chapters 28 and 29, but for now just know that high quality content is one of the biggest ways to increase your natural links. It helps establish yourself as a trusted expert, which will grow your audience.

You can also write blogs and turn them into sharable videos or podcasts for an extra boost of content that appeals to different audiences.

✓ **Be Active on Social Media**

The next way to increase your natural links is by being active on social media and taking advantage of all of the opportunities that arise. Social media is used by almost everyone in the world—people are addicted to it. This is why it's so important to build a presence on social media. If you don't think you'll have the time, consider outsourcing your social media efforts for the best results.

Social media is almost like a modern-day newspaper. The only difference is that it's electronic and incorporates an interconnected network of individuals, giving more importance to the term "word of mouth."

When a friend, family member, or someone you trust shares an article on social media, it's far more likely that you'll read it than if you needed to search for it. Social media puts your business out there for people to see, and the more people who see it, the more will share, and thus the more natural links you'll gain. This ideology may even land you in front of major influencers and give you much stronger natural links than ever imagined.

Good posts on social media spread like wildfire, so make sure you put yourself in the position to be caught up in the flames. We dedicate an entire section on social media and will help walk you through it later on in the book.

When you create content, make it easy for people to share by including social media share buttons on your website and all pages. Create a profile for Facebook, Instagram, Twitter, LinkedIn, Pinterest, Google+, and YouTube, join groups, follow influencers, post content, and be active.

✓ **Get Discovered**

There are a variety of ways you can get involved in natural link building. Just because it is natural doesn't mean you can't actively do things to support it. Some suggestions and ideas include:

> ✓ E-mail Blasts: We'll talk more about this in a future chapter; however, when you blast out your content to your e-mail list, it will increase the changes of gaining internal links as people may mention it on their website, blog posts, social media, or other places they post content.

> ✓ Round-up Lists: Search out in your industry websites that do "round-up lists", which are lists that include quotes and links to experts in an industry. For example, we may search out sites that have done "Top 25 Quotes from SEO Experts" and e-mail that site offering up a quote for a link.

> ✓ Contribute To 3rd Party Sites: Different from guest posting, consider becoming a contributor to third-party sites. The best of these are invite only—for example, Brendan is a contributor to Entrepreneur.com, but even lesser known sites can be helpful. See if there are sites in your industry that you can regularly contribute content to and insert links either in that content or at least in your author by-line.

The bottom line here is getting out there so people can discover you, as it will naturally lead to more links for your site.

✓ **Maintain Consistency**

Finally, when you're trying to take advantage of natural link building the best thing you can do is be consistent. You might not see success right away, but if you post high quality content and are active on social media, you'll eventually see results. Aim for a few times per week and remember that timing is everything.

We understand that natural link building is difficult and often frustrating, but it's necessary to boost your off-site SEO efforts. While you're working on building up your website and credibility, don't neglect relationships. Find people in your niche or industry and work on developing personal or professional relationships with them. Sometimes, it's not about what you know, it's about who you know.

Combine these techniques with manual link building for the best result. In the next chapter, we'll let you in on a few secrets for getting "easy" links fast.

Marketing Masters Pro Tip: Create Tools That Foster Natural Links

One thing we often try to identify for clients is a scalable way for them to attain natural links. Some ideas of this include a widget that people would use and embed that links back to your site, a badge or award you can offer to other websites which creates a link back, or a helpful calculator or tool that has a link back to your site that people would want to use/share.

Think outside the box of ways you can provide help and value in your specific industry, and it could be a fantastic way to gain a huge amount of natural links back to your site!

Chapter 27: How to Get Easy Links

In addition to building links manually and naturally, there are a few other ways you can get easy links. We're not talking about Black Hat SEO link building strategies, but rather easy to implement link-building strategies that are at your fingertips. Start off by creating a list. Think about all the vendors, partners, suppliers, customers, and consultants that you do business with, either now or in the past. Write down their names, contact information, and relationship to you. After you've finished, take a look at your list. Using these contacts, you can get a substantial amount of easy links.

Reach out to those you've done business with and let them know that you've written a high-quality testimonial about doing business with them. It's more powerful to give a testimonial, since businesses will showcase that on their website or specific pages with a link back to your business. We've seen this strategy generate dozens and even hundreds of high-quality links for our clients.

You can also contact all your vendors and see if they would be able to link back to your site without a testimonial. This way, their prospective customers will be able to see how their products are being used in different businesses. It can help them increase their sales, and it helps you get external links.

In certain circumstances, offering free products or services in exchange for reviews can also generate links. Recall what we talked about in Chapter 25—never offer these things directly in exchange for a review. This is a direct violation of multiple search engines' SEO guidelines and can hurt more than help. Instead, if your product or service is good, those who review it might be so kind as to link to your site in one of their posts.

You should also take notice of the people that are mentioning your business, but not linking to your site. Reach out to them directly and see if they wouldn't mind including a link in an already published piece of content—this is much different than flat out asking to be mentioned.

Consider doing interviews or podcasts to get links. Almost every time you are interviewed or featured on a podcast, you'll likely gain a link back to your site. And surprisingly, many new podcasts (and even some established ones) are desperately looking for great guests for their shows.

If you implement all the previously discussed techniques to build your backlinks, you should see a significant rise in your rankings on SERPs. As we mentioned, be consistent, foster relationships, and continue to publish high-quality content that is worth reading.

Chapter 28: Generating the Right Amount of Content

After learning a bit about optimizing your on-site SEO and building links to your website both manually and naturally, you're probably curious about how to develop the perfect content. While there are a few different opinions as to what perfect content encompasses—besides captivating, high-quality writing—every marketing professional agrees that it revolves around three things: the right frequency, the structure of the content, and the right length.

When we talk about frequency, we're talking about how often you will be posting new content to your website, usually in the form of a blog. If you don't already have a blog, it's time to start one. It doesn't have to be big, but a blog gives you a platform to generate content that will help your overall SEO efforts, establish yourself as an expert, and provide a perfect place for people to link back to your site.

Make sure when you start a blog, you have it on your website's domain and not on a 3rd party domain like Blogger, Wordpress, or some other site. This will ensure your domain name gets credit for all the hard work you're about to do.

While most people think that a blog should be handled with the mentality "go big or go home," it doesn't have to be that way. The important thing—as with anything in the scheme of marketing—is consistency and reliability. It's a marathon, not a sprint. If you're just starting a blog, it's unlikely that you'll see much of a difference in terms of traffic and conversions from just a few posts, but if you develop a blog content strategy and stay with it, big things can happen. In fact, marketers who blog consistently on average will acquire 126% more leads than those who do not.[li] In our experiences, this number is even higher.

The reason for this success is that people love routines. As much as they hate to admit it, routines are an integral part of our lives. When our favorite companies or businesses have a routine that we can easily integrate into our own lives, it makes it that much easier to continue to read, listen, or watch new releases. But how often should you release this new information? A lot of people think they need to be giving their readers something new every day, or at least a few times a week. We think that's overkill, as do most of the highest influential bloggers.

In reality, all you need to do is release one to two new blog posts per week.

Pick a day of the week and maybe even a specific time, and each week publish your new content on that day and/or time. Don't miss a day, unless you announce it to your audience with a good reason to do so. If you have a crazy schedule or hectic lifestyle, get a content calendar and use your website's platform to release content automatically. WordPress has this as a built-in feature, and you can program your blog posts for the entire month or year if you'd like, or there are external applications you can use. Stay consistent and give it time.

Your readers aren't the only ones who will appreciate this. Google will actually reward you for posting consistently. Why? It consistently gives your readers—and the Internet in general—updated, new content that evolves as we do. Google favors this constant flow of information and rewards your website with better rankings. SEOblog published content that sums it up well: "If you're posting content regularly, you're more likely to keep positing, and thus Google can feel better about promoting your site as a good intellectual investment."[lii] Having a consistently published blog that emits strong, valuable content is an easy way to kill multiple birds with one stone. Getting a grasp on scheduling is fairly simple, but knowing how long to make each post and how to structure it is a different story.

Now don't be afraid to post more often, even as often as once a day, but make sure you remember that consistency and quality is much greater than quantity.

Chapter 29: Generating the Right Structure and Length of Content

You've got your content calendar created, researched long-tail keyword ideas for weekly blog posts, and now it's time to start writing. The best way to start is to have a plan. Understand how you'll want to structure your blog post and aim for a certain length with strategically placed keywords throughout. Each industry and niche will be different because each type of audience has a different reason for reading. Some may want in-depth technical analysis, and others may want a one-sentence summary that they can take away and use in their everyday lives.

The truth about blogs ends up being the same—people are busy, and more often than not, they skim through your blog. In fact, 43% of people admit to skimming blog posts.[liii] We wish we could say that every single word of your content will be read and cherished, but as you can see, that's not always the case.

This is why the structure and length of your blog is so important.

You want to appeal to those who will actually read your content *and* the dedicated skimmers each time you post a new blog. So how do you do that? Create a system and stick to it. We suggest sticking to the basic anatomy of a blog post, which includes an awesome headline, catchy picture, introduction, lead in, your main points, and conclusion, followed by an invitation for feedback and any related post and comments.[liv] Be practical and always ensure that everything you're writing points back to the value you're delivering in each post. The above anatomy follows the AIDA formula—an effective writing model to persuade and engage your readers. Structure your post so that it grabs the Attention of your readers, creates Interest in what you're saying, fosters Desire, and encourages Action.

As you write with that structure in mind, remember what we mentioned about skimming articles and blog posts. While you still want your posts to have good, strong information that is valuable to your readers, you can appeal to both worlds by implementing a lot of white space. Make it easy to scroll and easy on the eyes. Use multiple sub-headers, bulleted or numbered lists, easy to digest sentences, and bolded or emphasized text. The easier you make it for your readers, the more likely they'll come back. It also increases the chances of people actually reading your entire post.

Now the hard part comes. How long should your blog posts be? If people are skimming, what's the point in writing thousands of words instead of publishing short summaries of the important things? There is a point, and that point is stronger SEO.

Google favors longer articles, and churning out short, generic posts won't do you any good if you're trying to grow in the SERP rankings. The ideal length is *at least* 1,000 words per post. The longer your post, the more information Google can gather and analyze for your rankings. Longer posts make keyword placement easy and natural, increase the amount of internal and external links you can include, and give you a better way to incorporate relevant images. All of which influence your SEO efforts.

If you want to see better results in less time, structure your blog for easy readability and aim for a minimum of 1,000 words. If you have more to say, go for it! Don't limit yourself to 1,000 words. Sometimes, more words are better and can even help you outrank your competition.

Marketing Masters Pro Tip: Analyze the Competition

One of the easiest ways to answer the question of "How long should my blog post be" is to take the keyword you are targeting in that post and Google it. Take a look at the 5 top results for that keyword and see how long their content is.

In a study done by several expert SEO companies, they found that the vast majority of the time, the top content on the first page of Google has the most in-depth and longest content ranking displayed first. This is not to say that quality is not also highly important, but it is hard to escape the reality that Google loves long content.

If your 5 competitors for a keyword have 500-word posts, then writing 1,000 words will definitely put you ahead of the competition. If the competition has 3,500-word posts, then 1,000 words likely won't put you on the first page.

There is more to ranking than just length, but it is important, and it's critical to know what your competition is doing for a given keyword.

Chapter 30: How to Measure Your Success and Adapt

Now that you have a solid toolbox of SEO strategies that will help you propel forward in the SERPs all you need to do is implement them. As with anything you do to grow your business, make sure that you're measuring your success along the way so you can make changes as you go. When you measure your results, there's always room for improvement. We believe the first step in this process is creating your very own, personalized SEO dashboard. You can do this using Google Analytics and the built in SEO tools. Simply head over to your "Dashboard" and create a new one for SEO. You can add widgets for almost anything, including your users, bounce rate, revenue, goals, keyword searches and success, landing pages, pages per visit by keywords, and organic visits. Make sure that your website is linked to Google Analytics and they will take care of the rest.

Moz, a great SEO resource for both beginners and experts, has a great article on another 5 ways to measure your success, which we will walk through below:

1. **Search Engine Share of Referring Visits**[lv]

   This involves paying attention to where your traffic is coming from—either direct navigation, referred traffic, or search traffic. This helps you easily identify where you're excelling and where you have weaknesses.

2. **Search Engine Referrals**[lvi]

   Keep track of where your traffic is coming in terms of search engines. While most people use Google, Bing and Yahoo still exist and they have, albeit minimal, differences in their SEO guidelines. Compare how much traffic you're getting from each search engine so you can better optimize your site. If most of your audience is using Bing to visit your site, but you're not ranking well, you may need to adjust your SEO efforts to better reflect their algorithms.

3. **Visits Referred by Specific Search Engine Terms and Phrases**[lvii]

By keeping track of which keywords are successful and which aren't, you'll be able to better focus your efforts and appeal to your target audience more. You can also track searches being made for your niche that are getting the most traffic, which can help you align with what people want to read. Google Analytics can help you track these things by creating "goals" for you with specific rules.

4. **Conversion Rate by Search Query Term/Phrase**[lviii]

The main goal of all your SEO efforts is getting more conversions. This results in profits, and is the bottom line in business. Check your rankings and track your conversions using Google Analytics or your preferred application. Figure out which keywords are bringing in money and which aren't, then adjust. When you pay attention to this information, you open up a world of possibilities.

5. **Number of Pages Receiving at Least One Visit from Search Engines**[lix]

Finally, keep track of how many pages search engines are actually indexing. In other words, it's important to know how many of your pages are showing up on SERPs. The more pages that end up in the results, the more opportunities people have to visit your site. Look at your site's overall architecture and sitemaps in relation to these numbers and make changes as you move along. It's a process, but as long as you continue to work on it, you'll succeed.

You can use these methods and data to track your efforts in both on-site and off-site SEO factors and export them into easy to read PDF documents or e-mails. Remember to take notice of any keywords that are doing well, how many conversions you're getting from each blog post, and whether your organic traffic rises over time. If there are any areas where you're not seeing success, adapt and try again. It will take time to find something that works for you, as each industry is different, but if you pay attention to your efforts, you will be rewarded.

There are also a variety of 3rd party tools to assist in tracking metrics not available in Google Analytics. Agency Analytics is a fantastic tool for tracking and monitoring keyword rankings on Google as well as other key advertising metrics. Their software checks your placement for hundreds of pre-entered keywords every day, and provides you with intelligence on which direction your keywords are trending over time.

Moz offers a fantastic tool called Open Site Explorer, which allows you to examine and research your backlink profile and keep track of what links are the most important to you. Then, you can plug those links into Agency Analytics, which will actually monitor the links and alert you if a link ever is removed or goes offline.

And lastly, Google Webmaster Tools is a fantastic tool for keeping track of actual search queries. Since Google Analytics no longer provides keyword data for users logged into Google accounts, Webmaster Tools is your best bet to gain valuable keyword insights into what terms people are using to find your website.

Part 3 – Digital Advertising

Digital advertising is a booming industry, outpacing television advertising in recent years for the first time. Unlike organic SEO where you are doing work to get "free" organic traffic from search engines, digital advertising encompasses all forms and varieties of ads ranging from search engine ads to video ads, banner ads to e-mail campaigns, and everything in between.

There are always new and unique forms of digital advertising popping up online, each one having its own unique pros and cons.

Digital advertising requires a dedicated budget towards the ads, but beyond that requires a great deal of planning to ensure your investment will pay off and deliver an ROI.

Even if you don't want to hire the experts for your digital ad campaign, at the very least you should consult them to help you establish a plan, as digital advertising isn't as easy as just throwing some money towards ads. Well, it can be that easy, but the ROI likely won't be maximized without an experienced digital marketing consultant helping formulate a proper plan.

Digital advertising is multi-pronged, often encompassing a variety of ad mediums, platforms, and placement types, which have to work together to form a cohesive campaign. If you throw off one piece of the puzzle, it will often lead to wasteful spending and an undesirable number of conversions.

In this part, we'll dive into some of the most common types of digital advertising, and offer some tips and tricks to get the most out of your ad spend and maximize the effectiveness and ROI of your digital advertising campaigns. We'll focus a good deal of information around Google Ads as it is the most widely used platform for most small to medium sized businesses running digital advertising campaigns, and also incredibly robust.

When used together with other marketing strategies in this book, digital advertising can offer an outstanding ROI and even help improve the ROI of your other marketing efforts.

Chapter 31: Understanding the Different Types of Digital Advertising

The basic premise of marketing is simple: promote your business through a targeted product or service. It doesn't matter if you use print advertising, radio advertising, or digital advertising; the goal is the same. However, with the rise in the use of technology, the Internet, and social media platforms, digital marketing has gained traction as one of the best ways to get in front of your target audience. Forbes published a statistic from eMarketer in 2019 indicating just how relevant digital advertising has become. They concluded that in 2018, digital spending in the U.S. would be $94 billion—in comparison, TV would total $72 billion.[lx] The largest portion of that $94 billion digital spending will come from advertising, which accounts for $48 billion.[lxi] Digital advertising has pushed past televised advertising, which is almost unfathomable considering the history of commercials. The world is shifting, and if you want to be successful you need to shift with it.

That's where digital advertising comes in. It's a big umbrella term, encompassing every kind of advertising you come across on the Internet. It could be a banner, pop-up, sidebar, social media, e-mail, or more. To give you more clarification, we're going to walk through the different types of digital advertising that you may come across on a given day.

Search Engine Ads & Ad Platforms

This type of digital advertising uses a bidding process against other companies to purchase keywords that will help push your page higher in the rankings of SERPs. It's worth noting, however, that these ads are totally separate from organic listings and bear no impact on one another.

They're textual advertisements that are usually on the top or sides of Google, Bing, and other search engines.[lxii] Google Ads is the most popular platform to use, but other search engines offer this as well. All search engine ads are on a Cost Per Click (CPC) basis, also referred to as pay per click (PPC). However, most platforms including Google Ads also offer other ad placements such as digital banner ads, video ads, map ads, and more. For these, the most common cost distributions are Cost Per Action (CPA), Cost Per Mille/Thousand (CPM/CPT), Cost Per Click (CPC), and Cost Per View (CPV).

Cost Per Action (CPA) is a type of advertisement where the publisher gets paid only if someone makes a sale as a direct result of clicking on an advertisement. It's nice because the risk falls on the publisher instead of your company, but it's often not as lucrative as other options.

Cost Per Mille/Cost Per Thousand (CPM) is a bit different. The price paid by the advertiser depends on how many people visit the site each day—measured in thousands—and the number of pages where the ad appears. It's a bit less common, primarily used for businesses that are highly competitive and that use very common keywords. They end up paying more per click due to the popularity of keywords, which is a major reason why businesses don't predominantly use this method. It's also riskier than CPA or PPC, but it does give your company a boost in visibility.

Pay Per Click (PPC) is the most commonly used type of digital advertising, primarily because you only have to pay for the ad if someone clicks on it. The Cost Per Click (CPC) will differ depending on the publisher, but equates to how much each individual click will cost you. Take the time to determine what your maximum CPC is for each ad if you want to see a positive ROI. The nice thing about PPC is that it's found all over the Internet and social media, so it gives you a wide range of options. For instance, if you decide to use PPC with Google Ads, you can bid against other businesses on keywords that you think will be popular with your target audience. The more popular it is, the more expensive it is—the higher the CPC is. The goal is to keep your CPC as low as possible while maximizing traffic and conversions—another great reason why long-tail keywords are essential.

PPC is great because it can do a lot of different things for you. It can help you get more targeted traffic, give you immediate traffic, reach more customers, and target local customers.[lxiii] It is considered the quickest, cheapest way to reach a large, targeted audience. It's easy to track success using PPC, and it's easy to fix anything that's not working. Plus, it's cost effective and adjustable for any budget. You can use bid modifiers for location, times/dates, and devices to help reduce spending and target strong keywords that will resonate with your audience. It's a fairly simple process that can be done in Google Ads, but you need to review all of the information specific to your campaign to ensure you're making accurate adjustments.

The above types of payment/cost structures are primarily applied to Google Ads and Bing, but you can also apply CPC to things like digital display ads, native advertising, and others, although it's rarely done.

The two most common Google Ads advertisements are text ads and responsive ads. They're most commonly used by Google Ads and appear at the top, bottom, or side of a website. For text ads, your focus is the text. You get a headline, descriptive sentences for a description, and no images. Use strong keywords to grab your audience's attention and be brief, yet compelling. For responsive ads, your focus is still the text, but you can include an image. Responsive ads make a strong impact because they're visual and tend to leave more of an impression on your audience. Google will "automatically adjust their size, appearance, and format to fit just about any available ad space,"[lxiv] so just choose your images and the rest will be taken care of.

Display Ads

These types of advertisements are clearly displayed on a third-party website. When you visit a website, display ads are noticeable advertisements that are often related to the content of the third-party website or your previous search history. They're used in specific areas of a website that the owner has designated for paid advertising, and are the most common type of digital advertisements. There are countless ways for your company to use display ads, most often as a banner placed either on the top of a page, the bottom, the sides, or running throughout the content.

However, as digital marketing has evolved, you can now create your display ads with more personality than before.

You can stick to a basic banner with text, static images, and some sort of CTA, or you can infuse them with video, flash advertisements, floating banners, and more. You can also purchase pop-up ad space, which is also considered a type of display ad. Depending on your needs, your budget, and your audience, display ads can be the perfect option. Display ads "are more suitable for long sales processes than for selling high volumes."[lxv] It's also important to understand that when you use display ads, you want to make sure your images, videos, and all-around design captivate the viewer. Avoid using stock images or texts. Show the world your brand through these ads and make sure your audience can quickly and easily understand what it is you're advertising.

Native Advertising

If you've seen a sponsored listing or post, you've seen native advertising. They float through your feeds or recommended pages based on your search history, and almost seem like they were posted by one of your friends or pages that you follow. Native advertising can be helpful when relevant to the page it is on. For example, if you're reading an article already about "How to save money on car insurance", rather than a car insurance company plastering an ad on that page, they could natively advertise their cost comparison tool, which saves drivers 20% on car insurance. It is seen as more trustworthy and authoritative than just a traditional banner or display ad placement.

Remarketing/Retargeting

We'll talk about this in more detail later, but this type of digital advertisement basically takes your current audience—the ones who have visited your website—and drops a cookie on their device so you can follow them as they travel around the Internet. Your ads will continue to appear to them on different websites to remind them of your product or service.[lxvi] This is a fantastic tool in conjunction with all advertising as it helps increase ROI through getting targeted people back to your website.

Video Ads

Video ads are like mini-commercials made for the Internet and are a great alternative to attract customers to certain products. You have a lot more freedom with video ads. You can go the traditional advertising route, or you can make a video that teaches someone something. You can tell a story or demonstrate a product. It's all about subtle advertising that attracts attention, rather than persuading people to act. You can run video ads primarily on social media and YouTube.

Social Media Ads

We'll talk more about everything social media in its own section, but it's worth mentioning here because of the relevance of social media in today's world. Everyone is on Facebook, Twitter, Instagram, LinkedIn, Reddit, Tumblr, Pinterest, or some sort of social platform. This makes social media the perfect opportunity to convert people into customers. Plus, social media ads are easily customizable and can be targeted toward different audiences. In fact, almost every platform allows you to specify your target audience's demographics, region, profession, education, interests, and more. There are no limits to what you can achieve with social media advertisements, and you can use them on Facebook, LinkedIn, Instagram, Twitter, Pinterest, and more.

Another bonus of social media advertisements is the potential for people to like and share them, as well as comment and interact with them, thus giving you a greater reach and more potential conversions. Social media advertising should use more visual aspects to draw customers in and elicit a feeling of connection, along with catchy headlines that make people want to learn more.

There are many types of digital advertisements, and each has their own benefit. As we begin to dive deeper, we should first take a look at when we should be using each type in our marketing efforts and campaigns.

Chapter 32: When to Use Digital Advertisement

Before you start implementing different types of digital advertisements at every opportunity, you need to first define your advertising and business goals. Consider them individually and take time to brainstorm and write them down. When you start with a specific set of objectives, you'll be able to better choose which type of digital advertising to use, measuring your success more efficiently down the road. Your goals can be anything from increased brand awareness to selling more products, or you can define a list of multiple goals. As long as you take the time to define them, and write them down, you'll be off to a good start.

Having these goals will not only help you measure success more effectively, but you'll also have a better understanding of when you should be using different types of digital advertising.

As we just discussed, SEO is integral to every business' online success, but it is a long-term investment in your marketing. Digital advertising can be implemented immediately, and can give the fast results you need to see your business grow. Digital advertising gives you the ability to target a specific audience right from the beginning, regardless of how well you rank, and see almost immediate results. If you have a working website and a product or service to sell, you could start using digital advertising today and see results this afternoon.

Digital advertising can be targeted to reach the exact people you need it to reach, without anything extra. Using different platforms and different social media channels, you can segment your advertising efforts based on demographics, geographic location, interests, and more.[lxvii] This allows you to effectively reach your audience without much invested time commitment. It's another reason why the real key to success with PPC advertising is correctly identifying and properly targeting your audience. It's how you get people to click. There are different kinds of PPC ads, and each one depends on your business type and preferences. You can use campaigns through Google Ads that put you at the top of the search results or at the top of popular websites. You get similar exposure of SEO efforts without having to wait years for your efforts to pay off.

SEO and digital advertising are two independent marketing strategies that are important in their own way, but aren't mutually exclusive. SEO and digital ads can support one another. Imagine being the #1 organic result and the #1 ad for a given keyword.

What's great about PPC digital advertising is that there's no minimum on spending. You can try it out with the smallest of budgets and let it prove itself. PPC gives you minimal risk with the potential for maximum reward in a quick and painless manner. With that said, results can vary depending on your budget. What works with a $10 per day budget won't be the same as a $100 or $1,000 per day budget or more. The beauty is that you can easily cut what isn't working, and scale what is working.

In a nutshell, you should use digital advertising when you need fast, immediate results and are okay with paying a premium. Because of the speed, convenience, and targeting options of digital ads, they will often times cost more for traffic than other advertising mediums, but should deliver strong results due to their flexibility and customization.

Chapter 33: Optimizing Advertising by Device

Did you know that your ad metrics tend to be dramatically different for mobile, tablet, and computer users? Not only are there different buying behaviors on each device, the way your ad is displayed can be starkly different from one device to the next. Tailoring your advertisements for each device will save you money on your ads, increase your conversions, and make sure that you tailor your calls to action appropriately.

Consider this example: You know the ads that pop up on news sites that have a tiny, microscopic "X" in the corner? Those ads are no problem on a laptop, just point and click. But closing one on a smartphone, or even a tablet, can cause customer frustration and even fallout. You might end up still paying because someone clicked on your advertisement, but if it was an accident, you just paid to annoy a potential customer, and even potentially leave a bad impression for your brand. It's therefore important to differentiate mobile ads vs. tablet ads vs. desktop ads.

Or perhaps you have a product that requires research before buying. You may run Google search ads and find that your conversion rate is 5% on desktop but only 0.2% on mobile. In this case, you may want to set a negative bid adjustment for mobile or even omit mobile all together so you are not paying as much for mobile clicks as you are for desktop clicks.

When it comes to mobile advertisements, you're going to want to tailor them to the mobile experience. One of the simplest ways to do this is to have a "click to call" feature. This means that when someone clicks the ad, the option to call the number appears on their phone. It doesn't give them time to put it off, and it makes it extremely easy for those who want to take immediate action. People browse while they're on their mobile device for one of two reasons: boredom or necessity. Tailoring your digital advertisements on smartphones to be different from those on laptops will give you better results. Your display ads should be different so they can be easily seen, and your pop-ups need to encourage less reading and more action. You might purchase a banner ad for people browsing on a laptop but focus on video ads for those on smaller devices. The important thing to understand is that every digital advertisement is not created equal, depending on the device through which it's being viewed. It's important to have the right creative difference for each device, including your verbiage, type of ad, and CTA.

Now, that's just one thing to pay attention to, but the most important thing, and we can't say this enough, is to invest the time and money into optimizing your website experience for mobile. Your website needs to be fast and easy to navigate, and shouldn't have ad placements that interfere with the user experience. People don't have the patience to sit and watch a blue line banner ad stay stuck in the same place forever. They'll just move onto the next website, which will often belong to your competitors.

In Google Ads, you can use the bid modifiers we discussed to decrease bids 100% and remove ads from your mobile devices. This comes in handy for the tiny "X" example mentioned above and other device specific actions. On the other hand, you can increase your bids for mobile devices by XX% if you find that mobile users are converting better than desktop. This all relies on you, your knowledge of your business, and the quality of your ads, along with the amount of time and resources you have at the ready to create an entirely separate PPC campaign optimized for mobile and the results that come with it.

Although they can save or make you a ton of money, bid modifiers "don't act in a vacuum. That is one of the core challenges of enhanced campaigns. You can have modifiers for device, time, and even geography all firing on one keyword. This can make adjusting keyword bids extremely difficult as the data gets more blurred with each automated adjustment."[lxviii] Your analytics need to be on point and very detailed to hit your sweet spot. But once you do, you'll see a world of difference.

Case Study: The Importance of Mobile

We didn't think we would say this as soon as we are, but apparently, we're getting old. We recall a few years ago fighting the shift to mobile, thinking that in certain industries and situations, people would never convert on mobile. For example, filling out a credit card application online, is something that we thought would always be done at a desk on a computer and not on a mobile phone.

To our surprise, we've been proven wrong. In 2019, over 85% of the clients we work with have more mobile traffic than desktop/laptop, and even in industries which require research or have a lengthy "checkout" process, users are converting equally or better on mobile than desktop.

While this still shocks us, it's something we've learned to accept, and rather than be stubborn, we embrace this through driving more mobile traffic, enhancing mobile websites, and focusing on where the data is leading us. Remember to always analyze your data, as it will always be unique vs. industry averages and lead you to the best decisions for your advertising situation.

Get yourself prepared for mobile, or get left behind.

Chapter 34: Branching Out to Other Types of Advertisements

In Chapter 31 we talked about all the different types of digital advertising that are available for use. If you're like most people, you tend to stick to what you know, which is often purchasing Google Ads, display ads, and growing an e-mail-marketing list. These are great tactics that every business should be using, but you need to branch out if you want to see more success.

To successfully branch out to other types of digital advertisements, you should first and foremost focus on profit and exposure. Improving your click through rate—how many people click on your links—may be one of your goals, but if your audience isn't acting, you may want to reconsider your advertising. Since almost all types of digital advertising can be done on a budget, start out with your resources spread out. Invest in a few different strategies and keep track of what's working and what's not. If you've never made a video ad, try it. Share it on social media. Attach it to your e-mails, website, or signatures and see what happens. Run some YouTube ads with it. The main thing to remember is that you want to spread out. It's risky to keep all your eggs in one basket.

You should also pay special attention to what's happening in the offline world. We've seen a lot of businesses fall behind because they get tunnel vision and focus on primarily digital advertising, but truthfully everything's changing. Digital advertising is expanding to reach our lives even when we're not connecting to the Internet. Don't believe us? When's the last time you saw a digital billboard? How about one of those digital traffic signs? A digital store sign for, say, the grocery store or mall? All are considered digital advertising since they can be changed remotely based on the time of day, passing traffic, and date. In fact, these types of advertisements are managed similarly to how you manage a Google Ad—which is why they're considered digital advertising.

Old school offline advertising—newspapers, billboards, television advertisements—is slowly starting to make its way into the digital world, and it's becoming more and more attractive for people to migrate back towards. As these offline advertising methods become digitalized, they come along with immense data, which was part of the main lure towards digital in the first place.

Speaking of which, you should be using both static ads and dynamic ads in your efforts. Static ads are unchanging. Once you upload them, they stay the way you originally designed. They're good for low maintenance brand awareness and are budget friendly. Everyone will see the same ad, or one of a few similar variations, regardless of their demographics and interests.[lxix] Unfortunately, if the same audience sees them time and time again, it'll become annoying, and some viewers may even become immune to their effects[lxx].

This doesn't mean stay away from them completely; it just means that you want to add a bit of diversity to your ads.

Running a few static ads and a few dynamic ads is a good way to combat this. Dynamic ads reduce the chance of people becoming immune to a message and can lead to more conversions. Why? Because they "use content from your website to target your ads to searches."[lxxi] They are targeted and segmented toward different audiences based on what people are searching for. You can choose to target your ads based on different landing pages from your standard ad groups (all the webpages you're currently running ads against), different categories, and your page feed.[lxxii]

Dynamic ads can be personalized based on a user's cookies and increase the chances of you turning a visitor into a customer. You can display products, prices, phone numbers, different images and CTAs, and more. Dynamic ads can follow consumer behavior, which means that you can adapt with your visitors based on whatever they're searching for or what websites they're visiting. Dynamic ads can be purchased through ad platforms that distribute your ad across various targeted websites.[lxxiii] The only problem with these types of ads is that they are harder to create and require more stability in a website, so you won't be able to use them if you offer a different deal each day.

Again, the important thing to remember is that you want to use multiple avenues of digital advertising to better appeal to your target audience. Try to use a combination of the above, in addition to the different types of digital advertising we discussed in Chapter 31. Doing so will give you a greater chance of increasing your ROI. Implement your digital advertising, measure for results, and then adapt until you find something that works best for you.

Chapter 35: Understanding the Types of Keyword Matching Available

Unless otherwise stated, when we talk about keywords and digital advertising, we're referring to anything you run through Google Ads, Bing, or Yahoo. Like we went over in Chapter 31, PPC advertising uses a bidding process against other companies to purchase keywords that will help push your page higher in the rankings of SERPs. When you're doing this bidding, you'll need to choose a "keyword match type." Google Ads describes a keyword match type as something that helps "control which searches on Google can trigger your ad."[lxxiv] Each match type has a different parameter that will tell Google how aggressively or restrictively you want to match your advertisements to keyword searches.[lxxv]

The three main types of keyword matching are broad match, phrase match, and exact match. Google Ads also uses a negative match and broad match modifier, which we'll also review. Each of the types of keyword matching has its own advantages and disadvantages, but after learning more about them you'll have a better understanding of when to use each one.

When you use a broad match type, you end up giving your keyword more potential traffic because the parameters are very general and include a lot of different search potential. When you use a narrow match type, your ads will be shown less, but to a more targeted group of people—people that are more likely to act. We recommend starting with broad match keywords, running your ads, and then discovering which actual search terms work best for you. From there, you can add those terms to your campaign in a more narrowly targeted manner to have greater control over your campaign in the long run.

Broad Match

Whenever you are creating a PPC campaign through Google Ads, broad match is set as default unless otherwise changed. This means that your ad will show on searches for a keyword or phrase, even if a user's search includes misspellings, synonyms, related searches, and other relevant variations. [lxxvi] It gives you a higher opportunity for visibility but also means that your audience isn't as targeted so you might not see as many conversions. You can take broad match a step further by adding a modifier (+) to the keyword.

Let's look at an example. If you add the keyword "Designer" to your Google Ads set as broad match, your ad would show up if someone Googled "Designer," but it would also show up for "Graphic Designer," "Concrete Designer," and "Designer Handbags." You can quickly see how broad match is exactly that—broad—and often requires some controls or parameters to ensure your ads show up only for relevant searches.

Phase Match

This setting needs to be customized and changed from broad match, but still allows for some variation from exact wording. If you use a keyword and someone searches for that keyword, with additional words either before or after, your ad will still show up. However, according to Google Ads, "if a word is added to the middle of the phrase, or if the words in the phrase are reordered in any way," your ad won't appear. Your phrase needs to be connected by the searcher. This type of keyword matching will target a specific audience more than broad matching, but not as much as exact matching, giving you a middle ground of the two extremes. This is good for new businesses that might not know their customers well but want to try and narrow them down.

Let's look at an example. If you add the keyword "Graphic Designer" to your Google ads set as phrase match, your ad would show up if someone Googled "Graphic Designer for Free," "Cheap Graphic Designer," and "Graphic Designer in New York." These may or may not be what you are trying to target, but the main difference is that if someone Googled "designer" without the word "graphic," your ad would not appear.

Exact Match

Finally, another one of the most important keyword matching you can set your PPC campaigns to is exact match. In this situation, your ad will only show if it matches the exact keyword or phrase that someone is searching for, or a very close variation. The main takeaway here is that search intent needs to be the same in order for an exact match keyword to show your ad. You can add or remove function words, like prepositions, conjunctions, and articles, that don't impact the underlying search intent.[lxxvii] This type of keyword matching gives you the most control in determining who sees your ad, which can translate to more visits to your website, and more sales. Exact keyword matching is perfect for businesses that know the search patterns of their targeted audience.

Let's look at an example. If you add the keyword "Experienced Graphic Designer" to your Google ads set as exact match, your ad would show up if someone Googles that exact phrase. If someone searches for "Cheap Graphic Designer," "Graphic Designer," or "Designer," your ad would not appear. You can see this provides a much higher level of control over who sees your ad, but in doing so, narrows your audience dramatically hence reducing potential search traffic.

Negative Keywords

While those are the three main types of matching, another important topic to understand is negative keywords. Negative keyword matching is when you basically tell Google Ads what you don't want to target, therefore excluding specific keywords from displaying your ads. This can help you avoid confusion for similar keywords or unrelated search phrases. You can use negative keywords across broad matching, phrase matching, and exact matching, but be careful. Too many negative keywords can cause your ad to reach fewer customers, and can even be omitted depending on placement and length of a search.

Let's look at an example. Let's say you add the keyword "Graphic Designer" as a phrase match but you also add the negative keywords "Free" and "Cheap." This will ensure your ad shows up when someone searches "Experienced Graphic Designer," but if they were to search "Free Graphic Designer" or "Graphic Designer for Free," your ad would not appear.

For best results, focus on implementing a good mixture of the three positive keyword matching techniques in your PPC campaigns while adding strategic negative keywords to ensure your ads are not appearing to the wrong audience.

Case Study: Finding the Best Keywords

Any good digital marketing agency is going to do keyword research at the start of an ad campaign to identify the best keywords to focus on.

We had a client in an industry where the keyword research was leading us nowhere. Hour after hour, we would research keywords, and the volume estimates came back at 0 searches. We looked at competitors, and none of them were running Google Ads, so we couldn't piggyback off any of their keywords, either.

We told the client we would run a 2 month experimental campaign on "broad match" for some very broad words. We ended up wasting about 90% of their budget, but we knew that would happen going in. The 10% that was successful helped us find some of the best keywords in this industry that we wouldn't have otherwise found.

Now, this may sound wasteful, but when left with no other options, this is a fantastic strategy and, over the last 3 years, has seen a fantastic ROI. Had we not been okay with wasting a little budget upfront, we never would have seen the strong ROI we have and continue to see for this client.

Chapter 36: How to Take Advantage of Ad Extensions

When you're using Google Ads for your search advertisement efforts, there are many different options available to take your ads to the next level. Whether you're utilizing a simple text ad or a responsive ad, you want your audience to have all the relevant information they need to take the next step. That's where ad extensions come in.

Ad extensions are simply extra snippets of information—including business location, phone number, business rating, current call wait times, images, or different links—that you can incorporate to your Google Ad while it's running to increase customer awareness/engagement.[lxxviii] You can either use automatic or manual ad extensions. Let's go over both.

Manual Ad Extensions

As the name suggests, manual ad extensions require you to personally fill in your business details, rather than creating a self-generated summary. While this might seem like more work, the benefits far outweigh the effort, primarily because manually entering the information gives you more control. You can customize specific fields and convey information in the simplest, most basic terms so you don't waste space. Some of the different types of manual ad extensions include: sitelink, callout, location, affiliate location, structured snippet, call, message, app, price, and promotion.[lxxix] To make sure that you understand each, we are going to briefly walk through them all. It should also be noted that you have the option to create different extensions for each of your campaigns, so that you can easily identify which extension is bringing you the most success.

- ✓ **Sitelink Extensions** – this involves incorporating additional links to the search ad you're currently running. You can include independent links to your website's different pages, testimonials, contacts, and more. It gives your audience an opportunity to follow a direct link that might be more relevant to what they're looking for. Mobile and desktop extensions have different limits—four and six, respectively—so make sure you take that into account when entering them. If you enter six, keep in mind that the last two won't show up on mobile searches.

✓ **Callout Extensions** – these are similar to sitelink extensions, but they allow you to include textual information below the link. This is perfect for direct CTAs and any additional relevant information.

✓ **Location Extensions** – these give your audience details on store location, hours of operation, and, if their location services are enabled, their distance from the store. It's imperative to use these types of extensions if you want to increase your in-store traffic. Set up a Google My Business Account and connect it to Google Ads. Whether you use this extension or not, this is a smart move for all businesses with a storefront.

✓ **Affiliate Location Extensions** – these are like location extensions, but are more commonly used for nationwide companies and brands. This type of extension will help potential customers find the best retail chains to buy your products.[lxxx] It will appear below your text ad information and will say "Available at Target," or whichever retailer you wish to advertise.

✓ **Structured Snippet Extensions** – these extensions give you three additional header lines of text so you can highlight additional, important aspects of your business.[lxxxi] You can include anything from courses, destinations, models, shows, neighborhoods, types, amenities, styles, and more. It really depends on what you want to add. Keep it clean and simple and focus on adding value rather than merely more words.

✓ **Call Extensions** – as you might guess, a call extension makes your business' phone number visible on your ad. This is beneficial because people won't have to click on your ad and spend time searching for your number. When a search is made on a mobile device, all the person needs to do is click on your phone number and it will automatically contact your business. If you use this extension, make sure that someone is always around to answer incoming calls.

✓ **Message Extensions** – younger generations are more likely to do business with a company they can text, instant, or direct message than those they can't. Make sure you're updating your technology and offer alternative ways of getting in contact. A lot of people are steering away from phone calls due to automation and time constraints. Luckily, you can enable message extensions so that any potential customer can send a message over e-mail or a phone call.

✓ **App Extensions** – if your business has a mobile app, you can display it directly on your Google Ads by using the app extension. Simply connect it and your thumbnail icon, name, and customizable call to action button will be shown directly below your ad.[lxxxii]

✓ **Price Extensions** – these are great extensions, but are only visible if you're in the #1 ranking place on a SERP.[lxxxiii] If you're selling a specific product or service and know that your pricing is competitive and appealing, you have the option to include it on your Google Ad. This is great because it mainstreams the process for potential customers and gives them a quick and easy way to compare prices. Keep track of your conversions using CPA to see whether using price extensions are helping or hurting your business.

✓ **Promotion Extensions** – when your business is running a special promotion, using a promotion extension will make it easy for potential customers to see. You can advertise ongoing deals, sales, price matching, or coupons, and they'll show up next to a price tag icon. This is a good way to stand apart from your competition, especially if you're in a highly competitive market.

In the past, Google Ads also had the opportunity to implement a review extension, where a strong public review was made visible on your ad. As of January 2018, this extension has unfortunately been discontinued and does not show for advertisers.[lxxxiv] Google is constantly both adding and removing extensions, so check their website often for the most up-to-date extensions available.

You can set up all the above extensions using a simple drop-down menu in Google Ads. For manual extensions, enter the information that you want to be highlighted. You can do this in bulk or for specific campaigns; it just depends on whether you want to use different information per campaign.

Automatic Ad Extensions

In contrast, there are also automatic ad extensions. This is something that Google does on its own to create a unique extension for your ad. If you want to avoid any surprises, you should use manual ad extensions, as they will override any automatic ad extensions that Google has put in place. You can also manually opt-out of each of the automatic ad extensions on Google Ads, or remove them altogether. However, the automatic ad extensions generate different content, which we'll review now.

✓ **Consumer Ratings Extensions** – like the above review extension that was discontinued, but without any written testimonials. This will generate your average rating out of 10 based on multiple different sources and surveys.

✓ **Previous Visit Extension** – this reminds your visitors how often they've visited your website in the past x-amount of days.

- ✓ **Seller Ratings Extension** – again, like consumer ratings, your seller rating is generated and represented visually with starts (out of 5).

- ✓ **Dynamic Sitelink Extension** – this will link your potential customers to a popular offering or piece of relevant content on your website.[lxxxv]

- ✓ **Social Extension** – depending on the different social accounts your website is linked to, this extension highlights some of your most relevant social information. It will change based on number of followers or likes, and may even include images of friends.

- ✓ **Dynamic Structured Snippets** – like structured snippets in manual ad extensions, these will show relevant information to your visitors. The main difference is that the information is automated based on what Google thinks is the most relevant.

Ad extensions play a critical role in making sure your ads receive valuable traffic and clicks. We've implemented them on campaigns that were previously running without them and have literally seen campaigns become 100x more effective and drive hundreds of thousands of new impressions just because the extensions help the ads stand out against the competition.

While there are many different options to choose from, you won't be able to implement all of them at once for each of your campaigns—Google just doesn't allow it. Instead, if you turn on all the extensions that you want to use, Google will keep track of customer behavior and "choose the best performing combinations of ad extensions to display."[lxxxvi] This makes ad extensions easy to use with a relatively non-existent risk, while increasing your click through rate and conversions. Not taking advantage of extensions is a huge waste of potential in digital advertising. Spend a few minutes setting up your manual ad extensions and turning off any unwanted automated ad extensions and you're ready to go.

Chapter 37: Utilizing Remarketing

In addition to the different types of ad extensions available, you can target different advertisements to people who have already visited your website. It doesn't matter how they got there—whether through Google Ads, display ads, e-mail marketing, a billboard—but keeping track of your website's visitors can give you a special advantage in marketing. You can direct special promotions, CTAs, and more toward those who've already shown an interest in your products or services.

Remarketing, sometimes referred to as retargeting, is simply a form of digital advertising that "enables sites to show targeted ads to users who have already visited their site."[lxxxvii] It gives you an opportunity to stay at the forefront of your visitors' minds by following them around and reminding them of your brand, product, services, or business.

It may seem a bit creepy, but it's how some of the most successful companies advertise.

Think about it. Have you ever been considering ordering a new pair of shoes, do a little mindless browsing just to see what's out there, and then find your Facebook feed littered with advertisements for the shoes you were looking at? If you don't understand how it works, it can throw you off. But remarketing is a common technique in digital advertising that many companies utilize. The conversion rates from remarketing are high, so you should be utilizing it if you want to increase your ROI.

So how exactly does remarketing work? Let's take a look.

The basic premise of remarketing involves adding a piece of code into the backend of your website. This is easy if you're already taking advantage of Google Ads, as they have a specific "tag" or "pixel" that you can copy and paste into your HTML code. This is simply known as the Google remarketing code. In the digital advertising world, it's well known that "you can customize the code for different pages to correspond to more defined categories."[lxxxviii] For each different code that you have, on each different page, you can direct certain visitors to specific remarketing audiences. We'll talk more about segmenting your remarketing lists in the next chapter.

Once you have these codes on your website, they will drop a cookie to every visitor that browses your page. This cookie will follow your visitors around as they surf the web, reminding them of your company, website, products, or services. You determine the criteria for people who receive this cookie, and can measure its effectiveness through CTR and conversions—both of which tend to be much higher with remarketing ads in comparison to display ads. In fact, "Remarketing audiences tend to have 2-3 times higher click through rates"[lxxxix] than other types of advertisements. The benefit of remarketing is that it allows you to show people who have already expressed an interest in your company a highly targeted advertisement, usually with a stronger CTA than a generic display ad or PPC ad, or with some sort of special offer to encourage a sale.

It's estimated that the Google Display Network can reach over 92% of Internet users.[xc] That means that your remarketing might not extend to Bing or Yahoo, but it shouldn't make too much of a difference since most of the world sticks with Google search or browses third party sites which use advertising through Google's Display Network.

This is an extremely powerful marketing tool because it gives you the opportunity for increased brand awareness even when people aren't physically on your site or social media page. The more exposure you have, the more highly recognized your brand is, which leads to higher trust, dependability, and sales.

You can set your remarketing ads to different parameters in Google Ads, including:[xci]

- ✓ The time someone spent on your site
- ✓ The frequency of a person's visits
- ✓ The bid amount for keywords
- ✓ The type of displays that encouraged action
- ✓ The geographic location of a visitor
- ✓ The demographics of your audiences
- ✓ The pages that have the most views

- ✓ If someone added something to their cart and never checked out—and what the item was

If you're just starting out, try remarketing to everyone who visits your website's homepage to understand how it works and increase the exposure of your ads. You can also use the basic information of your visitors to determine a generic type of audience that visits your website, and run ads to them using Google Ads and PPC. Remarketing is great in so many ways and can help you identify a target audience you hadn't considered before.

However, don't get lazy and keep your remarketing list as one general audience forever. As you start to get the hang of it and understand the backend of things, move on to segmenting your remarketing lists. This is where you'll see the biggest ROI. We'll go over how to properly segment your remarketing lists in the next chapter.

Marketing Masters Pro Tip: Remarketing with Little Traffic

Many small businesses only have a few hundred visitors to their website a month. Most of the large remarketing services only focus on brands with 6 figures of traffic or more per month. Google Ads allows remarketing for lists as small as 1,000 trackable visitors per list segmentation.

While segmenting your list is important (as we'll discuss in the next chapter), it's okay to run a remarketing campaign to every website visitor if that's what you need to do based on your traffic. The results may not be as strong, but they will still be far better than not doing remarketing.

Chapter 38: Properly Segmenting Remarketing Lists

Now that you understand what remarketing is and why it's beneficial, you should know that whenever you can you should avoid keeping your remarketing generic and avoid segmenting your lists. It restricts you in your messaging and leads to ineffective connection with your audience.

Segmenting your remarketing lists means that rather than sending the same remarketing ads to everyone who visits your website, you'll start to differentiate categories like behavior, search terms, and viewing history by separating them into sublists or new audience groups. This is a more direct approach, where you learn to better advertise to people who've shown an interest rather than just stumbled upon your site.

If you've put together a general remarketing strategy, now is the time for analysis and actions to bring your strategy to the next level. Take some time and think about which groups of people you want to target. Do you want to target people based on a product page they visited? How long they spent on your site? Based on their demographics? There are thousands of possibilities and you can create a segmented sublist for each of the groups you want to target.

Make a list of all of the different people and pages that you want to target on your website. If you're stuck, you can use Google Analytics to focus on areas that have heavy traffic. Creating a sublist for whatever the primary goal of your website is, along with the following five that are listed, is a good place to start. Google recommends five remarketing lists that every business should use:

1. **Homepage Viewers** – people who visited your homepage, but didn't move any further into your site.[xcii] Keep these messages and ads broad and use them as a general reminder of your company and what you do.

2. **Category Page Viewers** – these are the people who have taken a further step and visited a general category-level

page, but not specific products or services.[xciii] If they continue to a specific page, exclude them from the general category sublist. You can do this by creating custom combination lists in Google Analytics or Google Ads.

3. **Product or Offer Page Viewers** – people who took another step from category pages and viewed specific products or services, but never attempted to purchase them by adding the product or service to their cart or contacting your business to learn more. Use these ads to try and re-engage previous visitors to take action on whatever product they viewed. You can offer discounts, promotions, or general reminders to different visitors.

4. **Cart Abandoners** – this sublist includes people who made it as far as adding a product into their cart if you run an e-commerce site, but stopped short of completing the purchase, or made it to your contact page, but never actually contacted you. Target ads to try and get these potential customers to convert into real customers.

5. **Past Converters** – these are your favorite types of people: customers. They've previously made a purchase or submitted a lead form,[xciv] and if they were happy with your company, they'll probably come back for more. Target them using cross-selling ads or up-selling ads.

According to Google, the point is to "focus your remarketing lists based on how someone's interacted with your website or app.[xcv] Separate each action and treat them differently based off their unique journey throughout your website. This will yield the biggest returns, as you'll be able to determine each visitor's value and whether it's worth it to spend the extra money for targeted ads. When you break your visitors into these sublists, you can arrange them based on importance and adjust how much money and marketing power you'll put into these specific sublists. You can market to them with different ads or messaging, and even control the CPC or impression based on their level of interest in your product or service.

A good way to approach segmenting is to look at every part of your business and ask "why?" Why didn't that person checkout? Why did that person peruse twenty products and not make a purchase? Why did that person visit and leave immediately? Always ask yourself "why?" and try to put yourself in your visitors' shoes. Once you do this, you can create creative assets to upload and utilize to target that visitor. Perhaps offering them free shipping, a free consultation, or even utilizing your ad to differentiate your offering versus your competitors.

Once you properly segment your remarketing lists, you'll need to add the "tags," or "pixels," to specific pages on your website. Like we discussed in Chapter 37, these are the codes that will be used to put a cookie in the visitor's Internet browser and thus, follow them around. When segmenting your lists, you will put a different one on each page so that the audiences are properly targeted.

To optimize each of your remarketing campaigns, you can implement one or more of the following.[xcvi]

✓ **Ad Testing** — experiment with different messaging, ads, offers, CTAs, brand images, and videos. See what works and what doesn't and make the necessary changes.

✓ **Custom Combination Testing** — try making different custom combinations in Google Analytics or Google Ads to get more specific with your remarketing lists. Change around time spent on your site, time since last visit, frequency of visits, and more with the above Google recommended parameters.

✓ **Frequency Cap Testing** — don't overdo it and make yourself seem too pushy. Put a cap on how many ads follow each customer so they don't get annoyed with over the top digital advertising. However, you don't want it to be too low, either. Experiment, analyze, make adjustments, and move forward.

✓ **Bid Testing** — keep an eye on your bids to make sure you're optimizing your cost effectiveness and ROI, but also making a good impression on your visitors.[xcvii]

✓ **Landing Page Testing** — play around with what landing page your ads bring your customers back to and how well they connect with different visitors. Try a different landing page for each category, or change it up and take notice of any differences.

When it comes to remarketing, the more closely you understand what works and what doesn't, the sooner you'll be able to get a positive ROI. Now, while segmenting your remarketing list creates an audience list for specific people, you can also set up different types of audience lists in all your digital advertising efforts. We'll learn more about this in Chapter 39.

Chapter 39: Utilizing Different Audience Lists in Your Advertising

What we just discussed was essentially using different audience lists in your remarketing lists, but you can also do this with other types of ads. Google makes it very clear that "you can show ads to specific audiences according to their interests… by adding audience lists to your ad groups."[xcviii] You can set these up on Google as well as other platforms (e.g., social media, e-mail list, and others) to narrow down your targeted audience for each ad. Some people argue that getting the right message to the right customers is now more important than utilizing keywords.

First, we want to walk through a few tips to help you be successful when setting up audiences.

- ✓ Make sure your niche lists are large enough to have an impact on your audience. You can be too narrow, and it will end up wasting your time. Head over to your Google Analytics page to get detailed statistics about your sites' visitors, pages, and time spent.

- ✓ Make sure you input the correct settings when configuring your ad group level. There are two options: "target and bid" or "bid only," and using the wrong one for a specific campaign could lead to thousands of dollars in costs, the wrong targeted audience, and more wasted time. You can manage your alerts in Google Ads so that you have to double-check everything, helping to catch any mistakes before it's too late.

- ✓ Think carefully about how long you want your ad to run. When you set up a campaign that's not long enough, you might miss crucial data trends that can only be analyzed after a specific duration of time. The same goes for shorter cycles—if you create a 30-day list, you could limit your ad to exclude traffic from people who get paid at the end of the month.[xcix]

✓ Be careful when overlapping your audience list durations. If you do overlap them, be extremely careful and remember to subtract the lists from one another so you don't ruin your lists. If you don't, you can easily end up paying more than necessary for a particular person, as they'll be listed in numerous locations.[c]

✓ Make sure you exclude lists from one another, especially the people who have already moved through the purchasing process and have converted into customers. If you don't, you could come off as annoying or clingy.

✓ Always utilize a frequency cap. We talked about this a bit in Chapter 38, but a frequency cap limits the amount of ad exposure your audience lists will see. You can edit this on a per-day basis so that they won't see 25 of your ads one day and 3 the next.

✓ Don't forget to periodically check for broken code. Luckily, this is extremely easy to do in Google Ads. There will be an icon in your audience tab that shows you if your code is working. If it is, perfect. If it's not, try re-entering your code in Google Analytics and see if it refreshes.

✓ Use Google Ads remarketing whenever possible. They'll help you build up your audience lists and give you a more detailed idea of who's a valuable visitor and who is not. There are hundreds of different metrics that you can use with your display remarketing campaigns.[ci]

✓ Track seasonal audiences the same as you would track regular audiences. People purchase things based off what holiday is around the corner, and this shouldn't be a time when you avoid tracking their behavior. In fact, if you put in extra effort, you'll be able to target the same people the following year. Believe us when we say that this will be a huge selling point to busy audiences.

✓ Take the time to create a strategy. It might take some extra time, but when you work on your audience lists strategically, you'll see a much greater ROI and conversion rate.

There are several different audience lists that are listed on Google's support website, including the following.[cii]

1. **Affinity, Custom Affinity**: set different interests and habits for your audience based on history, products, or services
2. **Custom Intent, Life Events, In-Market**: based on what people are researching or planning
3. **Remarketing**: based off previous interactions with your business
4. **Customer Match**: based off what you know about customers' activities
5. **Similar Audiences**: new users that have similar interests to your current site visitors

You can use these audience lists in different campaigns, such as display campaigns, search campaigns, and video campaigns, but there are restrictions for each. For display campaigns you can use affinity, custom affinity, custom intent, in-market, and remarketing audience lists. For search campaigns you can use in-market, remarketing, and customer match lists. For video campaigns you can use affinity, custom-affinity, custom intent, life events, in-market, remarketing, customer match, and similar audience lists. Within each list you can segment even further, bringing your targeted ads to a very specific set of people. This type of segmented and audience building is good for increasing click through rates, conversions, and building a stronger brand.

While most of the campaigns and PPC we've talked about have focused on Google Ads, there are a few other platforms you can utilize for your digital advertising efforts, which we'll discuss in the next chapter.

Case Study: Using Audiences & Demographics to Massively Increase ROI and Reduce Wasteful Spending

There are millions of combinations of ways to use audiences and demographics on Google.

One of our favorite case studies on this is a B2B company in an industry full of consumer keywords. This client historically was paying for 90+% of their clicks to consumers who had a one-off need for their services and didn't even meet the minimum purchase requirements.

When Google rolled out a new tool for business targeting, we immediately jumped at it, setting up a test campaign targeting businesses based on their revenue.

The results were amazing. We went from seeing several hundred clicks a day to only a few dozen, but those clicks were all businesses, and highly targeted. Rather than spending a few hundred dollars per day on wasted clicks, we were now spending under $30 per day and getting about 3x more leads.

We then were able to set up a "Similar Audience" list, in which Google automatically identified people to show our ads based on those who had already been to our site/clicked on our ads. The results were truly amazing.

Properly targeting and picking the right audience can make the difference between success and failure of your campaign.

Chapter 40: Using Alternative Platforms for Your Digital Advertising

As you can probably tell from the past several chapters, one of the most used platforms for digital marketing is Google Ads. Google does an awesome job of connecting websites, analyzing data, and providing tools to make your life easier. However, with all the focus on Google Ads, people tend to downplay the other platforms available for hosting digital advertising. If you want to get the most out of your digital advertising strategies, you can't ignore the other platforms available.

These additional platforms can be beneficial if you need different targeting options, are trying to reach a different audience, or simply to increase the reach of your campaign and gain more exposure.

While each platform is different, they all share many of the same concepts and terminology as Google.

Here are a few alternative ad platforms to Google Ads.

✓ **Facebook**

Facebook advertising is like its own little Google Ads. You can use their platform for targeted marketing if you know who your market is, or you can use their targeting tools to discover your market. There are a ton of extra parameters that allow an in-depth digital advertising experience that shouldn't be ignored. Since it's used by almost everyone in the world, Facebook has a great team of experts that continue to improve both user and business experience. You can also run remarketing ads on Facebook to increase reach and target different demographics. One of our favorite things about Facebook is that unlike Google or other tools, most Facebook users provide a wealth of information about themselves such as their marital status, employment status, location, interests, and more. Facebook lets you target people based on this information, providing one of the most highly customizable targeting experiences available in digital advertising.

✓ Instagram

When Instagram was first released, there wasn't a lot you could do in terms of business advertising. It wasn't nearly as easy to integrate as Facebook was, but that's changed. You can actually link your Facebook and Instagram account so that your Facebook ad campaign is pushed through to connected social media sites, such as Instagram. Plus, the fact that Instagram is primarily visual-based gives you an opportunity to attract a whole different market—just ensure your posts are high quality and try to foster engagement. The larger your influence is, the better your marketing campaigns will be. If you'd rather go the sponsored ad direction, Instagram also has an option for you to push your content to users who will find it relevant and useful.

✓ LinkedIn

Most people who use LinkedIn started so purely for business connections, but it's grown to be much more. It's a great place to launch B2B digital advertising campaigns, and the business pages allow you to use the same targeted segmenting as Facebook. More people are going to LinkedIn just to scroll through their news feed and find relevant information than ever before.

✓ Pinterest

Pinterest uses captivating images to link content to a network of millions of users. The pictures tend to get higher click through rates than typical digital advertising since they aren't accompanied with a thorough description, and can give you some solid conversions. You just need to play around with it and see what works best for your specific industry.

✓ **Native Advertising**

With more and more content on the Internet, native advertising is becoming increasingly popular. There are a variety of platforms to run native ads on. For those who don't know, native advertising refers to in-content advertising streams. For example, if you were reading an article about "Tips For SEO" and at the end you see a section which says, "You may also like…" those are generally native ads. Native ads can be beneficial both for branding as well as direct lead generation.

As the sphere of digital advertising continues to evolve, don't limit yourself by only using platforms that can run through Google Ads. Branch out and try a few different options. You might be pleasantly surprised with the results. Or you may even discover a platform that works best for your niche at a fraction of the cost. Experimentation is always a critical part of marketing.

Chapter 41: Properly Tracking Conversions

Ultimately, your digital advertisement efforts (or any of your marketing efforts for that matter) won't matter if you're not tracking conversions. Sure, they might be doing some good for your bottom line, but without taking the proper steps to measure, analyze, and understand your campaign's successes and failures, you could end up wasting money and underutilizing areas with a capacity for higher potential. As Google states, "Conversion tracking can help you see how effectively your ad clicks lead to valuable customer activity on your website, such as purchases, sign-ups, and form submissions."[ciii] They measure the effectiveness of your campaigns.

This is why it's so important to start right away. If you don't start at the beginning of your campaigns, there is no way for you to go back in time and gather previous data. This means tracking your conversions on every platform that you're using, not just Google Ads. We can't stress this enough: tracking and measuring conversions are essential. They help you measure your ROI, the success of your keywords, and which are doing the best.

In addition to Google Ads and the platforms we discussed in the previous chapter, you should track conversions based on where they're coming from and what action was taken. This means setting up a unique code for websites, apps that you run, phone calls, and even sales made in the offline world. Track all of the customer actions you're using for conversions in your digital advertising efforts to get the best results and make necessary adjustments.

Most businesses decide to track a number of the following, but it ultimately depends on your type of business and your business' goals and the nature of your business. Be sure to track at least one of these conversion actions in your campaigns:

- ✓ Visiting a landing page for specific CTAs
- ✓ Filling out any forms or surveys
- ✓ Signing up for newsletters

- ✓ Contacting your company through a number of methods including phone or contact form
- ✓ Making a purchase online
- ✓ Requesting A Consultation
- ✓ And more

Remember, you want to track the main key performance indicators (KPIs) for your business, so take some time to determine what those are. Once you do, you need to move on, knowing how to do it. Luckily, Google Analytics makes tracking conversions easy. All you need to do is set up your goals, install the conversion tracking, and let the data roll in.

Let's start with talking a little bit about how this works. You'll start by logging into your Google Analytics page > Account > Property > View > Goals. Click on your goals, and from there you can set the different rules for conversion tracking.

Google Analytics gives you the option of using pre-configured templates: Revenue, Acquisition, Inquiry, and Engagement. These are great for measuring the big actions, but they leave out the details of how a customer came to make that action. This is why you want to go in and customize your own goals, so that you can track the 'micro' conversions.[civ]

First, let's talk about engagement-based goals. These are the micro-conversions that give you all the details you'll need for an in-depth analysis. For each one that you set up, you'll need to add different labels to tell Google Analytics what events to track. They are as follows:

1. **The Category**: this is the most general umbrella term for whatever it is you're tracking, whether it be an outbound link, a video, a file, or similar.[cv]

2. **The Action**: this is a description of what your visitors are doing within each of the above categories. Are they downloading a file? Making a purchase? Clicking on a specific link? Playing a video? Sharing your website or blog?[cvi]

3. **The Label**: this takes the action above and breaks it into even smaller snippets of information. This is where you get specific. As Neil Patel puts it, "if it's video playbacks you're tracking, this is where you note the video title."[cvii]

Now, let's move on to acquisition-based goals. These are your larger, more macro-conversion goals that will give you a broader view of the information you're looking for. In these goals you can track the destination (a specific URL), duration (how much time was spent there), page/screens per session (how many pages/screens were viewed), or event type (the action a visitor took). For example, if you want to track how many people made a purchase, you can enter the URL for the confirmation page that occurs after payment. Google Analytics will then track how many people view this page, and what the process was like, thus giving you an accurate number of how many people made purchases and how they came to do so. You can customize these goals even further by including:

1. **The Value**: this is where you indicate the value you charge for the action specified, whether it is for specific purchases, sign-up fees, or any other action. You can assign this fee based on profits, cost per lead, cost per click, and other attribution models. Again, it depends on your goals.

2. **The Funnel**: this is where you specify whether a conversion goal is tracked based on if someone hits every single page in a specific sequence to get there.[cviii]

After the initial setup, you can make sure that everything is working correctly by verifying it through Google Analytics. Let it gather data for a few days, then head back to your goals section and look at the overview. It will present you with all of the data gathered since set-up, but not from before.

Once you start to see results, you can determine what action you want to take. You can start to better understand how to gain new opportunities, fix any problems in your sales funnel, work on strengthening your conversion path, and analyze your visitors based on whether they made a purchase. Play around with your options and always work toward your business goals.

Marketing Masters Pro Tip: *Always, always track conversions*

It amazes us how many businesses spend 5 or 6 figures on digital advertising and don't properly track their conversions.

Sometimes, conversion tracking isn't easy, but there is always a solution. Even in the most difficult cases, unique tracking numbers, tracking URLs, or even a good old fashion CRM system can all act as forms of conversion tracking.

If you don't track what is actually converting, how can you possibly improve upon your digital ads? Anything you do will at best be a shot in the dark and lead to endless waste. Save yourself time and headaches and set up conversion tracking from day 1. It will ensure all your campaign decisions are based on data and not guess work.

Chapter 42: Using Automation in Your Digital Advertisements

In today's fast-paced world, it can be difficult to keep up. To run a successful business, there are so many different moving parts in the marketing arena alone, and if you want to focus on other areas of your business, you're going to need to bring in some automation. Even for digital marketing agencies, it's impossible to connect all the dots between time of day, device type, audience type, keywords, and countless other data points to understand on a micro level how to adjust bidding, budgets, and campaign settings.

At our agency, we do not utilize any automated tools when running digital campaigns. But that is mostly because we do this day in and day out, are extremely efficient at running campaigns and making changes, and have the time to do so. As a business owner, if you plan on running your own campaigns, you likely will *have* to utilize some degree of automation to keep up.

What we do use is the automation within the digital platforms themselves. This is an important distinction, as there is a countless number of third-party software that try to automate processes within campaigns, which in our opinion weren't built to be automated. The automation within each advertising platform, be it Google, Facebook, or others, is designed to be leveraged and used to the fullest extent possible.

When you use automation in your digital advertising, you're basically setting things up to work independently of a person or team, using technology or AI. By using algorithms and rules that analyze visitor behavior, statistics, and data, you can free up your time for things that need more human attention.

You cannot just set up a new campaign, however, and expect automation to kick in. Automation needs something to base the changes on, which is why conversion tracking is so important. Once you have properly set up your conversion tracking and in a 30-day period collected at least a few dozen conversions through manually running your campaigns, then it's okay to turn on some of the automation tools within the advertising platform to help further refine your campaigns.

This approach still requires a great deal of human intervention, however in our opinion this is the best way to leverage the strengths of automation without getting stuck in the common weaknesses. An experienced human touch coupled with the strong automation tools built into advertising platforms will help ensure campaign success.

Automation will assist in maximizing your conversions or your ROI, depending on the settings you enter. What this does is make micro adjustments based on billions of data points, ensuring that your bids are higher for those who are more likely to convert and lower for those who aren't. At the end of the day, it is a micro-managed ad campaign that will yield the strongest conversions and ROI. But remember, at least for the foreseeable future, automation can't be run without close monitoring.

Chapter 43: Creating Digital Ads That Convert

It doesn't matter if you are running search ads, display banner ads, video ads, native ads, or something else, your ads are ultimately what are going to drive action to bring that visitor to the next step in your conversion funnel.

If your ads don't drive action (generally speaking clicks), then your campaign will not succeed.

There are a multitude of different settings and adjustments to be made in a campaign, but simply put; your ads are perhaps one of the most important.

Lead Generation & Sales

If your ads are focused on lead generation, they need to convey a sense of urgency and drive action. Let's assume you are a company selling widgets. You might run an ad that says: *Best Widgets Available Online at Affordable Prices*

This is okay as it describes your product and explains that it is for sale. But a much stronger ad might say: *ABC Widgets – Highest Quality on The Planet – Shop Now for Limited Time Free Shipping*

This is a much stronger ad as it shares your company name to assist with branding and future impressions, conveys that they are the "best on the planet" not just best or good, and commands the viewer to take immediate action by shopping now for limited time free shipping.

Your ads need to be unique. You can't simply run the same ads as all your competitors and expect to see a strong click through rate. They need to drive immediate action, be edgy, and resonate with those viewing them.

This applies for all other ad types, be it banner ads, video ads, or otherwise.

Branding

Ads for branding are a little bit different. These ads should reflect your brand and your value proposition or core values. Their purpose is not necessarily to drive immediate action, but is to either support your lead generation efforts, or to help your brand stay fresh in front of current and prospective customers.

Branding ads are more difficult as each brand is unique.

In general, these ads strongly convey the brand's name, some strong value statement about the brand, and sometimes will have a more subtle call to action.

An example of a strong branded text ad might be: *ABC Widgets – US Made Quality Widgets in Thousands of Sizes – Sign Up for Our E-mail List to Receive Special Offers*

This gentler approach still has a call to action, while also branding that ABC widgets is US made and high quality as well as available in thousands of sizes.

At the end of the day, your ads are where your creativity can shine. It's important to remember that numbers drive everything in the world of marketing, so be sure to closely monitor the ad's click through rates to ensure they are as strong as possible, and more importantly monitor the conversion rate of each ad variation. We always run a variety of A/B testing with our ads to identify what works best, because even after doing this for over a decade, we are still surprised at where the numbers lead us sometimes.

Part 4 – Social Media

While the Internet shaped the 90's and early 2000's, social media undoubtedly has shaped the 2010 decade more than anything.

Whether you love it or hate it, social media has become a part of our everyday lives and culture. And similarly, it has shaped the world of marketing.

In this section, we're going to dive mostly into the organic side of social media, talking about do's and don'ts for managing your company's social media presence, which platforms you should be on, how to grow your audience, and how to measure and track results.

Like almost anything in marketing, social media is definitely an area where you can do as much or as little as you'd like. And it's also an area where no matter how much you do, there's always more to be done.

At the end of the day, we tell the brands we work with to focus on what is converting for them. In many cases, it isn't social media, so we allocate funds in to areas like SEO or PPC where they are seeing strong ROI's.

But even if conversions aren't strong, social media has become a necessary evil, and something your brand has to be on simply because of the fact that everyone uses it.

Chapter 44: The Importance of Using Social Media in Business

When social media was first developed, it was done so purely for entertainment purposes. However today people have integrated social media into every aspect of their lives, including making purchases, researching brands, connecting with influential people, increasing brand loyalty, and more. Social media has blurred the lines of business and pleasure, and if you aren't currently active on all the main platforms, you're missing out. Regardless of the industry you're in, social media is an absolute must.

Arguably, the main benefit of social media for businesses is that it allows you to connect with and reach different audiences. It's an easy way to build relationships, grow, and engage with your customer base, all while people see what your brand represents. Different platforms give various feedback on your target audience's wants, likes, and dislikes, allowing you to gather valuable data and adjust your marketing efforts. Having a social media presence allows you a unique insight into your potential customers, it helps your SEO, encourages more website traffic, and positions your business as a relevant and modern enterprise.

As of 2018, there are "3.196 billion global social media users, equaling 42% penetration."[cix] That's a lot of potential, especially if your business offers location-independent services or worldwide shipping. Of these 3.196 billion users, 71% of those who completed a business transaction, and had a good social media experience with the brand, will likely recommend it to others.[cx] Social media not only increases your reach, it also supplies an additional area for conversation among your customers.

Since the average person spends nearly two hours a day on social media, you have a strong window of opportunity.[cxi] You have endless opportunities to gain more exposure for your brand, advertise using posts, media, and video, which we'll discuss in Chapter 46, and garnish more conversions and visits to your website.

Social media has even started to impact the success of your SEO efforts. Since social links act as an independent link in search engines, they will appear when prospects make a Google or Bing search for your brand. They also act as their own mini-search engines where people come to search for relevant information.

While some people head to social media to learn, others check in without any clear purpose, aimlessly scrolling through their newsfeed. It's your job to catch their attention so that they take action that will benefit your business' bottom line. That's why you need to have a strategy in place—and be ready for it to change with the evolution of each platform. Be respectful of what you post, create the right presence, cultivate the right content, and monitor all your activity and results. We'll tackle each of these in the chapters to come.

Social media should be used throughout your marketing strategies, but only having one active platform won't cut it. Regardless of your end goal, you should be actively engaging on the following big five: Facebook, LinkedIn, Instagram, Twitter, and Pinterest. In the following chapter, we'll dive deeper into when to use each platform based on your individual needs and the demographics you're targeting.

Chapter 45: The Most Effective Social Media Platforms

Now that you've started to realize the necessity for social media in business, you should take some time to set up a profile on a few platforms. There is an overbearing amount of different social media platforms to choose from, which can be problematic at first glance. The hardest part is getting started, and knowing on which of the thousands of social media platforms to be active.

To start, we're going to walk through the big five social media platforms that all businesses should be using, regardless of their needs. How often you use each, and what type of content or actions you take, will depend on your business, industry, and overall objectives.

Facebook

This is the largest social media platform in the world and is equally beneficial to both individuals and businesses. There are over 2.23 billion monthly active Facebook users, according to recently released data.[cxii] That number makes this social media platform impossible to ignore. Information spreads fast on Facebook, which is why many news channels, government officials, and businesses have opted to create a profile. Use Facebook to post blogs, videos, advertisements, general updates, product releases, and more. You can also run specific Facebook ads, similar to PPC ads, which allow you to market to a specific demographic. These highly specific ads have been shown to increase conversion rates and work in line with your end goals. With the release of Facebook Live, you can host Q&A segments, interviews, or simply engage with your customers in a more intimate setting. Whether or not you will want to pay for additional advertising is up to you, but make sure you're monitoring your success to see whether your ROI is worth it.

There's also a tool on Facebook called Audience Insights, which lets you gather data from your followers. You can start to aggregate information based on their personal interests, behaviors, demographics, and general characteristics.[cxiii] This is a great way to get more information for your digital advertising efforts, as discussed in the previous section.

All in all, Facebook is very personal. If you want to be more customer-oriented, it's essential that you build a presence.

LinkedIn

LinkedIn was developed to act as a social media platform for professional social networking, job-hunting, and a place to display your skills, résumé, and interests. This platform is great if you're looking to grow your team or build a repertoire with other like-minded industries. With over 500 million members active today, LinkedIn is best used as a career management tool.[cxiv] As an established business, you can publish your blog posts, grow your influential networking team, and give or receive recommendations. There are also options for businesses to use LinkedIn's tools to generate sales leads through their internal advertising.

LinkedIn boasts four major opportunities when creating a business page: hiring, marketing, selling, and learning.[cxv] If you're interested, or if your company would benefit from a professional LinkedIn page, start by creating a company page using the free demo trial and continue to pay if you find it beneficial. A company page allows you to personally outreach to customers, grow your target audience, and get to know the people who may be interested in your services. You can stick with a free account, but there will always be more options with premium. Additionally, remember that LinkedIn showcases your company, along with your employees. Make sure that all your employees linked to your company account are professional and represent your business in a way that reflects your mission statement and the company's core values. The stronger your profile is, the more trust, authority, and connections you can build.

Instagram

A lot of businesses don't think they'd find a place on Instagram, given that it's primarily pictures and stories created from live videos. They're wrong. Instagram has grown as an invaluable business tool over the last few years, and since it's inexpensive and easy to manage, it should be included in every business' social media toolbox. Instagram allows your audience to connect with you quickly and get an overall image of your brand and what your company is all about. It connects to visual customers and allows you to develop creative, inexpensive advertisements. You can link your updated blog into your biography and mention your new post in a corresponding picture, feature products or services, and even show your audience the life of a typical employee. It fosters connection and engagement, and features like geotags and hashtags can help bring you to the forefront of your audience's minds.

Instagram Stories is a newer feature, which has pushed Snapchat out of the picture. Since these stories are temporary, you can showcase special promotions, offers, or just your day-to-day activities. There are a few advertising options on Instagram where you can sponsor posts, so make sure you consider that if you have something you think will grab a typical Instagrammer's attention. Try to avoid using influencers to market your product, as this has decreased in effectiveness over the years—we'll talk more about this in Chapter 48.

Twitter

In the past decade, Twitter has grown to be one of the greatest social media platforms for short, direct messaging. Since there is a limit to each post you make, people can quickly and easily see what you're offering, and you can work to build relationships with customers, partners, vendors, influencers, and the general population. It's all about instant connections and sharing ideas.[cxvi] Recently the character limit has grown, but it is still much smaller than Facebook and even Instagram. You'll need to be creative to reach your audience while ensuring your posts are easy to digest. It's also a good idea to include links whenever possible, as "link clicks account for 92% of all user interactions with tweets."[cxvii]

In terms of business benefits, Twitter allows you to grow globally and increase brand recognition. You can share videos, host polls, upload pictures, and share witty, relevant information. Twitter also has an ad platform, where you can "target particular audiences and reach them so they learn about your business and have an opportunity to become followers and engage with you."[cxviii] When you post anything, make sure that it is 100% grammatically correct so you foster credibility with your audience. Implement hashtags and geotags when relevant, and make sure that you monitor how often your business is mentioned—and what people are saying. It's a great feedback tool, in addition to the ad platform available.

Pinterest

Pinterest isn't a heavily business influenced social media platform, but if your business has captivating pictures and a compelling blog to accompany them, it can help your advertising and SEO efforts tremendously. Keep in mind that this platform is for a specific set of industries so don't jump in headfirst if you're unsure. Stick to the above four platforms, and potentially find a few other industry-specific platforms if you really want to go the extra mile.

To determine which platforms you will want to use and when, you can start by defining your goals—which we'll talk about a bit more in Chapter 47. The main thing to remember is that these social media platforms perform different functions, and are used by people for different reasons. Another thing to keep in mind is that there are, like we mentioned, thousands of other social media platforms. Some of them are industry specific or specific to certain business needs, and others offer users a very specific set of activities. If you'd like to broaden your social media to some of these other platforms, take the time to do some research and try not to spread yourself too thin. The above platforms are the ones primarily used by people of all ages and will give you the best ROI for your time.

Chapter 46: Different Ads You Can Use on Each Social Media Platform

Depending on the social media platform you're using, there are several ads you can implement. Since each platform offers different functions and users interact with them in different ways, all the ads are application specific. Here are the most popular social media platforms and a list of the ads you can use.

Facebook

The biggest opportunity in terms of advertisements is when using your Facebook Business profile. There are quite a few different options, which we'll briefly run through now.

- ✓ **Link Click Ads** – the most popular Facebook ads. They help promote your external website and send people to your landing page or blog posts.[cxix]

- ✓ **Video Ads** – an offset of link click ads with a video in the place of an image. They serve the same purpose, and the shorter the video the more effective it tends to be.

- ✓ **Boosted Page Posts** – if you have a particular ad that you want people to see, you can use Facebook's Boost Post to increase its reach. Like digital advertising, you can set up a specific target audience, bidding methods, and promote your post to a larger set of people.[cxx]

- ✓ **Multi-Product (Carousel Ads)** – allows you to add multiple images, videos, headlines, links or CTAs in one unit[cxxi], which can then be scrolled through by your visitors.

- ✓ **Dynamic Product Ads (DPA)** – think of remarketing ads and multiply that by 100. These types of ads use people's past actions, inactions, and characteristic to perfectly place a targeted ad into their newsfeed at specific times.[cxxii] It's automated through Facebook and easy to implement.

✓ **Facebook Lead Ads** – these help you generate new leads by offering downloadable content and signups directly in the Facebook application. This is perfect for people who want things instantly and don't want to wait for an external website to load.

✓ **Canvas Ads** – these are mobile-specific ads that allow users to engage with your content quickly, easily, and in a very interactive way.

✓ **Collection Ads** – this type of ad is similar to multi-product ads, but with a different formatting. Display multiple products in one post that is easy to see and take action.

✓ **Page Like Ads** – these are the ads that businesses use when they're trying to increase the amount of page Likes they have. Use a strong image that will attract the right audience, and include them on any of your ads for an extra CTA.

✓ **Page Post Photo Ads** – a post ad is simple and everyone on social media does this every day. All you need to do is post a captivating image with minimal text or a link for people to follow.

✓ **Page Post Video Ads** – the same as a Page Post Photo Ad, but with videos. It tends to be more engaging and garners more attention than images. Plus, if you post a popular video, you might get the chance to go viral. There is a built-in code that allows you to retarget subsets of visitors based on how much of your video they viewed, making it a great way to create audience sub-lists.[cxxiii]

✓ **Page Post Text** – again, the same as the Ads above, but in the most minimal sense. You should try to always accompany your posts with pictures or videos to get the most engagement.

✓ **Mobile App Ads** – this adds CTA buttons to the ads above that prompt your visitors to download your mobile app.

✓ **Event Ads** – if you have an event coming up, you can create a Facebook Event and advertise there. Use additional ads to boost your reach and target potential attendees. Don't forget to include geometric limitations so that you don't waste time or money advertising to people that won't be able to attend.

✓ **Offer Claims** – if you have a storefront and are looking to boost foot-traffic, you can advertise special offers for discounts, promotions, or BOGO.

✓ **Local Awareness Ads** – this also helps attract people to your physical store through location-based targeting such as "Call Now" or "Send Message."[cxxiv]

It's important to select ad types that are most relevant to your business and your target audience. Since each company is different, testing, monitoring, and adjusting will help keep your costs low and your ROI high.

LinkedIn

While there aren't nearly as many specific ads for LinkedIn as there are for Facebook, they can still be beneficial if you're using this social media platform.

✓ **Sponsored Content** – this type of ad helps to boost the content on your LinkedIn company page by promoting it to your followers, on specific newsfeeds, and in groups. You can choose to implement them in a Cost Per Click or Cost Per Thousand Impressions model.[cxxv]

✓ **Direct Sponsored Content** – like Sponsored Content, but with this you can personalize and test content in a news feed without creating posts directly on your LinkedIn company page.[cxxvi]

✓ **Sponsored InMail** – this type of advertising is similar to e-mail marketing, except you're sending personalized, private message to a user's LinkedIn inbox.[cxxvii] These messages can be anything you want, from simple helloes, CTAs, or embedded links. They're purchased using a Cost Per Send model.

✓ **Text Ads** – text ads on LinkedIn are used to run campaigns almost like Google/Bing search ads.[cxxviii] This is perfect for increased brand awareness and simple advertising on newsfeeds. Purchase them through a Cost Per Click or Cost Per Thousand Impressions.

✓ **Dynamic Ads** – these are highly engaging, and effectively drive traffic to your company's website or landing page.[cxxix] They are highly personalized and generated for each individual user.

✓ **Lead Gen Forms** – these are pre-filled forms using a user's LinkedIn profile information.[cxxx] This makes it fast and easy for people to fill out forms for downloadable content, e-mail marketing lists, or special offers.

Again, make sure to run tests and track your results when using these different types of advertisements. See what works best for your business and amend your social media-marketing plan to reflect the strongest ROI.

Instagram

Since Instagram is 100% visual, all your ads should be captivating, regardless of which ones you implement.

✓ **Picture Ads** – the most basic type of advertisement you can do on Instagram is picture ads. Turn each post into a Picture Ad by producing high-quality, relevant images. With the new Instagram updates, you can use your posts to get people to apply, book, call, order, and even download.

✓ **Video Ads** – with the release of the elongated 60-second video option, businesses can say even more. As long as you're not posting dull, irrelevant video, they will captivate your followers and help get you more likes, comments, and hopefully, conversions. Video Ads can also have a specific CTA button included directly below the content.

✓ **Carousel Ads** – like Facebook's Carousel Ads, Instagram offers a feature to upload more than one image in one post, with the ability to scroll through them. Again, you can implement a CTA button or direct link back to your website.

✓ **Stories Ads** – Instagram Stories came out as a reaction to Snapchat's 24-hour videos and have effectively pushed Snapchat back off the radar. You can use stories to show offers, advertise promotions, give how-to demonstrations, or just let people know how a day in the life of your company works. You can include options for users to "swipe up" for more detailed information or CTAs.

✓ **Canvas Story Ads** – just like Facebook's Canvas Ads, Instagram has implemented them into their stories. This allows you to build customizable advertisements in real-time that will increase your click-through rate up to a factor of four.[cxxxi]

Twitter

Finally, we want to give you some insight on how to use the built-in advertisements on Twitter. While you may think that there aren't many options for this simple, self-explanatory social media platform, there are more than you'd imagine. Check them out below:

- ✓ **Promoted Tweets** – these are tweets that an advertiser pays to display to people who aren't currently following them on Twitter.[cxxxii] They're labeled as being promoted, but are just as functional as regular tweets.

- ✓ **Promoted Accounts (Followers Campaigns)** – this lets you promote your Twitter account to a specific set of targeted users who aren't currently following you, but may find your account interesting.[cxxxiii]

- ✓ **Promoted Trends** – similar to Promoted Accounts but with current trends and topics. You can promote a specific hashtag that backlinks to a long list of organic search results, but you need to work with a Twitter Sales representative to purchase these.[cxxxiv]

- ✓ **Automated Ads: Twitter Promote Mode** – this is a flat rate advertising fee ($99/month) where a team will automatically promote your first 10 tweets of the day to a specific set of audiences.[cxxxv] This increases your company's brand recognition and can help you gain more followers.

Using Twitter's Ad Campaigns, you can set specific objectives, create ad groups and bidding budgets, and confirm where you want your ads to be placed. After launching each campaign, be sure to monitor it for success, failure, and any plateaus.

Now that we've thoroughly discussed some of the main types of advertisements available on the most popular social media platforms, we need to dive into more detail about how to make a strategic plan. We'll discuss this in the following chapter.

Marketing Masters Pro Tip: Less Is More

We took over a client account a few years ago from another agency when they decided to part ways with the client. This was a case where the client came to us in a mad scramble because their ad agency had fired them as a client (should have been a red flag to us from the start).

This particular client demanded that they use everything available to them. When we were performing our initial intake, we realized they were not only running ads on every social media platform possible, but they were running nearly every single type of ad and targeting, and doing all this on a mere $2,500 per month budget.

While these ad types and tools all serve a purpose, it's important to remember that they aren't one size fits all. A carpenter doesn't bring a saw, drill, pipe wrench, jackhammer, and excavator to change a light bulb. Similarly, it's important to use the right platforms and ad types for the right advertising goals and audiences.

In this case, we convinced the client to give us 3 months to make major changes to their advertising. We took them from 6 platforms down to 2, and from dozens of ad types down to 3. Their campaigns went from losing money every month for the business to seeing a 3-4x ROI, which isn't huge, but is a dramatic difference from something that was losing them money. Equally as important, their agency fees were cut by 1/3 because of the need for less management time on a more simplistic campaign.

Chapter 47: Creating a Strategic Plan for Social Media

While we've discovered more about the importance of social media, the different platforms, and the advertisements available, there's still a lot to be said in terms of creating a strategic plan. Many companies don't understand the true importance of planning, tending to move forward thinking they can simply wing it along the way. However, doing so is dangerous.

Since social media has infiltrated the lives of nearly everyone in the world, it's become a necessity in the business world. We've seen a lot of companies ignore creating a strategy because of the intimidation that surrounds the creation and management of profiles across multiple different platforms. If this isn't your area of expertise, you can always consider outsourcing and hiring a social media manager—someone who is hyper-focused on curating ironclad strategies. Depending on your industry, this might be worth the ROI, but if it's not within the realm of financial possibility, you can do it yourself.

1. **Set Goals**

   The first step in your strategic planning is setting social media goals. The easiest, most effective way to do this is to align them with your overall business objectives and company values. You should also ask yourself the *reason* you want to market on social media platforms.

   ✓ Is it all about getting sales and driving traffic to your site?
   ✓ Do you want to increase brand awareness?
   ✓ Are you looking for a way to generate new leads?
   ✓ Is it about highlighting what makes you different from your competitors?
   ✓ Would you like to build a stronger business-related community?

- ✓ Is it to build customer loyalty, and increase your customer base through social sharing?
- ✓ Do you want to learn more about your customers and why they do what they do?

Consider how social media has the potential to impact your business through one or more of these goals and take the time to think about them in detail. Pick a few based off your main business objectives, but don't go overboard. The next step is to expand these goals, make them actionable, and write out a plan for how to achieve them.

2. Make Them SMART

After reading this book, you should be familiar with the idea that goals will never be achieved unless they're SMART—think back to our goal setting in Chapter 11. For a quick refresher, that means that a strong goal needs to be Specific, Measurable, Attainable, Relevant, and Time-Bound. These same principles apply when setting goals for your social media strategy. You need to pick apart your chosen goals and break them down into small, segmented parts. Create goals for your goals.

If you want to get more sales through social media marketing, set a number of sales you want in a set amount of time. If you want brand recognition, set a goal that you want an increase in social mentions by 30% within a 6-month window. If you want to drive traffic, say you want your traffic to increase 20% as a result of social marketing over the next 3 months.

Making your goals as objective as possible allows for them to be measured. Otherwise, you'll have no idea if you successfully met them or not.

3. Construct a Plan

Once you've determined the objectivity of your goals, start brainstorming the actions necessary to successfully reach your goals. This will be an ongoing process through the rest of your strategic planning, but it helps to start immediately and make any amendments throughout the process.

If you've decided to focus on increasing social mentions, create a plan to accomplish it. For example, you can start to mention other influencers, become more active on social media, engage with your customers, create more meaningful content, and post more giveaways. Use numbers set on a specific timeline for action. Each specific action you create depends on your overarching goals, but again, they need to be measurable so that you can see what's working and what's not.

4. Research Your Audience

You'll reach your goals only through the actions of your audience and your customer base. Sit down and create a profile of each type of customer that you envision being attracted to your product. There is no point in appealing to the entire age 18-35 social media demographic. It's nearly impossible, and you'll end up wasting your time and money. Instead, really think about why each set of customers would be attracted to your products, what personal characteristics they have, their needs, and so on. Create a strong mental image of what they look like, act like, and think like. This will make it much easier to speak to them in a language they understand.

Once you've determined a few different potential personas, start to gather data. Don't assume that you're right. Look at social media analytics and how your marketing efforts in other realms are paying off.

5. Research Your Competition

As with everything in business, you should look at what your competitors are doing. This makes it easy for you to learn what works and what doesn't with your ideal target audience. Take the time to look at what the best two to four companies in your industry do with their social media. Focus only on the ones dominating the market, as they have more to teach.

Study their content and how it comes across to a visitor. Is it light-hearted, or is it more to the point? What kind of graphics do they use? Are their ads more transactional, or more about brand recognition? Conduct a competitive analysis so you can better understand what seems to work and what doesn't.

It's also important to take note of what platforms they tend to have the most success on. While you may want to advertise across all social platforms, if your competition is completely dominating Facebook, you should focus your efforts on where your audience is underserved.[cxxxvi] Don't skimp out on Facebook, but don't spend hours on end trying to beat out a company that's been succeeding for years. This strategy will also help you keep your budget in check.

6. Evaluate Your Social Media

Chances are, you already have a social media account on at least one of the platforms we've discussed. If so, it's time to take a step back and look at what you've been doing. Is anything working? If so, why?

Once you have a mental picture of your customers, your objectives, and where you'll be advertising, you'll be able to re-evaluate your standings and make the changes needed to start moving toward your goals. Think about the overall message you want to send and how to speak out to the customer personas you've created. Break those messages

153

down into smaller messages that will eventually convey the content of your advertising.

Use the previous chapters to help you focus on what type of advertisements you'll be using on each platform. Not every platform is going to be a successful advertising space for you. And even if you do have it in your budget to advertise on all of them, why waste the time, money, and energy if you're not going to see a strong return?

Remember, the best thing you can do is analyze your current situation and see where it makes the most sense to change. If you don't currently have an online presence, consider this a fresh slate. Start building a list of influencers in your industry, including bloggers, and follow them so you have a few people to start engaging with. As you build your profiles and your brand continues to develop, you'll gain recognition from people you've connected with that will help you increase your social media presence.

Determine what networks you want to use, how you'll use them, and make any improvements necessary to your current profiles. As *Hootsuite*, a popular social media management platform, recommends, "it's a good exercise to create mission statements for each network."[cxxxvii]

7. Optimize Your Accounts

Once you've determined which social media platforms you'll be using, and whether your previous accounts need updating, it's time to develop your profiles. Fill out all the details that each platform needs to create the most complete profile possible. Use relevant keywords, high-quality images, and make sure you're using the business page option for each. Walk through the steps and take some time to fully optimize each profile to be the best it can be. While this may be a bit intimidating at first, start with one and just take it step by step. Get inspired, check out success stories, and follow people that give you motivation. Remember, you can always go back and make changes to your business pages as you gain experience in social media management.

8. Create and Schedule High-Quality Content

Now that you've got everything set up and ready to go, you'll need to create high-quality content. We'll talk all about this Chapter 51, but for now let's go over some basics in addition to creating a social media content calendar.

The biggest rule here is to provide value, and that value comes in different forms depending on the customer. You have to think about print ads, videos, infographics, and so on in order to reach the learning styles of each individual customer. Depending on your analysis, schedule weekly releases of videos, text ads, images, infographics, and other types of ads depending on the platform. You can do this by creating a posting schedule using one of the social media management tools such as *Hootsuite*.

Have your content calendar reflect your previously defined goals, company objectives, and mission statement to get the most from your efforts. You'll need to create a calendar for each platform, and you can segment actions based on the immediacy of your goals. Think about content from your blog, other sources, interesting facts, education purposes, promotional material, stories, and personal interactions. As you move forward, you'll learn what works and what doesn't so you can make the necessary adjustments to your strategy. We'll talk more about monitoring, tracking, and adjusting in Chapter 52. For now, let's dive a bit deeper into what it means to cultivate your presence with the right content.

Chapter 48: The Truth Behind "Influencer Marketing"

Since the rise of social media, we've started to see people become famous due to their online presence. You may know influencer marketing as being "Instafamous" or famous on other platforms. This fame stems from people gaining a large number of followers, although it's unsure whether they should truly be seen as an "influencer" in their field. Just because someone has 10k, 20k, or even 1M followers does not necessarily give them credibility—especially because followers can be bought, and an active, engaged follower is different than a silent one.

According to Forbes, to be an influencer you need to produce a result from your followers—specifically, a change in thinking or behavior.[cxxxviii] True influencers are people who can sway the public's opinion through their previously established credibility and salesmanship. They're not someone who uses their 100k ghost followers on a social media platform to push product for personal gain. Influencer marketing, therefore, has lost its power.

This loss of power stems from three main reasons, all of which revolve around the saturation of what it means to be an "influencer" in today's social media world.

1. Influencer marketing has become so saturated, in the sense that every person in the world is attempting to do it, that there is a lack of credibility behind these individuals. They have no previous expertise. They're taking action and posting sponsored ads for the money, the followers, and the likes. Many don't truly believe in what they're recommending to their fans, and this decreases their credibility.

2. With so many Instafamous users available, businesses have started ramping up their marketing efforts using these people to promote a product or service. This means that people end up posting nothing *but* promotional content for multiple businesses—oftentimes with no relation to one

another—and it does the opposite of what you'd expect. It drives people away because people can't seem to connect to an influencer's values. It's simply too difficult for businesses to get legitimate brand recognition due to the over saturation and lack of continuity from these types of posts.

3. Finally, and arguably the most unfortunate reason against influencer marketing, is that those who are real influencers are spamming their followers. People who have grown their following and gained social media fame in legitimate ways have discovered that the more followers they have, the more money they'll make for each sponsored post. They sell-out and start posting promotion after promotion, and their previous followers take notice. People stop following them because, quite frankly, it wasn't what they signed up for. Rather than a feed full of inspiring pictures and videos from their friends and the people they look up to, they see ad after ad after ad. It's just as easy to unfollow someone as it is to follow them, and that's what ends up happening. People get annoyed and they opt-out. Simple as that.

With all of this being said, it's important to avoid getting caught up with paying influencers to market your products. Five years ago, this was a very successful marketing tactic. Now, with the over-saturation, it's become annoying to people who are trying to use social media platforms to get inspired, find recommendations, and connect with their peers. Instead of wasting your money on influencer marketing, consider focusing on the other points that we solidify in this section. Or if you must give influencer marketing a try, at least do it on an affiliate or commission basis so the influencer has the same incentive to sell your product or service.

Organic Influencer Marketing

If you want to understand the type of influencer marketing that actually makes a difference, look at this statement made by Forbes: "The best influencer marketing does not involve financial compensation... Good influencer marketing is centered on building sincere personal relationships with influencers and sharing useful, unique, exclusive or early information… An influencer speaks about your product not because they are being paid to do so, but because they want to—because they find your company interesting and the information useful to their readers."[cxxxix] You can compare this to how you would naturally build up your backlinks for a website. Stop paying for these things and instead focus on building a brand that people support.

Chapter 49: Social Media Etiquette

I'm sure you've heard some kind of social media faux pas over the past year. Whether it was one of Donald Trump's notorious tweets, Nike's ad release with Colin Kaepernick, or any of the businesses that tried to use sarcastic customer comments and failed miserably, there are simply things that you should avoid doing on social media platforms, unless you want to take a risk that you may not bounce back from.

Obviously, Donald Trump is still our president, so his tweets have not impacted him his position, and Nike is still a multi-billion-dollar corporation. On the contrary, when smaller, less established companies attempt to do this, it can prompt the beginning of the end. If you want to play it safe, you need to be respectful of the guidelines in place by different social media platforms as well as your audiences.

Remember, social media is used by billions of people. That's billions of eyes worth of exposure, which can be both positive and negative. You need to be careful what you post and how you respond to your audience, unless the direct purpose of your business is to stir the pot. Even then, however, you should be cautious and sensitive. Certain images you put forth and words you use can be interpreted as offensive.

Avoiding small, unintentional mistakes can be tricky, which is why you should double-check everything you post before submitting it.

For instance, avoid posting potentially offensive material that pertains to current political, social, racial, or cultural issues. Even when it's intended to be entirely positive, it can be misconstrued. If you are going to say something, make sure that it is in no way an opinionated viewpoint. Remember the Kendall Jenner commercial where she solved all the very current police-civilian relationship issues by handing a cop a Pepsi? Not a great advertising move. Even though you may not be in the position to understand every way that something could be offensive, you likely have people on your marketing team with the empathy and expertise to understand why certain things might get under people's skin. Racial tension, protests, and police activity are currently *major* hot button issues, so how that ad even made it off the cutting room floor still boggles our minds.

You should also consider your original hashtags and wording. Look at them from different perspectives and think about how your target audience would perceive them. There's a major millennial, feminist, gender-specific/neutral movement going on right now in the language that we use. So always keep that in the back of your mind. The current generation is one of the most politically correct we've ever been, and it's magnified tenfold by the presence of social media. Vera Bradley launched an #ItsGoodToBeAGirl campaign in which girls shared why they liked being girls. The problem is, "Vera Bradley's efforts to connect with young girls is well-noted, but the execution flawed. Not all women want to accessorize. Not all women belt their favorite song lyrics. Perhaps using more caution when incorporating the hashtag #itsgoodtobeagirl in a 21st century marketing campaign would have been helpful—a strategy in which its approach seems almost … backwards."[cxl] Another example was DiGiorno Pizza. They "thought it was capitalizing on a fun, popular trend when they used the hashtag "Why I Stayed" to advertise pizza. The brand didn't realize that the hashtag was being used as a way to raise awareness of domestic violence in the United States. Thousands of angry responders let DiGiorno know their mistake... DiGiorno suffered some lasting damage to their reputation"[cxli] because of it.

If it fits with your brand, be light-hearted, make jokes, but always be aware of current social issues like women's rights, stereotyping, and casual racism. One recent example was an astonishingly offensive tweet sent out during the Golden Globes, asking, "Where are the English subtitles?" while Americans Ferrera and Eva Longoria were on stage… speaking English.[cxlii] Think about what you're posting before taking action, especially since you're running a business. Personal and professional profiles are vastly different, but the results are even more catastrophic when companies rather than individuals make mistakes.

A huge red flag is using a tragedy, like natural disasters, as an opportunity to boost sales. For example, a company in San Antonio called Miracle Mattress posted a video promoting a "Twin Towers" sale. In the video, the store manager implores customers to "remember 9/11" by getting "any size mattress for a twin price." At the end of the commercial, store employees scream and fall back into two stacks of mattresses, symbolizing the fallen Towers, with the manager turning to the camera and saying, "We'll never forget." Again, how that made it through the lines of marketing professionals and onto TV doesn't make much sense to us.

Another example was during Hurricane Irma. Lularoe consultants were holding countless "Hurricane Sales" because one of their popular shirts is named "Irma." These started popping up a week or so before the hurricane was due to hit Florida, right after Hurricane Harvey had devastated Texas. Lularoe encouraged and even provided consultants with graphics for "Hurricane Irma Sales." They thought that since the hurricane shared a name with one of their popular shirts, it would be a good sales tactic. It wasn't.

Most consultants sell through Facebook groups, and the ones foolish enough to fall for this stunt were blacklisted by many customers who took personal offense as their families prepared for a state of emergency. The sales for both consultants and the revenue for the company took major hits. The consultants are independent contractors, but with the company pushing the initiative, they blindly went along with it and likely ruined their reputation.

As a general takeaway, if you want to ensure you're being respectful when using social media and would like to improve your overall etiquette, consider these tips:

1. Be professional and use common courtesy.
2. Always use spell check and aim to be grammatically correct.
3. Only post pictures that represent your brand, company, and culture. Avoid unprofessional, revealing, embarrassing, or overly negative pictures.[cxliii]
4. Separate your business profile from your personal profile, and keep your personal life private.

5. Don't spam your followers.
6. Avoid adding fuel to the fire in controversial debates, issues, or reviews.
7. Use an appropriate amount of punctuation, hashtags, and Emojis. There is fine line between appropriate and overbearing.

Having good social media etiquette will benefit your reputation, and your audience will take notice. Remember that practice makes perfect, and if you make a mistake, always apologize and focus on moving forward.

Chapter 50: How to Grow Your Audience and Overall Presence on Social Media

After your strategic plan is in place and you've educated yourself on some of the guidelines for social media platforms, it's time to get to work. Your next goal is growing your audience on each platform that you're using to increase your company's overall social media presence. This is important because when it comes to social media, the larger your audience, the bigger your reach. While you can pay for sponsored ads to appear in the newsfeeds of people who don't follow you, if you don't have a large presence, they may not view you as a legitimate company. So, to really get ahead, check out some of our tried and true tactical tips to grow your audience.

✓ **Follow the Right People**

While your ultimate goal is to increase your company's followers, you need to start somewhere. Spend some time doing research on influencers in your space. This includes both smaller bloggers and the big guys, and maybe even a few of your competitor's social media pages—even if it's only to learn what works and what doesn't. Once you start to follow people in your niche or industry, be sure to comment on their pages, respond to questions, and take notice of how they're acting. When you get your name out there, even if it is on another person's social media site, people will get curious about who you are and will visit your page. If they like what they see, they'll follow you. This is similar to getting more backlinks for your blog by commenting or guest posting on other websites.

✓ **Include Your Location**

Include your location in all your profiles, especially if you have a storefront. Build connections with other local businesses, news sources, and city accounts. If they see that you're in their area, for the most part they'll be happy to follow you back. Re-tweet, share, or re-post information they've shared to show them you're a team player in building up local businesses. Just make sure that the content is relevant to your business' bottom line, otherwise you may confuse current or future followers.

✓ **Share Valuable Content**

If there is a product or service that you believe your audience will love, it won't hurt to tweet or write a quick blog post about it. Social media is all about enhancing the lives of your audience and followers, and showing them that your company has a culture and daily life in addition to business. Sharing content from influencers in your niche, or similar ones, can help add value to your growing social media. Mention both small and large brands and connect back to their site. You might get some new followers because on most social media platforms, you can see who re-tweeted or shared something from the original post.

✓ **Create High Quality Content**

In the next chapter, we'll dive into all the small details of creating the right content for your social media platforms, but you should keep in mind that high quality content is crucial to growing your social media presence. The great thing about high quality content is that it helps your business in so many ways, without any extra work. It will not only lead to more social media followers, but you'll improve your SEO efforts, create value, and establish yourself as an expert in your industry. You can also "extend the life of your own blog posts and content by posting multiple times in one day, and then a couple times over the following week. Never be afraid to schedule an older post!"[cxliv]

If you've heard of viral content, you know that it is the golden ticket to becoming well known on social media.

164

Viral content is content that is shared thousands of times and has millions of views. It's content that's so good people can't help but pass it along. Aim for this with all your posts.

In addition to high quality content, don't forget that each social media platform is unique and should have its own unique content. Don't just copy and paste one post across all your platforms—change it up with images, videos, hashtags, different wording, or links. Test out what works and what doesn't, and get into a habit of posting to please your audience.

✓ Use Hashtags

Hashtags are great because they facilitate popular searches and make it easier to be found. They can add a sense of reliability and help propel your campaign forward, but at the end of the day the real value lies in how they connect you to new audiences. If you use a popular hashtag, people who are searching that specific phrase will see your company, page, or post appear in the results on different social media platforms. Don't go overboard, but things as simple as #ThrowBackThursday can help people find you.

✓ Don't Focus on Sales

Social media is a place for engagement and information, not hard sales. Businesses who focus solely on making sales suffer. People simply don't care about your internal goals as much as you do, especially if you don't have a previous establishment in the online world. Focus on adding value for your audience and the sales will come naturally. It's okay to use promoted posts every now and then, but don't make them the sole purpose of your social media profiles.

✓ Engage and Respond

It's a well-known fact that responsiveness matters, especially on such a public sphere as social media. The faster it occurs, the better your publicity will be— regardless of whether the original comment, question, or complaint was positive or negative. The truth of the matter is that people want to be acknowledged. The more you respond and engage with your audience, the more people will see your company in a good light. This is because you can amend your responses to showcase your strengths, and downplay any weaknesses. If there was a problem with shipping, or the product wasn't what they expected, publicly announcing your regret and apology, while simultaneously offering a generous solution, shows your commitment to customer service. It's a win-win.

✓ Limit Your Profiles

Sometimes it doesn't make sense for a certain company to be highly active on Instagram or Pinterest or Twitter. See what works for you, and don't spread yourself too thin. Focus on dominating a few platforms rather than trying to be everywhere at once. It'll save you a ton of energy right from the beginning.

✓ Host Giveaways and Promotions

One of the best ways to increase customer engagement, grow your audience, and get noticed is by hosting giveaways, promotions, or exclusive offers. Show your audience that it pays to be your friend on social media, and reward them for their loyalty.

✓ Be Realistic

There are multiple opportunities online to pay thousands of dollars for promoted posts, advertisements, and even social media managers. While you should include a budget for these types of things, don't put all your money into social media. It's a great asset, but it shouldn't be your primary area of marketing concern.

Work these tips into your social media strategy and daily operating techniques and you'll start to grow your audience in a legitimate, organic way. Now let's look at how to master the art of crafting content for social media.

Marketing Masters Pro Tip: Don't Focus on The Numbers

Your number of followers is irrelevant. It doesn't make you money and it doesn't grow your business.

We always recommend new businesses on social media do something to get an initial boost. No one wants to follow a page with 2 followers. Do whatever you have to—be it ads or otherwise—to get your initial few hundred or few thousand followers fast. And after that, never look at that number again.

The reality is that some of the brands we work with who have 3-5k engaged followers are getting far more out of social media than brands with 50,000 junk followers.

This is a true case of quality over quantity. We can say that over and over to people, but the reality is, most entrepreneurs have an ego as big as their brain, and this just never seems to sink in.

Channel all your efforts into growing an engaged and relevant audience, and spend less time worrying about the size of the audience. I guarantee this will lead to stronger results for your business.

Chapter 51: Cultivating Your Presence with the Right Content

After you've outlined your goals, chosen social media platforms on which to grow your business, and developed your strategy, you only have one major action item left. It's time to create content that you'll be sharing on social media. The great thing about this is that if you've been working on developing content for your blog, you already know what you need to do. Remember, the biggest consideration is how you're going to provide value to your audience, which will take different forms depending on your target audience and the social media platform you're using.

The main thing we want to stress in terms of social media content is to avoid strictly posting sales posts. People don't follow businesses to fill their newsfeeds with advertisements. They follow them for their unique expertise in a topic, their overall culture, and the value of the information that you provide. Share your business' blog posts, similar articles or posts from your influencers, and always include a lot of visuals—especially when using Facebook, LinkedIn, and Instagram. Provide links on Twitter and re-tweet relevant information. For each of your target customer personas, look at their interests, previous activity, and social media behavior to get a better idea of what they would like to see on your page. You could even use a social media poll to get direct answers from your current followers.

From the topics, create a small list containing a hierarchy of articles that should be added to your content calendar (we'll dive more into content calendars later in this chapter). Pay close attention to the posts that generate interest and those that don't, and make changes accordingly. Content is dynamic, and your target audience will help you understand what they want to see. Always post content with your followers in mind.

At all costs, avoid taking any shortcuts when it comes to content cultivation and building your online presence. Just like we've learned about SEO, digital advertising, and link building: shortcuts never pay off in the long run. One popular shortcut some businesses and influencers use is paying for followers. Sure, it may be easier than spending hours and hours researching influencers in your space and growing a natural following, but you'll end up losing money in conjunction with having a group of followers who will never engage with your content—not exactly the point we're trying to push with social media. Plus, when real followers see that your followers are all but real, they're going to question the quality of your brand, and whether they want to be associated with it.

Create a Social Media Content Calendar to Schedule Your Posts

We mentioned earlier that you should be adding articles to your content calendar, but we didn't elaborate. If you're a pro at social media, you might already be implementing one. If you're like most of us, it's a new term. A content calendar is a scheduling tool that you can use to automatically post content to each and every one of your social media platforms. Since it's automated, you can consistently churn out content so your audience comes to anticipate new releases on certain days and times of the week.

We recommend using a content calendar tool like *Hootsuite* or *Buffer* for all your scheduling needs. They are invaluable when it comes to running a business and proliferating a social media presence. Social media content calendars are crucial for busy executives and, frankly, any business. It allows you to never miss an important date—think holidays, launches, campaigns, and more. You'll be more organized, and it streamlines collaboration, saves time, and allocates your company's resources in an efficient way.[cxlv]

Taking the time to develop your social media content calendar each month needs to be part of your overall social media strategy. You can use your company's blog posts, influencer posts, articles that would be valuable to your audience, infographics, how-to articles, webinars, surveys, interviews, product updates, illustrations, relevant photography, videos, or anything that you think they might enjoy. When you post mostly valuable information, you can also throw in a sales post every now and then. Just make sure that what you post includes high quality content and is relevant to your audience, and you'll be on track for success.

To ensure that you're posting relevant information, take the time to fully understand your audience. Luckily, this is a reoccurring theme when it comes to marketing, so you should already have a strong handle on how to do this. The key with social media is keeping track of what content resonates and what doesn't, so you'll need to monitor your success through likes, shares, re-tweets, comments, and engagement. We'll dive into this in more detail in Chapter 52.

If you want to use the same content across multiple different platforms, you need to make changes so that the post is appropriate for the platform. For instance, Facebook's layout is completely different from Instagram and Twitter, so physically they must be changed. You need to consider your wording and imagery based on which of your target audience uses which platform. For example, hashtags are huge on Instagram and Twitter. But on Facebook they aren't as successful, and can even be viewed as annoying. Likewise, Instagram is all about images and short, powerful statements. Twitter is all about words and links, and Facebook does best with memes, images, links, and video.

You can share the same blog post two to four times a day during peak hours in various parts of the country/world, just mix it up a little by changing the headline, the image, or even creating a video of the same content if possible. In other words, get creative. Avoid using duplicate carbon copy posts. It feels spammy and gets annoying pretty quickly.

Another thing to consider is posting user-generated content. User-generated content is "any type of content that has been put out there by unpaid contributors, or using a better term, fans. It can refer to pictures, videos, testimonials, tweets, blog posts, and everything in between and is the act of users promoting a brand rather than the brand itself."[cxlvi]

Now, as you can imagine, there is a huge difference between a company boasting its products are great and a real customer organically saying that your product is great. In fact, check out these statistics:

- ✓ 84% of millennials report that user generated content (UGC) has at least some influence on what they buy.[cxlvii]
- ✓ 51% of Millennials state that UGC from strangers is more likely to influence their purchase decisions than recommendations from friends, family and colleagues[cxlviii]
- ✓ 68% of 18-34 year-old social media users surveyed were at least somewhat likely to make a purchase after seeing a friend's post.[cxlix]

Word-of-mouth always has, and most likely always will be, one of the most important ways we reach our audience. So, if you receive a great testimonial, or tweet, or Facebook post, or Instagram post, don't be afraid to repost it. Yes, it's self-promotion, but it's real, straight from the mouth of people who are benefiting from your company.

As long as you're consistently posting high quality content that resonates with your audiences across each social media platform, you'll see an increase in followers and audience engagement. The key is monitoring your activity and making any necessary changes, which we'll tackle in the next chapter.

Marketing Masters Pro Tip: Use Google Alerts for Social Media Content

Take a list of your 5 closest competitors, 5 largest competitors, and 5 keywords that describe your business, and set up a Google Alert for them. For those who don't know, a Google Alert is a daily or real time e-mail that sends links to articles found on Google search that contain the keywords you put into the alert.

You can use this tool to keep an eye on your competitors and what they are doing, but more importantly, to gain content and ideas based on what they are posting.

When you get those alerts, scan through them, and either rewrite, reword, comment on, or straight post those articles into your social media calendar.

Some of the best social media posts we have posted for our clients have come through this method, and it's a quick and easy way to gain access to tons of social, sharable content.

Chapter 52: Monitoring Social Media the Right Way

As with all your marketing efforts, to have the greatest impact you need to monitor your actions. Social media isn't exempt from this rule. To get the most out of your social media strategy, make sure that you begin monitoring your profiles the right way from the beginning. It's not as difficult as monitoring some of your other marketing tactics, but it is just as important. By using social media monitoring tools, you can understand the impact you're making on your audience, see what works and what doesn't, and analyze the data to better propel your business forward with an actionable agenda. It allows you to capture powerful insights into your customers, competitors, and industry influencers in ways that digital advertising and research can't.[cl]

Let's look at some best practices you should be implementing to monitor your social media profiles across all active platforms.

First, you need to engage with as many of your followers as possible. As you grow, this will be daunting, but engagement goes hand-in-hand with increased brand awareness and recognition. People take notice. In fact, "70% of people are more likely to use a brand's product or service when they reach out or respond on social media."[cli] When you make customers or potential customers feel like they're interacting with a hands-on company that cares about their needs, they're far more likely to choose you over a competitor. This includes both positive and negative comments, questions, or posts in general. While it might be difficult for you to respond to some of the negative things you will see, you need to understand that it will happen. Even the best brands receive this kind of attention, and so long as you respond publicly in a manner that both addresses the original poster and the issue at hand, people will take notice.

Next, get a system in place that allows you to monitor activity and analyze results. This is best done with one of the many social media tools available on the Internet. There are hundreds of different options, including *Sprout Social, Brandwatch, Buffer, Keyhole, MeetEdgar,* and *Hootsuite,* which is our favorite. *Hootsuite* offers numerous different tracking and monitoring tools that offer insight as to how your social media efforts are paying off. It connects all of your different social media profiles to your account and manages everything in one place. This tool is perfect for any company looking to mainstream their strategy, schedule and curate content, and track and prove your social ROI.

To successfully monitor your social media efforts, you need to follow key conversations, social streams, and keywords—all of which can be done using *Hootsuite*'s built in features. It almost gives you a backend view of social media, one that makes it easy to see where you're getting engagement and where you're not.

You can also use Google Analytics to look at your ROI for any purchased social media ad-space. When you see that there are a few posts that are generating a lot of excitement among your followers, you can use the boost feature across all the major platforms to push your post, picture, or tweet to get more exposure. This feature means you don't actually have to pay to boost anything until you see what's getting the most attention. Once you boost the ones that are getting more attention, analyze them and ask why you believe they resonate more with your audience than others. Ask yourself: What was the common ground here? What was it about this ad that resonating more with my target audience?

As you continue to monitor your social media platforms and gather more data, you can start to analyze your activity to track trends and measure growth.[clii] This is easily done through *Hootsuite,* but can also be done with a little work through each platform's backend or Google Analytics. There are a few key metrics that you'll want to keep a close eye on.

1. **Examine Follower Growth to Identify Anomalies in Audience Behavior**[cliii]

   As you start to grow in followers you can keep an eye on their behavior to notice any similarities and differences in behaviors, trends, and engagement. If you have any outliers in your data, you can research the underlying cause and take note as to whether it was positive or negative. From there, you can begin to repeat the behavior that worked, or avoid the behavior that didn't.

2. **Look at Impressions to Spot Irregularities in Reach**[cliv]

Look at your analytics pages to see how many people are able to see your social media updates. Due to certain algorithms in place, your reach might not be as wide as you'd hope. Look for days where you've had irregularities in reach and see what you posted on those days and how often. Again, take notice and make changes to reflect the days when you reached a larger audience.

3. **Monitor Engagement to Find Peaks and Valleys in Interactions**[clv]

As we mentioned earlier in this chapter, engagement matters. Analyze your engagement rates to see what type of content resonates with your audience and what causes them to ignore and keep scrolling. Maybe posts with pictures are doing better than links, or vice versa. Use your social media's analytics dashboard to keep a continual eye on this until you find a balance that works.

4. **Review Clicks and Traffic to Reveal Inconsistencies with Website Experience**[clvi]

The difference between a click and website traffic is that traffic leads your audience to your actual website, and a click indicates that someone took initiative to visit your site but exited before it finished loading. Keeping an eye on these will help you understand whether you're having problems with your website or if your loading speed is too slow for social media satisfaction. If you find huge inconsistencies in this data, check Google Analytics to review your network referrals and get an overall snapshot of each of your profile's referred traffic rates.

5. **View Mentions and Sentiments to Assess Overall Brand Reputation**[clvii]

Mentions are when someone else on social media writes your company's name or tags you in a post, regardless of if it's in a positive or negative way. Keeping track of this data is called social listening and gives you a good look into what people think about your brand. You'll need to use an external tool, like Brand24 or *Hootsuite*, to measure this data, but it is essential in understanding how your social media presence is doing. Using either of these apps, you can create a report and see how many positive and negative comments were left, as well as how many likes, shares, and total comments were made regarding your brand. Use this data to make changes to what you post and how you respond.

When it comes to social media, you can choose to monitor and analyze your data in whatever way works best for you. If you want to save some time, money, and a decent amount of stress, consider signing up for a social media monitoring tool like *Hootsuite*, or by outsourcing your social media to a professional. You can also use the provided social media analysis tools on each platform, but doing so individually may take a bit longer than using a tool.

Finally, as a closing note on social media, we want to reiterate that even if social media isn't a big part of your marketing plan, you should still at least do the bare minimum and have a presence somewhere. It's damaging to have absolutely no social media profiles and to only post once a year, so make sure you create a profile and follow the tips we've outlined in this section. Additionally, while it's important, social media is not the end-all-be-all, and you shouldn't spend all your time and effort there. Don't get too caught up in your social media numbers—there's a lot more that goes into marketing than likes.

Part 5 – Rich Media

Rich media in our view is any sort of content that is beyond text. Rich media can be visual banner ads, videos, podcasts, infographics, whitepapers, case studies, and so much more.

We've devoted an entire section to rich media because at the end of the day, marketing is about getting a step ahead of your competition.

Words on a page are often quick, easy, and overly saturated.

Rich media, however, is fun, sharable, memorable, and creates an impact. It creates a deeper connection between consumers and your brand, and will have a lasting impact.

Depending on your business, some types of rich media will work better than others, but every business should be utilizing some types of rich media in their marketing.

Chapter 53: Understanding Rich Media

So far in this book we've discussed many different marketing tactics that are used in today's business world—both online and offline. We understand that text and content have the potential to persuade an individual, pictures can transport potential customers into a "what-if" scenario, and that having a website will give you more opportunities than you could have imagined. However, with the evolution of the Internet and technology comes a changing desire from users. People don't want to simply read or look at information anymore. They want an interactive experience, accompanied by an immersive design. That's where rich media comes in. Google defines rich media as, *"A digital advertising term that includes advanced features like video, audio, or other elements that encourage viewers to interact and engage with the content."*[clviii] The main takeaway here is that it is interactive, functional, engaging, and immersive media. However, it's important to understand that rich media isn't only used in advertising anymore.

Throughout this section, we'll walk through different ways you can use rich media to enhance your business, including through content marketing, digital advertising, and mobile marketing.

From the definition above, we can begin to understand what encompasses rich media. It's creative media that engages your visitors in a way not achievable by standard display media, primarily due to the depth, quality, size, and complexity of the source. Using advanced HTML technology, rich media uses multiple levels of content in one place, employing videos, games, live streaming, applets, tweets, and more.[clix] It's an enhanced form of user experience, and more businesses continue to head in this direction.

Rich media is an extremely powerful tool to have in your company's marketing toolbox, and can help take advertisements, content, social media, and mobile efforts one step further. Rich media engages potential customers through stronger CTAs and more interesting, immersive content. For example, rich media ads receive 267% higher CTR than standard banner ads.[clx] It's clear that engagement increases with rich media, but what exactly does that entail?

As we continue to technologically advance, rich media is expected to grow in importance and become even more relevant than it is today. If you've had the chance to watch Netflix' show, *Maniac*, you can understand the potential. If you want to stay one step ahead of your competition, start implementing it in your marketing strategy as soon as possible. In the following chapters, we'll dive deeper into how you can do this, break down the different types of rich media, and discuss the best way to set up campaigns.

Chapter 54: The Benefits of Rich Media

With some understanding of rich media under your belt, you can probably start brainstorming its potential benefits. As you saw in the previous chapter, rich media exponentially increases CTRs for advertisements, but that's just the beginning. If you weren't already convinced to start implementing rich media ads into your marketing strategy, check out some of the undeniable benefits.

1. **Stronger CTR**

   Like we mentioned in Chapter 53, rich media ads receive 267% higher CTR than standard banner ads.[clxi] As rich media is extended to social media, content, and mobile devices, we expect results to follow.

2. **Greater Interactions**[clxii]

   Since rich media is, at its core, interactive and engaging, your audience will spend more time on your site. The immersive features of rich media draw people in and keep their attention for much longer periods of time than static media. This not only helps with conversions, but helps build your brand recognition and accompanying message.

3. **More Space**

   Since rich media is dynamic and interactive, a small usable space can be transformed into a completely limitless opportunity. Whether you're alternating images, enabling audio functions, or implementing an on-page game, you'll have much more space than typical media.

4. **Increased CTA**[clxiii]

   The level of increased interactions and visual space means you have a higher opportunity to offer more CTAs throughout one piece of media. You can use multiple platforms and features to focus your rich media, which gives you more opportunity to get the personal information you need to turn visitors into customers.

5. **Stronger Track-ability**[clxiv]

Since rich media uses more advanced technology, it allows you to "track different levels of engagement and interaction, including important metrics like the number of expansions, multiple exits, and video completions."[clxv] This helps you keep a closer eye on spending habits in comparison to the ROI of your marketing efforts.

6. **More Creativity**

The possibilities with rich media are endless. Literally, if you can dream it you can build it. Since the technology is so advanced, rich media allows you to stretch your company's creative capacity to the limit.

7. **Better Mobility**

Since rich media can be used to increase mobile device engagement (more on this in Chapter 56) you'll experience a stronger user experience across devices. "For example, you can embrace how viewers interact with devices, using swipe actions to rotate cube banners."[clxvi]

While the benefits of rich media continue to grow with its evolution, there are still reasons to start using it in your marketing strategy today. In the next three chapters, we're going to explore just how important it is to use in your content marketing, digital advertisements, and mobile marketing.

Chapter 55: The Importance of Rich Media in Content Marketing and SEO

One of the common themes throughout this book has been that the content you create for your website, blogs, and social media needs to be strong and valuable to your audience. When the Internet first became popular, words were enough. Now, with an increasing amount of video, interactive games, and other rich media being used across the Internet, you need to step up your game if you want to stay relevant. People don't want to visit a blog filled only with words. It's boring and isn't captivating enough for them to justify spending time there. They want to be engaged and offered a wide range of stimuli with every page that they visit.

Luckily, you don't have to be boring anymore. It's easy to implement rich media into your content marketing strategy, and you should be doing this every step of the way. In addition to all the benefits we outlined in Chapter 54, using rich media in your content marketing increases the chances that people will share your content with friends, family members, or coworkers. Rich media makes your content stand apart from the competition and is critical if you want to be successful in today's business world. Let's walk through some of the best, most effective types of rich media you can immediately implement in your content marketing strategy.

✓ **Video**

As the original rich media source, videos are here to stay. In fact, according to Forbes, "video is projected to claim more than 80% of all web traffic by 2019 and 87% of online marketers are currently using video content in their digital marketing strategies."[clxvii] Streaming video allows you to reach almost all of the available senses of your audience. It gives your brand and business a voice, face, sound, and feel that can resonate with your viewers. They increase retention rates and can foster stronger brand recognition over time. Videos have the potential to tell a story, draw people in, introduce new products, provide educational material, and more. They can be used in your blogs, on your website, across social media, and even in e-mail communication. It gives you the opportunity to present yourself in a way that you want people to see you, and, so long as it's captivating, it will help you grow your audience. If it's something that people can't get enough of, it could go viral and give you more business than you could handle within a period of 24 hours. Especially since 59% of company decision makers would rather watch a video than read an article or blog post.[clxviii]

✓ **Podcasts**

Podcasts have grown in importance as we migrate toward a hands-free world. They're like listening to your favorite radio talk show, but without commercials and any breaks in the story. There are podcasts for almost everything you can think of, and if you are in an industry where a podcast will benefit your audience, it's time to get involved. Around 30% of your customers are likely to be auditory learners and will benefit much more from podcasts and audio help.[clxix] People can also listen to podcasts at times when they wouldn't be able to read your content, such as during commutes, while walking around their favorite city, or even during workouts. This broadens your content reach tremendously and helps demonstrate expertise. When you write a blog post, recycle it into a podcast to reach more people.

✓ **GIFS and Cinemagraphs**

If you have a Smartphone or use the Internet, you've probably used a GIF or cinemagraph at some point in your life. These are those short, animated images, sometimes including text that people have started using in replacement of traditional communication methods. They are extremely effective at grabbing attention, and with an every-growing library, there's millions available to choose from. They can be uploaded into your content, attached to a social media post, or even featured on your website. They're easy to put into your content and can massively amplify your message and encourage sharing.[clxx] Insert a few into your content where you're trying to stress a point and your engagement rates will more than likely double.

✓ Stories

Almost all of the social media platforms that dominate the Internet have an option for you to post a story. These are pictures or videos that last for up to 24 hours and can be viewed by your audience as many times as they wish. When you release a new blog, product, or just want to say hi, create a story for your audience to view. Not only does this help user engagement, it helps boost brand awareness and can foster customer loyalty.

✓ Live Streaming

Similar to stories, you can now create live streams for your audience. A great way to incorporate these into your content marketing is by walking through a how-to blog or product description. Live streaming allows viewers to ask questions and get immediate answers, which is perfect for people who crave instant-gratification. After you've finished the streaming, you can archive it on your website for people to watch if they missed it. Create a blog post or social media post and let everyone know that you'll be doing a live stream of the content at a later time and date.

✓ Infographics

Long blog posts can be hard for some readers to digest, even if they're separated using short sentences, large whitespaces, and pictures. Look over your content and see if you can insert an infographic that either explains what you're saying or accompanies your underlying point.

Infographics draw in the attention of audiences and help to increase the number of shares and engagement you receive. Make sure the infographics you create, or use, are high quality and actually relevant to your content to be effective.

✓ Ebooks and Whitepapers

Look at the content you produce. Do you have enough information around a specific topic that would warrant an Ebook or whitepaper? If so, write one. It's a great way for your company to offer an interactive asset for your audience. If you sell them, you might be able to turn a small profit. Otherwise, you can offer them for free as incentives for joining a mailing list, answering a CTA, increased engagement, or simply for being a loyal customer. Ebooks and whitepapers will build your credibility as an expert, and help to further build trust in you and your brand.

✓ Interactive Content

This category includes everything from online polls, quizzes, interactive infographics or charts, content sliders, games, and more. It's the type of content that people will need to click, or mouse over, for the next action to occur. With interactive content, you can take your content and break it down into smaller and smaller pieces for people to navigate, rather than being displayed on one large, scrolling webpage. This is perfect for how-to guides, confusing explanations, or even to offer an array of images. Find something that works best for your company and test it out.

It's critically important to provide high-quality, consistent video, audio, and written content to build your brand, but, as with anything, it will take some time to perfect. Try utilizing a few of these types of rich media and see what works. If it boosts engagement and increases click through rates, keep doing it. See what works for your company. The goal is that by incorporating rich media into your everyday strategy, you'll start seeing a higher level of engagement across the board. Just make sure that all your content is complete with social media sharing buttons, as well as quick share buttons to copy the original hyperlink. Include relevant CTAs for rich media and, as always, keep your brand consistent.

Marketing Masters Pro Tip: Be Unique & Use Rich Media to Stand Out

Today, it's become the norm for people to do the basics when it comes to SEO. There are only 10 results on the first page of Google, and if you want to be one of them, just doing basic SEO and writing blog posts likely isn't going to cut it.

Rich media is a great way to stand out, create more content, and help consumers engage with your brand. We started working with a very well-established company who had been working with another marketing agency on SEO. While their rankings were definitely above average, they weren't hitting the home runs they were looking for.

We came in and recommended 3 forms of rich media—video, a podcast, and long-form blog posts—and within a year, their SEO rankings skyrocketed and traffic was up, as well.

Rich media is truly a great way—both for SEO and for general marketing—to stand out and differentiate yourself vs. your competitors.

Chapter 56: Utilizing Rich Media in Your Advertising

We've already gone through all the different types of digital advertisements you can use in your campaign, but now it's time to talk about rich media. Rich media advertising offers businesses a whole new opportunity and consistently boosts click through rates (CTR) while increasing conversions. It encourages interaction from your audience, and the responsiveness necessary fosters conversions. They're highly impactful and customizable, which is one of the reasons they've grown in popularity in the past decade and aren't going away anytime soon. "According to eMarketer, categories like video and rich media will account for the largest share of digital ad spending in 2016—a sum worth $30.4 billion. By 2019, with an estimated 68.1% growth, digital ad spending will total $44.6 billion."[clxxi] When you look at these numbers in comparison with your ROI, there's a lot to be excited for.

Due to their interactive design, rich media advertisements create complex ads that elicit stronger user response.[clxxii] This means that they offer more benefits to businesses, including the following:[clxxiii]

1. Increased Engagement
2. Flexibility in Creativity
3. Better Use of Space
4. Higher CTR
5. More Diverse Audience Communication
6. Increased Brand Awareness
7. Maximize Short Attention Spans
8. Advanced Analytics

To figure out which types of rich media advertisements to use in your next campaign, check out all the options available.

Banners

Banners are the most basic form of rich media advertising, so they're a good place to get your feet wet. Banners can include videos and can even offer downloadable content. There are also banners with floating, or interstitial elements, which draw the customers' attention in even more. The floating elements can include more embedded rich media, such as videos, and calls to action.

Dynamic Creatives

According to Google, dynamic creatives "use a linked management profile that can change creative content on the fly, either manually or based on content rules."[clxxiv] Dynamic creatives are all about personalization and, according to Forbes, that's an important detail to remember, as "94% of senior-level executives believe delivering personalization is critical or important to reaching customers according to a recent study conducted by PWC's Digital Services group."[clxxv] You want to stay up to speed with what's currently resonating with your audience, so it's important to consider dynamic creatives in your rich media advertising.

The way they work is through analyzing the user through algorithms; making the ads they see more personalized. This makes the journey far easier for the customer. It can span anywhere from the types of books people tend to purchase to commonly visited restaurants. It even proves beneficial for people who frequently travel. It was found that "a live data feed with properties or origin/destination combinations, pricing, and availability, creates and serves any combination of unique creative based… 47% of travelers say personalized ads save them time and effort, proving that tailored messaging is key in influencing the path to purchase."[clxxvi]

Expanding

Expanding rich media ads provide more content in the sense that once a user hovers over it, there's a call to action, such as "Enter your zip code to find the finest restaurants near you right now." It can also include embedded video that either plays automatically, or requires the user to click, and videos are a great way to reach a variety of audiences, which we will discuss later.

Interstitial

"A creative that either floats on top of a page's content or appears as a full screen ad during natural transition points in mobile apps, such as during launch, loading, and video pre-roll."[clxxvii] Basically, interstitials are when you click on a page and there's a pop up with a call to action (usually to sign up for a newsletter) that either disappears when you scroll, or continues to block the content on the page until you either sign up or click "No Thanks." Try to use a respectable amount of these and don't overdo it, as some visitors will be deterred from your site if you use too many.

Lightbox

Lightbox is exclusive to Google and works on both desktop and mobile. After two seconds of hovering over rich media or by tapping the screen, lightbox pops up and covers most of the screen with featured content. This type of advertising is best when you have a lot of rich media to offer customers, such as videos, podcasts, or games. Since it takes up the entire screen, more than one call to action should be offered.

Multi-Directional Expanding (MDE)

This is when an ad will expand to the right or left (wherever it has more space), and featured rich media content will pop up. For example, if the ad is for a movie, once it's clicked it will pop open to reveal the trailer to the movie, which will usually play automatically. The specifics are up to the advertiser, although automatic play is widely recommended as clicking on the ad is viewed as "permission" to see what's next.

Push-down

A push-down involves bumping the content of the website down and replacing it with rich media ad space, usually in the form of a video. In this case, the developer has the option once again for it to automatically push down, or for the user to initiate the push down by clicking on it.

Video

As far as Google goes, videos are either displayed in the VPAID or YouTube Masthead formats described below. We recommend implementing video as often as possible, as it's the type of media that has shown to get the largest ROI for engagement, conversions, and shares.

✓ **VPAID**

VPAID stands for Video Player-Ad Interface Definition. A VPAID creative is "displayed in a publisher's in-stream video player (like the YouTube player), and typically includes video content. Studio supports VPAID linear creatives, which appear before, between or after the publisher's video, and fill the entire video player."[clxxviii]

✓ **YouTube Masthead**

A YouTube Masthead will be a banner with rich media content, most likely video, advertising your product or service for 24 hours. This is beneficial because of the tremendous exposure gained from YouTube Users.

We recommend going through these rich media advertising options and determining what will work best for your company. Run a few campaigns, test the results, and make any changes necessary to increase your ROI.

Chapter 57: Utilizing Social Rich Media for Mobile Marketing

Social media, as we know, has become a tremendous platform for any marketing campaign, but even more so when we're talking about rich media. Consider your daily newsfeed. Images, videos, games, advertisements, and even polls outrank simple posts, and the algorithms are quick to favor something with rich media. This is one of the reasons that Facebook has created the opportunity to transform a simple text post into a picture with customizable colors, backgrounds, and emojis. This, paired with the viral video phenomenon, is reason enough to make sure you're implementing social rich media, especially when designing your mobile marketing campaign.

It's beneficial in more ways than simple exposure, particularly with social-mobile friendly adverts, like "store locators when your prospect is close to your retail location. Or easy-to-claim mobile coupons that remind your customers to claim when you are within the vicinity of a store."[clxxix] Not taking advantage of these opportunities is wasting untapped potential to increase your reach, conversion rate, and ROI. Social rich media for mobile marketing isn't much different than the regular rich media we've already discussed, the primary difference being the addition of social media insights to how you use your media. Since over 75% of the time spent on social media is on a mobile device,[clxxx] you should be focused on mobile optimization first and foremost.

So how, exactly, do you do this? We have a few tried and true suggestions.

First and foremost, avoid anything that requires your visitors to need a Flash plug-in. This does not work well on mobile and leaves your audience with a blank screen. Instead, implement the HTML5 code that is used for rich media on desktops.

Next, you need to understand the importance of grabbing someone's attention. People scroll mindlessly through their social media feeds on their phones during breaks, while on public transportation, before bed, and more. The fact that we're attached at the hip to our devices makes it quick, easy, and distracting. The average person sees hundreds of posts on social media each day, and unless something seriously catches their attention, they aren't going to give it a second look.

This means you must try and appeal to as many senses as possible: text, interaction, video, high-quality graphics, and more. Most importantly, you *do not* want the user to click your ad and leave the social media platform they're currently on, because if it starts redirecting, most people just close the ad. You want to make it easy for them to just hit that back button and return to scrolling through their newsfeed—hopefully after they've taken your desired action.

Therefore, one of the most important parts of succeeding with social rich media on mobile platforms is being able to see your content through the eyes of your audience. You need to understand exactly what gets their attention, how to engage them, and how to foster action. At the beginning of your marketing strategy, this might take a little trial and error, but through tracking browsing behavior and the success—or failure—of your marketing efforts, you'll get a stronger idea of what works and what doesn't. For example, you're able to track how many people watched the entire video, how many shared it, how many were compelled to visit/call your store or website, and which types of videos and images seem to garner the most attention.

When launching your social media campaign, rich media should be at the forefront. This is your megaphone to the world—don't silence it with boring content. Keep users engaged, make them interested, and give them offers that are hard to refuse. Do this, and you'll be far ahead of your competition. Not only will it increase your engagement—8x more than standard banners[clxxxi]—but it will increase brand loyalty and all-around traffic to your website.

Marketing Masters Pro Tip: Repurpose Rich Media on Social Media

Just like you can repurpose blog posts on social media, you can also repurpose rich media as well. We recommend your website be the hub of all your content, whether that be rich media or otherwise. Post all your rich media on your website and then also post it on your social media. You'll get twice the bang for your buck for the content you produce, and keep your social media followers engaged and interested in your brand.

Chapter 58: How to Properly Execute a Rich Media Campaign

Now that you have a comprehensive understanding of what rich media is and how you can use it to enhance your content, advertisements, and mobile marketing strategy, we wanted to give you some insight on proper execution.

The first step in this process is evaluating what types of rich media will represent your brand with the biggest impact. This is going to take some experimentation, but as with most of the marketing tools we've discussed, don't try to jump in and implement everything at once. Think in terms of your audience. What do you think they want to see? What meaning or value do you need to deliver to reach them?

Rich media does a good job at increasing awareness of your brand and helps your audience members move from prospect to customer. To get the most out of your strategies, differentiate your efforts based on where you are using rich media—whether it's in your content, through advertising, or to increase mobile marketing reach. This will give you the best results in terms of campaign deliverance and performance. A great example was the advertisement done for the movie *The Hobbit*, which implores users to take a journey created entirely in HTML5. Through this journey, visitors are introduced to the characters, conflicts and landscapes through an exciting, responsive game-like video.[clxxxii]

While this is an intense example, primarily due to a much higher marketing budget than most of us can afford, it shows the full potential of rich media. With that in mind, it's important to set your budget prior to taking any action. Your focus should be getting the highest ROI with your rich media strategy, which can equate to more click through rates, conversions, website visits, e-mails, and more. It all depends on your underlying goal. You might not have the money a giant production studio has, but you can still have the creativity with the right team that has the right skills. Because when it comes down to text vs. rich media, consumers only retain "10% of [text], but [they] will remember 95% of the video."[clxxxiii] Additionally, close to "52% of consumers are more confident to make online purchases after watching video ads."[clxxxiv] We think those are some convincing statistics.

When you're initially lost in the beginning, wondering where to begin, look back to what's been most successful in your other efforts. If you've used video, you've probably seen a lot of success with it. Due to compelling statistics mentioned above for engagement and recollection, we recommend using video rich media in each of your campaigns. Make sure whatever you produce is valuable, memorable, high quality, and unique for a potential conversion to run out and either purchase your product or talk to their friends about your company.

By and large, the rich media tactics that seems to be the most effective are the ones that take up most of the screen, on both desktop and mobile. Though at first it may seem like an inconvenience to the user, many people welcome and enjoy videos, *particularly* if they're appealing to their interests.

So, this is not something that can be rushed. You should test your video out on focus groups, groups within the company, friends, family, whomever you can, and ask them important questions, like: how did the video make them feel? Did the video make them want to purchase the product or learn more about the company? Did the presentation of the video feel invasive or annoying? These are all the questions that will make or break a rich media advertising campaign.

As you move forward, you must always return to the user's journey. In the infancy of your business, you're not necessarily looking for a major call to action. You want your video to portray your vision of the brand to pique interest in the user. You're looking to create that feeling of recognition, like those fostered by Volkswagen and Coca Cola. So, right from the beginning, that's what you're trying to accomplish.

Later, you'll want your rich media to offer a firm call to action. This is when you kick into high gear. Focus your goals on click through rates and engagements so you can start to nurture those into conversions. Your approach to rich media might be different in terms of demanding an immediate call for action, but the feel of the brand you've already established should be continual.

The main thing to remember throughout this entire section is that rich media isn't exclusively about advertising. You'll want all your content to include some form of rich media to appeal to different learning styles, along with posting on your social media. You can approach each campaign similarly to how you would an advertisement, but remember to avoid any "sales heavy" media unless it directly relates to your content.

Marketing Masters Pro Tip: What Should My Rich Media Topics Be?

Clients often struggle with ideas for what to turn into rich media. Two of our favorite ways to do this are through combing through old blog posts and creating rich media out of them, and using FAQs for rich media.

For the blog posts, it's as simple as going through your already well-researched, long-tail focused blog posts and modifying them to incorporate rich media. Maybe you do a podcast episode about the topics to dive deeper, perhaps a short video, or it could be as simple as going back and editing the post to add more content and incorporate graphics and infographics for key facts.

For FAQs, compile a list of the top 25 questions that you are asked the most frequently by customers or prospective customers, and turn those into rich media. Take those questions and do a podcast series on them or video series. Create beautiful infographics answering the questions in a visual way.

The sky is really the limit when it comes to rich media, and if you don't know where to start with your rich media campaign, use these two tips to kick things off!

Part 6 – Web Design / Development

Website design and development plays a tremendous role in your marketing. All too often, companies leave their websites to their information technology (IT) department.

While the technical aspects of your website should involve your IT department and developers, a website should never be left in the hands of IT. Your website is your biggest marketing tool and your 24/7 salesperson, and it needs to be treated as a function of marketing.

Your website is the first impression that anyone has of your company. And unfortunately, you never have a second chance at a first impression.

Your website must be done correctly right from its inception. Your website is your only 24/7/365 first impressions to the world.

From the aesthetics to the content to the rich media, your website has to shout your brand and value proposition from the rooftops.

Beyond this, it's important that the functions that are handled by IT and developers by done with marketing in mind. From SEO friendly coding to page load speeds to conversion optimization and everything in between, the technical aspects of your website also play a tremendous role in your marketing.

Chapter 59: The Connection Between Marketing and Web Development

Before we dive deeper into marketing and digital web development, we want you to understand the critical connection between strong web development and marketing coordination. When you first decide that you want to build a website, you'll start looking for an agency to help you. While there are a lot of things you want to look for, one of the first should be how much they know about marketing. If the company developing your website doesn't have a strong marketing background and offer marketing services themselves, you've either found the wrong company or you should be prepared to create your own marketing team, with consultants that will be highly involved in the development of your new website.

Why, exactly? Because your website's end result will depend on functionality, marketing strategies, brand alignment, and much more.

From the beginning, your web development will be much more effective if it's done with marketing and conversions in mind. A fully informational website functions much differently than a business website, and this needs to be clear from the beginning. This is why it's so beneficial to choose a web development company that has a strong marketing background. They know what they need to do to give you a website that not only looks great, but allows you to run campaigns, post blogs, and make marketing easy. From years of experience, they have an intuition that brings together the best of both worlds.

Since your website is the foundation of all of your marketing efforts, it's no surprise that this is so important. Lacking the proper foundation will, at the very least, cost your business money, or, at the worst, cause your business to crumble. Many business owners aren't well-versed in either of these areas, so bringing on a company that understands how to give you a marketing-focused website will make all the difference. The two work together to produce websites that are filled with high quality content, persuasive copy, directed information, and clear calls-to-action.

They'll also make sure that it's easy for you to make changes once they've completed the initial build. If you work with a web developer that has no marketing experience, you'll end up with a website that you can't regularly update with blogs, new case studies, images, or testimonials. IT people work on the backend of things and don't necessarily have the same interpersonal skills that marketing-minded people possess.

In addition, many of the marketing concepts we've discussed and will continue to discuss in this book can be very technical in nature. Your website needs to be coded right from the ground up to do well organically. It needs to have the right site structure, coding, tagging, and be built with SEO in mind. It has to properly integrate advertising tags, strongly converting landing pages, have good load speed, and much more.

It's no surprise that this means you should never take the cheap route. Cheaper usually equates to poor-quality and harder maintenance. Focus instead on finding someone who can build you a website that is optimized to rank well *organically*, perform well with ads, and resonate with your audience. This is the key to your success. You have to give it time to work.

Many clients often ask if they can use a DIY website builder like Wix, SquareSpace, GoDaddy, or others. The answer is simple— you get what you pay for. We have converted dozens if not hundreds of businesses out of these budget-friendly solutions and into real custom websites, and we have yet to this day had a business owner who has regretted the investment.

Marketing Masters Pro Tip: Do It Right!

We'll keep this short and sweet. Do your website right. There are so many things that can go wrong during a website development project. Hire a company that has good references, testimonials, and a solid design, development, and marketing background.

In the past decade plus, we have seen the good, bad, ugly, and horrendous when it comes to websites. And we've seen business after business struggle because their website isn't built right. It could be as simple as a redirect that wasn't set up right that is literally costing thousands or tens of thousands of organic visitors per month, or as complex as a site completely built wrong, but no matter what the issue, at the end of the day it is going to cost you money.

Make a good investment and trust a proven professional with your website. You'll be glad you did.

Chapter 60: How Often to Revamp Your Website

After you've developed a strong foundation—a website built by marketing-minded people—you'll likely move your focus to other parts of your business. Your website gets crossed off the to-do list and likely doesn't get revisited until a few years later when it's time to revamp it again.

That's okay. We expect people to do this. However, it's important to continually revisit your website to make sure that everything is working the way it should.

For instance, if you ask yourself when the last time your website was revamped and you think back to four years ago when it was first built, you're a little overdue. Web design technology and trends change quickly, so it doesn't take long before your site looks old and outdated. Since your landing pages and website are the first impression people get from your company, you need to make sure that you're doing a bit of housecleaning every now and then. If your website looks like it's out of date, people will probably think your company is, too.

When you first begin and create your long-term business plans, make sure you plan accordingly to invest in revamping both the front- and backend website updates at least every two years.

This doesn't necessarily mean that you need to go in and give your website a complete and total overhaul, especially if things are working the way they are intended to. Instead, it means that you need to make sure you're keeping up with what's new in your industry. Look at what your competitors are doing and whether they're seeing success. If you find them updating their website every year, it's probably because it better aligns with the changing user experience and needs. Follow suite. If your website looks like it was created when Minesweeper was still the #1 game, it's time for a complete facelift. Remember, your website is your foundation and you need to make sure you're offering optimal user experience if you want to see the biggest ROI.

With that being said, if your website is performing well, there may be no reason to fix it aside from a few modernizations. Keep in mind that according to a study performed by Stanford University, a whopping 75% of people judged the credibility of a business based on how visually pleasing their site was.[clxxxv]

On the contrary, if your conversions have dropped, or you've struggled getting them from the start, that's a good indication that it's time to start asking some real questions regarding your website.

- ✓ Have you done everything possible to optimize your website for SEO, including hiring a professional?
- ✓ Does your website offer good user experience? Is it easy to navigate? Can your visitors find answers to common questions without hassle?
- ✓ Do your competitors' websites have any noticeable differences that might indicate stronger user experience? Are they aesthetically similar to yours?
- ✓ Do you have clear, concise, and easy to see calls to action?
- ✓ Do you have social sharing buttons for all of your social media profiles?
- ✓ Within five seconds of arriving at your website, will visitors know what your company does?
- ✓ In addition to the user experience, consider various user journeys and whether your site caters to different ones.
  - ✓ How did they get there?
  - ✓ Why are they there?
  - ✓ What are their needs?
  - ✓ Is it easy for them to find a solution to their problem?

Answering these questions will give insight as to how often you need to go in and revamp your website. In addition to focusing on user experience, don't forget about all the technological aspects that surround web development. A simple checklist includes questions such as:[clxxxvi]

1. **Is your website fully working? Are you getting visits, just not conversions?**

If your website is working and you just aren't getting conversions, it's because people aren't finding a compelling reason to stick around and take action. Check your keywords, CTAs, and overall design.

2. Has the technology recently changed?

Browsers update constantly in order to work properly across different devices. This means your site needs to change along with the browsers. Likewise, devices change, screen sizes change, and technology changes. Wearables, smartphones, and tablets are common today and weren't nearly as prevalent just a few years ago when many websites were built.

3. Have your business goals changed?

When your goals change, your website needs to change. It's as simple as that.

4. Is your website outdated?

If you have old stock photos that elicit absolutely no relatable emotions to your business, you're probably scaring people away rather than drawing them in. Make sure you're evolving with increasingly rich media and interactive content.

5. Can you no longer make updates?

Super old websites were made solely using HTML and CSS, but now a myriad of backend languages is used to create and maintain websites. If your website is unable to update, it's probably because it's reached its capacity and you need new backend code. Additionally, if your website's platform uses outdated scripts or user interface, you're far past the point of needing an update.

If you want to stay relevant in your industry, you need to make sure your website doesn't lose its value. Like we said, as a rule of thumb, give yourself a facelift every two years. If you objectively enjoy looking at your website, chances are others will, too.

We also wanted to briefly mention the importance of weekly tweaks. As we discussed in the SEO section, there are a lot of changes that occur in algorithms. Taking the time to make small weekly tweaks will help you stay relevant. It will also mean that when it comes time for a redesign, you won't need to do a complete overhaul. Post content regularly, update case studies, add testimonials, and make sure your products and services are current.

Chapter 61: Making Updates on a Monthly Basis

Like we briefly mentioned at the end of Chapter 60, it's important to keep up with the evolution of your business through website updates. We recommend doing this on a weekly basis, but if you don't have the time, at least make monthly updates. We find that very few businesses implement this strategy, but in doing so, you will find that you receive more conversions and have fewer problems when doing your bi-yearly website revamps.

Making monthly updates helps to keep your website and the technology involved current. It's not difficult, especially if you continually do this throughout the year. Every month, spend some time analyzing and identifying key areas of your business' website, app, and any other developmental project, with the goal of finding areas that need updated. If you find any, update them immediately. This is much simpler than letting your site sit for years. You'll avoid having to rebuild from the bottom up while maintaining customer value.

There are many programs, such as *Jira* by Atlassian, that allow tech teams and beta users to report bugs and areas that may interfere with the optimal user journey. This is a great way to keep track of issues that appear over time, without having a full IT crew in your pocket.

Security is a huge concern in today's day and age, and keeping all your technology, website server, CMS, and any website add-ons up to date will dramatically minimize the chances of a security break or hacking.

In addition to regular monthly updates, if you want to go above and beyond you can have a specific area of focus within your website where you test out new key features or rich media. Smaller updates and revamps throughout the year are essential to avoid spending hundreds, potentially thousands, of dollars on a complete redesign. Whether you're expanding your product catalog, updating the user interface for your blogs, or simply changing your image gallery, a little here and a little there is a great way to spread things out. This way, when it comes time for your website revamp, you can tackle all the big things that you might not be able to handle in-house.

This strategy helps businesses focus internal efforts on what they need now, rather than what they want in the future. It's a way to constantly improve your customers' experience while still having the time you need to devote to them in other ways—such as social media engagement, customer service, and product development. It also helps keep your employees sane, rather than loading them up on work a few times a year, or once every two years. Most importantly, making monthly updates means your technology is always up to date.

There are certain things you should be monitoring at all times (or have someone on your team who does). Uptime is free, and it measures how well your website is performing. You'll also want to check your site's time to first byte (TTFB), a.k.a., how long it takes your site to load. Our attention spans have grown so short that "Most Internet users are impatient: 40% abandon a website that takes more than 3 seconds to load."[clxxxvii] So the time in which it takes your page to load can mean the difference between a sale for you or one for your competitor.

When you first start out with your monthly updates, always begin with the sitemap you'll be focusing on. From there, choose the areas that are absolutely necessary to update so you can get more conversions. Create a detailed task list and delegate accordingly with a reasonable time allotted to get things done. Regularly set goals, analyze results, and make changes. This process will help you keep everything up to date as your business changes, and your web visitors will certainly appreciate it.

Marketing Masters Pro Tip: Little Changes Add Up Over Time

Many of our most successful clients have us on a retainer to consistently keep their website updated.

Starting with the technical aspects, including the server, CMS, plug-ins and other add-ons, we also ensure that the information, content, videos, and graphics are all up to date.

Updating a site in bite-size pieces makes the large web revamps much easier and more affordable, and it also ensures your site is pretty much always kept up to date.

Chapter 62: Using the Right Technology Based on Your Audience

During our initial conversation with new clients, it's rare if they don't mention wanting a mobile app. Whenever we ask why, specifically, their response is almost always because a competitor does or because everyone else has one. While yes—as we'll talk about in chapter 67—keeping up with the trends is important, you shouldn't follow actions just because everyone else is doing it.

Instead, you need to choose the technology your company uses based on your audience. This includes website-specific technology for your backend business needs, best practices for web design and development, and appropriate platforms.

When we talk about backend needs, we're primarily focusing on your content management system (CMS). This is a program, or set of programs, that work together to create, organize, and manage all your digital content. WordPress is a popular example of a CMS that's easy to use and responsive, but it's not for everyone. Instead, you want to focus solely on finding a CMS that will benefit your business and drive sales. If you have the wrong CMS for your business, you're going to miss out on many benefits, and it's very difficult to switch once you've gotten your website functioning. From the beginning, we want you to know that choosing a CMS system will take a lot of time, but it's worth it.

At the very minimum, it should have redundancy in IT, automatic backups, easy marketing integration, flexibility to deliver product catalogs and listings, and an easy editorial system. It's also important to find a system that boasts top of the line security and can be easily customized by your team. If not, you're wasting money. You need a content management system that can be handled internally, rather than having to contact a web developer every time you want to post a new blog or update your whitepapers.

The rest of the details will depend on the needs and goals of your business. You may want more personalization features, content scheduling, included analytics, calendars, or features specific to an e-commerce store. Since businesses are vastly different from one another, there is no clear-cut equation for what CMS system you should use. Put aside the time to research, knowing that it will be worth it down the road.

Once you know what you want in terms of features, find a high-quality, reputable company that will help you build your website. We've seen hundreds of businesses shop based on price, leading to a website that's extremely difficult for them to use. They didn't put in any research, the web developers created something based off a cookie-cutter site, and now they've spent money on something that you can't use. Instead, make sure your CMS *and* your platform is going to do what it needs to do. This is most often done through having a custom website built from scratch, maintaining a strong line of communication between you and the developer regarding needs and intended use.

With that being said, you'll also need to know which type of platforms you'll be using. This way, you can communicate to your developer prior to your initial website build and have everything ready to go from the start.

Business platforms, like ecosystems, are "dynamic and co-evolving communities of diverse actors who create new value through increasingly productive and sophisticated models of both collaboration and competition."[clxxxviii] They help facilitate communication between business owners, employees, and the public, or customers. They help make exchanges and condense networks of individuals into a manageable area. Each serve different purposes, so the ones you implement will depend on research into competitor behavior, your industry, and an understanding of your audience's needs. Without this research, it is impossible to know what your strongest investment will be.

There are three main platforms to focus on: aggregation, social, and mobilization. Aggregation platforms help connect people to necessary resources to answer a question or facilitate a transaction.[clxxxix] If you've ever had to do a research project, you've needed to find high-quality scientific articles. A common place to go was JSTOR, a large online database for scientific research. JSTOR is an example of an aggregation platform.

Social platforms we've already covered, and include Facebook, Twitter, and LinkedIn. Smaller, sub-categorized platforms also fall under this category. They help foster a deeper emotional bond, rather than just a transactional relationship, and increase social interactions.

Mobilization platforms work with the goal of moving people to act together—whether on a common interest, goal, or policy.[cxc] These have a much broader reach but tend to create long-lasting relationships, since they require continued action over time.

On a final note, there are certain features that every website needs to have if they want to be successful, regardless of their industry or goal. Some of these features include:[cxcicxcii]

- ✓ A Logical Roadmap
- ✓ Fast Loading Speed
- ✓ Crucial Business Information
- ✓ Contact Information
- ✓ Clear Navigation
- ✓ Tracking Enabled for Analytics
- ✓ Strong SEO Capabilities
- ✓ Strong Security
- ✓ A Good CMS
- ✓ Optimized for Conversions
- ✓ Social Media Integration
- ✓ E-mail Marketing
- ✓ A Mobile-Friendly Version
- ✓ FAQ Section
- ✓ Strong Hosting Platform

This list will help you prepare for your initial conversation with your web developer. Knowing the purpose of your website before building it is the best way to take advantage of all the available technology. Just make sure you always focus on user intent and your audience.

Chapter 63: Proper Website Structures

Your website structure is critical to helping visitors navigate your site and allowing search engines to properly index your content.

Sitemaps were extremely common five years ago, but most digital marketing professionals today no longer use them. Why? Having a proper site structure eliminates the need for a site map in most applications. As long as search engine spiders can effectively and efficiently crawl and navigate all the pages on your website, there isn't a need for a sitemap.

This all starts with having a proper site structure. The best way to design a site structure is to draw it on a whiteboard.

You should start in the center with your homepage, and have all of your subpages cascade from there. You'll generally have three levels of pages on your site:

- ✓ Homepage
  - o Tier 1 sub pages
    - ▪ Tier 2 sub pages

For example, on a website selling clothing, that might look like:

- ✓ Homepage (Main landing page)
  - o Tier 1 sub pages (Product categories such as "Shirts")
    - ▪ Tier 2 sub pages (Product pages such as "Superman Graphic Logo Shirt")

The homepage is just that—the main landing page of your website. This will live on the root of your domain, such as TheMarketingMasters.com.

From there, you will likely have a series of tier 1 sub pages. These are main pages which generally fall as headers across your navigation menu, such as your About page, Services page, Blog, and Contact page.

Below those, you'll have tier 2 sub pages, which are sub pages to the sub pages. These may be things like your Brand History,

Leadership Team, or other pages that might fall below a tier 1 page like the about page.

Some companies have additional sub tiers, and they can go as deep as needed, but it's important to follow an organized hierarchy as you get deeper and deeper into your site.

It's also helpful to use breadcrumbs, a navigational trail across the top of the page, to help both visitors and spiders know where they are in your site. Your URL structure should also follow the hierarchy of your website, for example a tier 2 sub page for Team might look like TheMarketingMasters.com/about/our-team.

Once you have this mapped out, it's important to interlink all these pages with one another. If you talk about your team on the Service page, hyperlink it to your team page. These links will further help visitors and spiders be able to navigate your website.

It sounds simple to plan a site structure, but it's amazing how many companies do this wrong. It's also easy to botch the structure when additional pages are added after the fact. Make sure your site always has a strong site structure and navigation in place, and it will help ensure your visitors and search engine spiders can easily navigate your site to find the information they are looking for.

Chapter 64: Effective Website Tools to Help with Your Marketing

In today's day and age, there seems to be a tool for everything when it comes to your website and marketing. In fact, we are at a point of tool overload, where too many tools are bogging down website load times, bogging down agency and internal marketing resources, and many of which are tracking things that don't really need to be tracked.

There are always needs for specialized tools, however in our option, these are the major website tools that should be implemented to help with your marketing:

- ✓ **Google Analytics** – Used to keep track of all your website visitors, traffic sources, and their interaction with your website

- ✓ **Google Webmaster Tools** – Used to keep track of technical website elements and SEO; This is the only tool which provides direct insights, recommendation and feedback from Google

- ✓ **Heatmap/Visitor Recording Software** – A tool to help identify how visitors are interacting with specific pages on your website

- ✓ **Chat Software** – This is not required, but will definitely help increase conversions on your website

- ✓ **Google Tag Manager** – An organizational tool which will help organize all of your tracking codes and tools on your website and also help your website load a bit faster

That's really it. There are of course going to be specialized needs in which other tools will need to be deployed onto a website, but for the vast majority of circumstances, these tools are all you need to properly track your marketing efforts on your website and make changes accordingly.

Don't get bogged down in data overload. Sometimes too much data is as bad as or worse than too little. These tools will provide a good amount of information and all the key statistics you need from your website in order to make intelligent marketing decisions.

Chapter 65: Landing Pages for Advertising

Landing pages are critical part of your website. A landing page is a dedicated page with a purpose of driving conversions. When it comes to running ad campaigns, whether on Google Ads, social media, or otherwise, it's important to send those visitors to a dedicated landing page or landing pages which are optimized for conversions.

Ads should really never point to your homepage and rarely should point to a sub page on your website. The reality is that these pages are designed for natural and organic traffic. Ad campaigns give us the opportunity to send visitors to a very specialized page based on your ad preferences, keywords, segmenting, and/or targeting.

A landing page aesthetically should match the design and branding of your website. Technically, they should be easy to manage through your CMS and usually are not accessible except by direct URL. Functionally, their goal is to convert, so they should contain strong calls to action, just the right amount of text, copy that drives conversion, and should be constantly analyzed and improved upon.

When you build a website, you should be sure to incorporate at least one if not a few different landing page templates which can easily be modified to run your ad campaigns. This strategy will ensure fast changes can be made to improve conversions.

Marketing Masters Pro Tip: Landing Pages Truly Do Improve Conversions

We inherited a client who was running ads but driving them right to the homepage of their website. When we went into their Google Ads campaign, their quality score was a 2/10, and cost per conversion was over $500.

With some minor campaign changes, we created landing pages for each of their main keyword phrases, and over time increased their quality score to an 8/10 and drove down their cost per conversion to under $75.

Landing pages truly help with conversions, relevance, and quality scores, and will improve every metric as it relates to an ad campaign. Make sure you take the time to set them up, as it will save you money in the long run and help drive stronger results.

Chapter 66: Landing Pages For SEO

Landing pages can also be critical for SEO. There is a true art to setting up landing pages for SEO so as not to come across as spammy or violate Google's guidelines.

Landing pages for SEO are often called doorway pages. Here's what Google has to say about doorway pages:

Doorways are sites or pages created to rank highly for specific search queries. They are bad for users because they can lead to multiple similar pages in user search results, where each result ends up taking the user to essentially the same destination. They can also lead users to intermediate pages that are not as useful as the final destination.

Here are some examples of doorways:

- ✓ Having multiple domain names or pages targeted at specific regions or cities that funnel users to one page
- ✓ Pages generated to funnel visitors into the actual usable or relevant portion of your site(s)
- ✓ Substantially similar pages that are closer to search results than a clearly defined, browsable hierarchy

The unfortunate thing is that doorway pages work and when done correctly pose a minimal risk to the site's overall SEO. We're not saying to go Black Hat here, but we are suggesting pushing the boundaries within limits.

When you engage in keyword research, you should map out specifically which keywords will be targeted on which pages. Any keywords that don't have a page should be created as an SEO landing page. These pages, unlike the ad landing pages, should be incorporated into your website's overall navigation in some way and internally linked to. The purpose is to treat these pages as if they were a natural part of your website, even though you felt they weren't necessarily needed when building your site and their sole purpose is to help drive SEO traffic. That isn't to say the pages should be useless; they should contain strong content and information about whatever keyword they are focused on, but in reality, likely wouldn't exist were it not for SEO.

Caution needs to be taken when creating these pages. You don't want to create dozens or hundreds of them, and you don't want to create new variations for closely related keywords. For example, if you want to rank for the term "Colorful Widgets," you could create a page about this, but you probably wouldn't want to create a separate page for each color widget. Similarly, if you were trying to rank for "Texas BBQ Manufacturer," you wouldn't want to create a doorway page for each city in Texas.

There is a fine line that needs to be followed when creating these pages so as to ensure you don't push the envelope too far, which could result in a penalty from Google.

Chapter 67: Staying Up to Date with New Technology

Web development is a continual game of staying up to date. Just when you start implementing a new technology, something better comes along. It can be tough, especially for businesses without an internal development team, but it's important if you want to stay relevant in your industry. When we say important, we want to stress that this doesn't mean spending every waking second making sure all your technology is updated and ahead of your competitors. If you did that, it'd be impossible to run your business.

Instead, focus on staying up to date with the trend, as opposed to chasing them down years later. We couldn't tell you how many companies have come to us, 10 years after mobile apps have been around, saying, "I think we finally are ready to develop an app." Yes, it's good to have, but you've surrendered years of potential benefits by putting it off. When big, new trends come out, it's important to take notice and understand why you need it now, not years down the road. That's where working with a reputable marketing agency and development company can help.

With that considered, not every single web development trend is going to apply to your industry. It depends on the needs, wants, and demands of your customers, along with how they use technology for satisfaction. For example, if your company has a Podcast, you'll need to pay special attention to any new things happening in that arena, which will be vastly different from new technology released for social media, other forms of rich media, and digital advertising.

Keep your eyes and ears open for new technology, and if you see something developing, jump on the bandwagon.

If you want to go the extra mile, we recommend following experts in your industry—either through blogs or social media. Occasionally check in with your competitors to ensure that you're not falling behind. Just be aware of the ever-changing web development around you.

You should also attend specific web development conferences and foster personal relationships with people who are constantly kept in the loop. Whatever you do, just don't fall behind. Make sure you act sooner rather than later to keep yourself ahead of the competition in an increasingly competitive world.

Marketing Masters Pro Tip: Be Careful Not to Get Sucked into Technology Scares

We truly believe honesty in business is unfortunately becoming a rarity. It's important to have a trustworthy development partner who can help you navigate the waters of what technology you should be utilizing and when.

We've had countless clients attend conferences and trade shows, and be sold on the latest and greatest fad, or told their marketing is suffering because they are missing X, Y, and Z, only to spend money on these things and see no return.

The reality is, many technology companies are focused more on their own bottom line than yours. Their sales pitch may not always be in your best interest.

Even as the owners of a marketing and development agency, we are constantly bombarded with at least a half dozen e-mails per day from other companies telling us "Something is wrong with our website" or, "Our marketing ROI would be much better if we had a mobile app." The reality is, these are just template e-mails that are blasted out over and over, playing a numbers game that a business owner will eventually respond with interest.

Find a good, reputable, trustworthy marketing and development agency and keep them close to you. Their honest advice will help steer you in the right direction and potentially save hundreds of thousands of dollars in poor technology decisions.

Part 7: E-mail Marketing

It's hard to find something that has changed communication more over the last 25 years than e-mail.

Life without e-mail was an entirely different world, and with the e-mail revolution we are all constantly connected to one another, for better or worse.

As such, e-mail has become one of the most commonly used ways to communicate marketing materials to an audience. While there is tremendous value in e-mail marketing, there is a right and a wrong way to go about it, and a fine line between marketing and spamming.

This is one area that we tend to err on the side of caution and avoid ruining a brand's reputation through poor e-mail marketing practices.

In this section, we'll dive into the most common and successful ways to utilize e-mail marketing and provide actionable tips on how to maximize the results of your e-mail marketing campaigns, how to properly manage your e-mail subscriber lists, and how to optimize the content you send.

Chapter 68: Understanding E-mail Opt-in Lists

We've discussed digital marketing and touched upon offline marketing, so now we're going to spend some time focusing on e-mail marketing. Every day, businesses use e-mail to communicate with each other, vendors, and most importantly, their customers and target audiences. It's an easy way to add a personal touch to your marketing strategy and offer value to your readers. E-mail marketing can be extremely effective, but only when it's done well, in a strategic manner.

One of the main aspects of e-mail marketing is your e-mail opt-in list. An opt-in list is when people sign up, or opt-in, to receive informational, educational, promotional, or other types of e-mails. E-mail opt-in lists are built many ways, but most include questions like, "Would you like to receive more information from [company name]?" or, "Would you like to sign up for [company name's] weekly/monthly newsletter to receive updates on [product/services]?" Using a short form—online or offline—they willingly enter their details and provide their e-mail. There is usually a disclaimer that states, "By submitting this form, you agree to receive e-mail marketing from [company name]." This method helps businesses and customers stay in line with the rules and regulations.

There are two types of opt-in lists: single and double. According to *Mail Chimp*, a single opt-in list is when a contact fills out your signup form, clicks submit, and their information is saved to a list.[cxciii] This is the most common type of opt-in list, and is frequently used by most businesses across the globe. A double opt-in list is when a contact goes through the above steps with an added confirmation step. After clicking the submit button, an e-mail is sent to their inbox and they follow the confirmation link to solidify their sign-up. This is advantageous, because it helps to lower invalid or fake e-mail addresses people might use to sign up. When you set up your lists, you can choose from either option. Both single opt-in lists and double opt-in lists are different than purchasing e-mail lists, which is when, according to *Hubspot*, you work with a provider to "find and purchase a list of names and e-mail addresses based on demographics and/or psychographic information."[cxciv] The main difference is the lack of consent, but we'll dive into more detail about purchased e-mail lists in Chapter 75.

Opt-in lists are important because they're voluntary partnership agreements. You gain permission to send e-mail to customers and prospects. Your audience is saying that they want to hear from you, and you have the opportunity to provide value and build your brand's recognition, make sales, and foster relationships. You can send special promotions, newsletters, event reminders, and whatever else you think they'd enjoy seeing—in reasonable amounts. The details of your content matter, and will be essential in keeping your current subscribers opted-in.

When it comes to e-mail marketing, opt-in lists are literally your most valuable assets!

Chapter 69: Well Known Ways to Grow Your Opt-in List

Many businesses start trying to build their mailing list without an understanding of what it really means to opt-in. For example, someone entering their e-mail to purchase something from your website is *not* opting in. All they opted to do was make a purchase. On the contrary, if you have a little box they can check that says something like, "Would you like to receive e-mail updates from us?" or, "Would you like to sign up for our newsletter for 10% off your next purchase?"—anything along the lines of asking permission to e-mail them—*that's* an opt-in.

All of the e-mails that you have access to aren't part of your opted-in e-mail list. The change occurs when they give their permission to send them mass e-mails. This can be difficult work, especially for new companies. Building opt-in lists will take time, especially sizeable ones. Luckily, there are some pretty easy ways you can start encouraging people to opt-in. In this chapter, we'll look at some of the well-known ways to grow your opt-in list, and in Chapter 65 we'll discuss a few of the more creative ways you can use. Just keep in mind that you want to implement numerous strategies so that you can build your opt-in e-mail list with every chance you get, including:

1. **Add an Exit-Intent Popup**

   When people visit your website, it's usually purposefully, or it could be because they were led there. However, over 70% of people who wind up on your website and then leave will never return.[cxcv] That's why an exit-intent popup is so valuable. It's a popup that appears with an opt-in form before visitors are about to leave. You can do this easily with a little coding and help lower the amount of people that will never return to your site.

2. **Article Opt-Ins**

When people take the time to read an entire article, it's because you've grabbed their attention and kept them engaged with informational and valuable information. Reading an article to the very end is a bit uncommon these days, so if you have people making it there, you're well ahead of the competition. Take it one step further by including an opt-in form at the end of the article. Since they took the time to read all the way through, they'll likely be interested in what you have to say in the future. Include a powerful CTA and an easy opt-in form.

3. Turn Popular Posts into Lead Magnets[cxcvi]

A lead magnet is the same thing as a giveaway or free promotion. All you need to do is offer them something *free* in exchange for their e-mail address. A popular post is a good vehicle for this, as it is an obvious source of value and creates a good initial impression of your company. You don't need to create a fancy eBook or video series. Simply take one of your most popular posts and turn it into a PDF that's easily accessible. Make sure you make your lead magnets instantly accessible so people immediately see the value of providing their e-mail address.

4. Display Testimonials

When prominent people give your business testimonials, proudly display them. Put them on your homepage and create a specific testimonial page to feature them, along with the rest of your testimonials. This shows people that your company is legitimate and valuable to your customers. People are much more likely to give their e-mail addresses to businesses they trust, and testimonials help build that trust. Use the testimonials and embed an opt-in form to grow your conversion rate tremendously.[cxcvii]

5. Keep it Simple

Opt-in forms that ask your visitors to provide unnecessary information are a surefire way to send people running. No one wants to fill out an opt-in form that includes their birthday, and when people are required to provide their phone number, it usually sends a red flag. Telemarketers already bombard us, so our phone numbers have become a precious resource. Instead, only ask for things that you absolutely need. Every information field you add to a subscription box reduces opt-ins by 11%![cxcviii] At the bare minimum, you should ask for a first name, e-mail, and the opt-in check box. If you're a B2B company, you might need to ask for their title, the name of their business, and their phone number, but only if you have to. Keep it simple and only ask for what you absolutely need.

6. Paper Sign-Up Sheets

Although there's a major focus revolving around online marketing, paper is still a relevant and effective way to grow your business and opt-in list. Whether you have a brick and mortar location, an event, or a tradeshow, have a paper opt-in form available. Just make sure that the benefits are clearly stated and include a call to action. This opt-in method is an easy way to grow your business that requires little to no monetary commitment.

7. Add an E-mail Sign-Up Button

The people you e-mail aren't necessarily on your e-mail opt-in list. If you make e-mails publicly accessible, the people that view them could be from a variety of different places. This is especially important when people find your e-mail valuable and pass it on to their friends, coworkers, or family. Make sure you have an opt-in button at the bottom of your e-mails so that people can easily add themselves to your list.

8. **Take Advantage of Events**

Regardless of the type of event, or whether you, or an honored guest, are hosting it, take advantage of the opportunity to network in-person and build your e-mail list. If you're a host, you can use event registration to ask people if they want to join your e-mail list. Since they already need to provide their e-mail address and accompanying information, adding a simple checkbox doesn't negatively influence the process.

9. **Use Industry Tradeshows**

Tradeshows usually mean you have some sort of company booth with information and important takeaways for your customers. The same can be said about certain conferences and industry specific events. If you have the opportunity, make it easy for people to add themselves to your e-mail list. Use a tablet or a simple piece of paper to gather relevant information while you're networking.

10. **Look to Your Existing Database**

Finally, a lot of prospects for your e-mail list are already right under your nose. Ask your family, friends, coworkers, neighbors, or regular contacts if they would like to help get your e-mail list off the ground. If you provide good content in addition to the personal relationships, they'll be more likely to spread the word and encourage their friends to sign up.

Now, let's move on to some of the more unique, less used ways you can grow your e-mail opt-in list.

Marketing Masters Pro Tip: Opt-in everyone!

We mentioned earlier that someone has to opt-in to receive your e-mails. This means you shouldn't blindly add someone's e-mail to your opt-in e-mails just because you communicated with him or her in the past.

However, we do believe you should add everyone to your opt-in e-mails.

But the trick is in how you do it.

Anyone you interact with should be added, but prior to adding them, send them a double opt-in e-mail. This means they need to click "Confirm" to receive your opt-in e-mails before they actually will receive them.

This added step confirms they are indeed opting in to receive e-mails, and will help keep your e-mail list clean, strong, and legal.

Chapter 70: Unique Ways to Grow Your Opt-in List

After you've implemented all the straightforward ways to grow your e-mail opt-in list, it's time to move on to those that might take more work. Since your e-mail opt-in list can be grown in differing ways, we recommend using as many of them as possible to get the best results. As long as doing so doesn't make your website or content seem spammy, there's no reason not to go the extra mile. Here are some of our favorite unique ways to take your e-mail opt-in list to the next level:

1. **Spruce Up Your Lead Magnets**

   You already probably have a few different options that you could offer your audience as lead magnets. Maybe you have a comprehensive checklist of all the things you need to include in your homepage, or step-by-step instructions on how to launch your very first digital advertising campaign. Whatever it is, see how you can make it better. Go the extra mile. See what your competitors offer and make sure yours is better, or includes more items on the checklist. Upgrade your blogs into condensed PDFs for easy readability offline, or create bonus toolboxes exclusively for people who've opted-in.

   Some other great ideas to improve your lead magnets include: building a cheat sheet, providing a list of resources, creating a starter guide or a full guide, create a printable, offer a challenge, provide exclusive interviews, send out case studies, create a mini eBook, make templates, offer free trials or courses, provide infographics, and more.[cxcix] The main focus is making improvements from simple, free downloadable material. It might take some time, but people notice extra effort and will be excited to see what your e-mails offer.

2. **Offer a Downloadable Whitepaper**

One great way to help grow your e-mail list is to offer a downloadable whitepaper. If you're not familiar with whitepapers, it's a business's way of giving "a persuasive, authoritative, in-depth report on a specific topic that presents a problem and provides a solution."[cc] Companies use whitepapers to help explain, promote, or solve problems. It is not the time to pitch your products, but rather to show facts and evidence that help deepen the reader's understanding.

Whitepapers are powerful tools to use as lead magnets. They will need to be crafted carefully, with relevant, up-to-date information. Creating a whitepaper might take a little more work than some of the previously discussed lead magnets, but immediately shows your audience how you can give them valuable information. Somewhere on your website, blog, in your e-mails, on social media, or wherever you want to focus your opt-in buttons, include a form for the free, instantly downloadable whitepaper in exchange for their permission to send future automated e-mails.

3. **Make it Entertaining**

One of the best ways to increase opt-ins is to make the process of signing up entertaining. Instead of a boring fill-in-the-blank form, consider hiring a developer to create a mini game or quiz. It's engaging and will leave a lasting impression in your audience's mind. Additionally, quizzes can further educate your readers about any products or services you offer without coming off too pushy.[cci] It's a great way to increase awareness about your company or a new product. Think *Buzzfeed*-style when you go to develop these, and make sure there is more than one outcome—some people will play more than once and might end up frustrated if they keep getting the same outcome.

Games or contests are better tailored around events since they can increase the effect of a simple promotion. The opportunities are truly endless. However you decide to transform your opt-in buttons, making them a form of entertainment is a surefire way to increase engagement.

After you've started building your e-mail list, it's important to have something legitimate to offer your subscribers. This can be as easy as creating a newsletter. You just need to make sure it's a newsletter worth reading. We'll teach you how to achieve this in the next chapter.

Chapter 71: The Importance of Creating a Newsletter and Keeping it Consistent

Many businesses wonder whether they should craft a weekly or monthly newsletter. They aren't sure if it's worth the effort or if it helps drive conversions. Despite these considerations, we want to stress the importance of creating a newsletter for your business. Newsletters give you an opportunity to provide valuable information to a targeted audience that has specifically asked for more information. They signed up for your e-mail opt-in list and understand what that entails. Your newsletter is one thing that they're anticipating, so you need to take the time to assemble something that's strong and organized, rather than a haphazard mess.

Newsletters aren't an opportunity for you to send something just for the sake of entering your contact's inbox. They're an opportunity to show your readers what your company can do for them. The importance of newsletters extends far beyond what you might think. Take a look at some of the many benefits of having a consistent newsletter:

✓ **Increase Brand Awareness**

Every time your newsletter lands in someone's inbox, you reach another member of your target audiences. Including your company's name and logo at the top of your newsletter will foster brand recognition and give new customers an idea of what your company offers. Rather than typical promotional e-mails, a newsletter helps paint a larger picture of your business. You can include links to your website, helpful pages, or your blogs. Just remember to be consistent and send them out at a scheduled time: weekly, bi-monthly, or monthly.

✓ **Demonstrate Expertise**

Your newsletter gives you an opportunity to show your contacts what you know. You can build confidence surrounding your company and deliver valuable information. Newsletters have the potential to help establish your company as a leader in your niche or industry. Make sure everything in your newsletter is accurate, relevant, and valuable.

✓ **Strengthen Promotions**

If you have a specific promotion running at any given time, newsletters can help strengthen them and extend their reach. They can assist in new product launches, information on offers, or future promotions. Special offers can be extended exclusively to newsletter recipients, which is a great way to keep people opted-in.

✓ **Nurture Relationships**

Newsletters also help with lead nurturing and customer loyalty. Sending a newsletter filled with useful information is a way to reach your clients/customers, leads, and prospects repeatedly, therefore establishing a relationship. People will anticipate and look forward to receiving your newsletter, because the information you provide is beneficial. Additionally, if your readers like your newsletters, they'll likely want to start following you on social media. A poll done by *Salesforce* found that "e-mails that include social sharing buttons have a 158% higher click-through rate than those that don't."[ccii]

Relationships are often forgotten or not nurtured in business, but they're very important. You don't remember your experiences that are simply transactional. You remember those that have a personal touch, the ones that go the extra mile.

✓ **Increase Coverage**

Newsletters allow you to increase your coverage further than your blog or regular content. You can clarify certain points or use them as an overview for information. The important thing to remember is that the more times you can connect with your audience, and the more coverage you have, the more conversions you'll see. According to *Salesforce*, "82% of consumers open e-mails from companies."[cciii] Take that number and make it worthwhile for both you and your audience.

We also want to discuss those companies that believe they *will not* benefit from having a newsletter. These are the types of businesses that offer completely free content and use social media for all their marketing needs. They don't see the value in a newsletter, which only reaches individual recipients, when they can use social media, where content is shared in rapid-fire fashion. While it's true that social media has unique benefits, we still argue that you do both. There's no harm in having a newsletter, so long as you are providing value, especially when people are making the conscious choice to receive it.

It's also important to have a newsletter that is well put together. Creating and crafting it should be an art. That's why it's important to use best practices to deliver an aesthetically pleasing newsletter that's the perfect length—no more than one PDF page—and filled with valuable content. Some best practices include:

- ✓ Keep a specific topic/theme for each newsletter
- ✓ Develop enticing subject lines
- ✓ Use formatting that is easy to read and digest—think lots of white space, lists, and multiple headlines
- ✓ Use headlines strategically
- ✓ Keep the copy short
- ✓ Keep information concise and follow expectations
- ✓ Create balance throughout the layout
- ✓ Make sure it's optimized for mobile devices
- ✓ Include exclusive offers, discounts, and coupons
- ✓ Make it personalized

- ✓ Link your social media profiles and include easy share buttons
- ✓ Be consistent with the delivery
- ✓ Avoid spammy content
- ✓ Keep a detailed analysis of click through rates, conversions, and more

A carefully crafted newsletter rewards with public relations, image building, and stronger sales,[cciv] while providing your audience with useful, valuable information. In the following Chapter, we'll explore into everything you need to know about how to offer valuable content.

Chapter 72: Offering Valuable Content

We believe that the best way of convincing people to stay on your e-mail opt-in list is by offering them valuable content. In the form of a newsletter, your content will give concise, easily digestible information that people will look forward to. We learned about the value of social media, but even the most popular businesses still need to share content through a newsletter. According to a statistic published by *FulcrumTech*, 90% of consumers prefer to get updates from e-mail newsletters, compared to only 10% who chose Facebook.[ccv] We've seen numerous businesses grow their reach, brand awareness, and conversions from creating a newsletter. As long as you put in the time to understand your target audience, it will be worth the effort.

Luckily, defining and understanding your target audience is common for a business owner. Think back to when you first created your business plan and needed to clearly define your audience for goal setting and brand development. Use the profiles you created and then write down a comprehensive list of topics that will make their experience, and association with your company, better. Consider topics that are valuable, helpful, educational, inspiring, entertaining, useful, or anything that will improve their lives.[ccvi] Keep everything well formatted, and remember that people love lists, white space, and information that can be delivered fast and easy to digest. Don't over-do it. If newsletters are too lengthy or wordy, people won't take the time to read them.

As a side note, your existing customer base, potential customers, your sales team, and even your employees will read your newsletters, so the content needs to reflect that. If you have specific internal needs, you may want to have both an external and internal newsletter.

Here are some ways to make sure you offer valuable content in each newsletter.

✓ **Stay Focused**

The beauty of newsletters is that you're sending information to the same people repeatedly. You don't need to send them an overwhelming amount of content right from the beginning. Rather, focus on having one specific topic for each newsletter. Otherwise it can get messy and disorganized, decreasing the value for your readers.

✓ **Have One Primary Call to Action (CTA)**

Think about this as expanding on your theme for each newsletter. While you can easily include multiple calls to action, you should focus on a single, primary CTA for each newsletter, something that falls in line with your topic. If you want to integrate more than one, make them more time specific, but don't let them steal the spotlight of your primary CTA. Add a side bar with the theme, "In case you have time..."

✓ **Stay Balanced**

Regardless of why someone signed up for your newsletter, don't over-do it on the promotional material. Focus on writing educational content that will help your customers, and the sales will come naturally. You can add small promotions here and there, but try and stick to 90% educational content and 10% promotional content.[ccvii]

✓ **Stick with Expectations**

People signed up for your newsletter because they expect it to be worthwhile. Stick to that expectation. Don't tell subscribers that your newsletter will give them everything they need to know to grow their business, and then create a newsletter selling your company's marketing tools. If you tell people what to expect, when to expect it, and how (e.g., in your inbox), then stick to those expectations. If you don't, people will unsubscribe.

✓ **Write with Your Audience in Mind**

Always direct your focus back to your audience. What do they need from you? Every time you create a newsletter, give something that can help them overcome their challenges. If your newsletter doesn't offer any value, they won't stick around or trust your brand.

✓ **Foster Authenticity**

Use a voice that is honest, transparent, and helpful. Be yourself and stay consistent with your voice. The more your audience reads, the more they'll build a connection with your company and your brand.

✓ **Integrate Your Business**

In your newsletter, consider sharing a new blog, case study, or whitepaper. Rather than just simply posting the link into your e-mails, write a short summary of your new content and include it—as long as it adheres to that week's theme. Bringing your business' culture into your newsletters will help people form a loyal connection. Consider using a weekly inspirational quote that resonates with your brands, or a weekly word of advice. Something unique to your business helps foster this connection.

✓ **Think Minimalism**

Keep things neat. Don't have different sized boxes all over the page or absolutely zero white space; it makes things look misaligned, cluttered, and busy. Instead, work on achieving a minimalism that is aesthetically pleasing and that works for your content. Use plenty of white space, keep the font, text boxes, and media consistent, and write specifically for your newsletter. Keep your copy short, sweet, and to the point. Your newsletter should send your readers somewhere else, not keep them glued to the e-mail for hours. Think of it as providing your audience with an appetizer for your business, and they need to head to your website or blog for the main course.

✓ **Be Visual**

You can still be minimalistic with media and rich media. Offer different types, such as videos, infographics, pictures, or anything you can think of other than straight text. "Adding a video to marketing e-mails can boost click-through rates by 200-300%."[ccviii] Just don't go overboard.

After you craft your newsletter, you'll need to determine your timeline. Are you sending a weekly, quarterly, or monthly newsletter? If so, pick a day and a time and stick to it. Maybe it's every Monday at 3:00pm, or the first Tuesday of the month at 12:00pm. There are many studies on the relationship of e-mail open rates and time. One study found that since there are so many marketing e-mails sent out Monday – Friday, those sent on Saturday and Sunday had more positive responses and higher open rates.[ccix] Use a scheduling tool to ensure that these go out, regardless of your weekend plans. The time of day also matters. The same study found that people were nearly twice as likely to respond between 8 PM and Midnight than any other time of day.[ccx] Whatever you decide, be consistent, and make sure you deliver your content in a timely fashion. If people start to anticipate your newsletter, they'll be happy when they receive it at the same time each week or month.

If you have different e-mail opt-in lists—for example, if you have a sales opt-in—make sure you deliver content to your customers at the right time in the right stage of their buying process. You can also use behavior-triggered e-mails. Behavior-triggered e-mails are exactly what they sound like. When a customer or webpage visitor hasn't landed on your page in a while, let them know. Facebook does this when someone hasn't logged in for five days. Another behavior-triggered e-mail from retailers is the "You left something in your cart, checkout now!" e-mail. These types of e-mails have a 152% higher click-through rate than regular e-mails.[ccxi]

Things to Avoid

There are various ways you can offer valuable content in your newsletter, but some techniques are better than others. To give you the information you need to succeed, we want to include things to avoid at all costs. Here are our top four recommendations on what to avoid.

1. **Excessive Length**

    People don't want to read lengthy newsletters. If they are looking for longer segments of writing, direct them toward your blog. No one wants to open a six-page long e-mail newsletter and sift through information for an hour.

2. **Too Many Goals**

    Just like using one theme per newsletter, you should focus on one goal per newsletter. When you do this, you're far more likely to lead your audience in the right direction. Too many goals make it feel like you're pushing and pulling from all directions.

3. **Overwhelming Number of Promotions**

    People are signing up for your e-mails because of the value they offer, not the discounts. Avoid sending e-mail just to show your audience your products. If you want to add promotions, speak conversationally about why you think a new product would benefit them and why you're excited about it, not just that they need it. Be genuine and avoid being too self-promotional.

4. **Stock Images**

    Whatever you do, avoid using common stock images. Your newsletter needs to be eye-catching, and common stock images aren't the answer. Plus, they offer little to no value for customers who are truly interested in your brand image.

Stock images have the opposite effect of what you want in a newsletter.

As long as you're offering valuable content to your audience, they'll enjoy receiving and reading your newsletters. But how can you make sure people who sign up for your newsletter actually open it? That will be our focus in the next chapter.

Chapter 73: Don't Let Your E-mails Be Treated like Spam

You can have the best newsletter in the world, but if no one opens it, it won't matter. Your e-mail campaign needs to be good. Not only because of the benefits of a strong newsletter, but because you need people to want to open it in the first place. We also understand that e-mails can unintentionally end up in someone's junk mail. There are some technical reasons that you might be flagged as spam, but it is avoidable. We love sharing these techniques because e-mail campaigns can be extremely effective, and they are extremely low in cost compared to other forms of marketing. This translates to a high ROI when successful. However, like we mentioned, you need to make sure your newsletter is seen to reap any benefits. Let's start by tackling the technical side.

The spam folder is every company's worst nightmare. You take hours to craft a beautiful newsletter, only for it to wind up in junk mail, never to be opened or admired. It's frustrating and discouraging, especially since you're sending content that they specifically opted-in to receive. So how can you avoid the spam folder? Below are some effective methods:

1. **Send From a Good IP Address**

    Your Internet Protocol (IP) address helps the Internet identify your company, computer, location, and more. It is how different websites, e-mail addresses, and accounts communicate with each other. When you send anything from a poorly scored IP address, it will immediately end up in the spam folder. Once you're filtered into the spam folder, it's more likely to occur in the future. This is because your IP address gets flagged, and will hold this flag despite your e-mailing efforts.

    To avoid getting flagged and sent to someone's spam folder, make sure you're sending your e-mails from a strong IP address. You can do this by teaming up with a reputable e-mail service like *MailChimp, Constant Contact, ConvertKit,* or *AWber.* Using one of these services eliminates easily fixed spam problems because all the mail goes through their IP addresses and servers. Since these companies want to maintain their reputations, they're very vigilant in checking your e-mails for spam flags prior to sending them.

If you'd rather send them independently of an e-mail marketing service, make sure that your IP address is either certified or extremely secure. Getting certified will give you a Sender Score Certified status, which ensures that your e-mails don't end up in the spam folder.[ccxii]

2. Send from a Verified Domain Name

Whenever you send an e-mail, make sure that it's coming from a strong source. The "from" field matters, and mailboxes evaluate the contents of an e-mail based on the legitimacy of the sender's e-mail address. Send it from an e-mail address such as, "name@yourdomain.com" and make sure that Google and/or your hosting website have verified your site's domain name. Once you choose an e-mail address for your newsletters, don't change it. Avoid using sketchy field names, for example "28941jdg18@yourdomain.com." Instead, stick with clear, trustworthy names like "contact@", "newsletter@", "feedback@", or similar.[ccxiii] You can even create an e-mail that mirrors a person so it looks like someone from your company is mailing out the newsletters. This gives them a more personal feel and tends to have a strong user response.

3. Keep Your HTML Clean

If you use sloppy coding, extra HTML tags, or a formatting code pulled from a rich-text editor, you will be far more likely to trigger spam filters.[ccxiv] If you're not familiar with coding or don't have anyone on your team who is, consider using an e-mail marketing service or talking to a marketing professional.

4. Avoid Excessive Links

We'll talk about the nature of your links more below, but for now just keep in mind that using excessive links sends a red flag to mailbox providers. There is such a thing as too many links, even if they're all from reputable sources. If you embed external links into your e-mail campaigns or newsletters, make sure they're coming from a reputable source. If you include too many links with low quality domains or spammy content, your e-mail could get flagged and end up in the spam folder.

5. Add a Confirmation Step

This is like the double opt-in form, but instead asks your new subscribers to make sure and add your newsletter's e-mail address to their address books. This makes it impossible for your e-mails to get flagged for spam and is an easy addition to your sign-up process. It also increases the likelihood that your e-mails will automatically be marked as "important" in their inbox.

6. Test Your E-mails

If you want to ensure that you're good to go on the technical side of things, test your e-mail campaigns. It's an easy way to see what works and what needs some help. You can do this by testing your e-mails to determine any minor tweaks you need to make to keep you out of the spam folder. This can be a little more difficult to understand, but it will increase the likelihood of a stronger ROI. In fact, "74% of companies who regularly test e-mail strategies report a positive ROI."[ccxv] Check with your e-mail marketing service for more specific instructions on how to test your e-mails.

If you follow those tips, you'll master the technical side of staying out of the spam folder. However, your content also helps to determine whether your e-mails are flagged as spam. It takes a little more work to have your e-mails opened, read, and digested by your audience.

1. Use Strong Subject Lines

The subject line of your newsletter is the first thing that people will see. It's important, and can easily be the difference between sending it to the trash and opening it to read. See what works well in your blogs, social media posts, or other e-mails, and try to mimic that type of language. Give a clear, concise, and accurate reflection of what's in your e-mail and make it compelling. Things like, "10 Ways to Stick to Your Goals," or, "Improve Your E-mail Marketing Today," are short, compelling, and offer a good preview for the reader. If you can, make your subject line personalized. E-mails with personalized subject lines are 26% more likely to be opened.[ccxvi] Only do this when it makes sense. Don't force personalization or you may end up in the spam folder.

Never be deceptive in your subject lines. Don't start things with "Re:" or "Fwd:" to suggest that you've already been communicating with recipients.[ccxvii] It's deceptive and will get flagged as spam if it's not correct. Don't tell people they've won something or qualified, either. Those are not strong subject lines.

2. Create Valuable Content

It all comes back to your content. If you don't have anything valuable to offer, you might not have the resources to put together a newsletter. Since we understand the benefits of a newsletter in your e-mail marketing campaign, we recommend working to find valuable content and then offering it only once a month rather than once a week. When your readers start learning that your business sends interesting, engaging, and informative e-mails, your open rates will increase tremendously. People get excited and look forward to your future e-mails.

If, however, you send information that doesn't hold any value, is already common knowledge, or is oversaturated with promotions, your messages will find their way into the trash.[ccxviii] Original content, a unique perspective on a common topic, pragmatic tips that can be implemented right away, and anything in list form are the types of content that are consumed voraciously. That's what you want to go for.

Include a nice balance of media and text, avoiding overly large e-mails. Don't write with an excessive amount of exclamation points, and avoid shouting at your readers with too many capitalized words. Your word choice also makes an impact, so avoid things like 'sale,' 'free,' 'rich,' or 'deal.'[ccxix]

3. **Stay Organized**

Organization is where lead nurturing and consistent updating of your CRM enters the picture. Keeping your lists of clients, leads, and prospects well organized and up to date is imperative. If you don't have the time to do this yourself, consider outsourcing it to someone or hiring a part-time assistant, especially during times when you're getting a large influx of new opt-ins.

Keeping your e-mail list properly segmented is crucial to your open rate. In fact, "39% of e-mail marketers that practice list segmentation see better open rates, 28% see lower opt-out and unsubscribe rates, and 24% see better e-mail deliverability, increased sales leads, and greater revenue."[ccxx] Taking time to make sure this gets done is a great way to ensure your e-mail campaigns are working.

4. Optimize Your Content

More and more people are using their mobile devices to open and read e-mails, so make sure that whatever you send is optimized for mobiles. This not only increases the likelihood of your content being read, it also helps different facets of your business, which we've previously discussed. Make sure your audience doesn't need to scroll right or left and that there are no oddly sized images.

5. Focus on Building Relationships

There are many e-mail campaigns that are sent with a notification to the receiver saying, "do not reply to this e-mail." This immediately let's people know that a real person didn't send it, making it difficult to contact the company. Instead, allow responses, or, even better, ask a question. This will help you build relationships in addition to finding new, valuable content for your next newsletter or e-mail campaign.

Following these tips will increase the likelihood of getting your e-mails opened and staying out of the spam folder. Before sending an e-mail campaign or a newsletter, sit on it for a day. Revisit it with a fresh pair of eyes and see if it's appealing, or if it seems pushy, inauthentic, or lacks real value. Check your e-mail address, the subject line, the preview, and the contents of the e-mail itself. Would it resonate with you if it landed in your inbox? As long as you avoid cutting corners and put effort into your e-mails, you'll start seeing an increase in your "opened" rates.

Chapter 74: How to Keep Your Subscribers

When you offer valuable content and actively avoid the spam folder, more of your audience will start to open your e-mails. Many of those who stay opted-in will do so because they love your content. The challenge becomes how to keep them happy enough to stay on your e-mail list. We've seen far too many companies grow their list tremendously, only to come back to us asking why so many people are unsubscribing or opting-out. In this chapter, we'll go over everything you need to do to make sure your subscriber list continues to grow.

Like we mentioned, the main focus is keeping them happy. People don't like when a company abuses their inbox, they don't appreciate misleading information or expectations, and they absolutely can't stand when they're receiving seven or more e-mails from a company in a given week. In fact, 54% of people who unsubscribed from an e-mail list said it was because e-mails were coming too frequently, while 49% said the content became repetitive or boring.[ccxxi] Some other reasons included irrelevant content, misleading expectations, a chance in the readers' needs, or finding the information in a better way. When people subscribe to an e-mail list, it's to make their lives easier and more streamlined, not messy and contradictory. If you want to reduce your number of e-mail list opt-outs, follow these guidelines.

1. **Give Them Control of E-mail Preferences**

   While you never want to over-e-mail anyone, some people have a different idea of how many e-mails are too many. When you give your subscribers the control to decide how many e-mails they receive, they will be much less likely to opt-out completely. Instead, they'll continue to receive and read e-mails and won't get annoyed with your company. When anyone decides to decrease the amount of e-mails they receive, simply re-segment them onto a lower-frequency e-mailing list.

You should also give your subscribers the power to control the types of e-mails they receive. While they may not want to see anything promotional, sending educational or informative information from your company will still increase brand loyalty and recognition.

2. Segment Your E-mail Lists

Segmenting your e-mail lists in general is a good way to avoid a reduction in subscribers. Segmenting your list can help increase personalization and make your e-mail campaigns relevant to specific subscribers. Doing this can help you increase your open rates, relevance, revenue, sales lead, and deliverability.[ccxxii] To get the largest ROI, consider segmenting your list based on the following[ccxxiii]:

- ✓ Engagement Level
- ✓ Reduced Subscribers
- ✓ Geographic Location
- ✓ Demographics
- ✓ Behavioral Data
- ✓ Persona
- ✓ Website Behavior
- ✓ Purchase History
- ✓ Cart and Form Abandoners
- ✓ Shopping Locations

3. Personalize E-mails

Personalization is related to segmenting your e-mail lists. The more personal you make your e-mails, the more people will resonate with your company. Everyone likes to feel they matter, and personalized e-mails are an easy way to show your subscribers that they do. Depending on your audience, you can use a more personal tone, include funny images or GIFs, or include information about your life or business culture to make them feel more connected. It doesn't have to simply be addressing them by their name.

Get creative, find out what your audiences like, and use that in your e-mail campaigns.

4. Include a "Re-Subscribe" Option

It's common for people to accidently unsubscribe. Make sure these people have an easy option to re-subscribe or they won't take the time to go through all the steps again.

5. Keep Regular Communication

Many subscribers become frustrated when content is randomly sent to them throughout the week, or even at different times of the day. We're creatures of habit, and consistent delivery is something that helps build trust and reliability. Make sure you're at least e-mailing your subscribers once a month to stay relevant, and more frequently if possible. Just remember, don't send an e-mail just for the sake of sending one. Make sure everything you send is valuable to your readers.

6. Focus on Value

We've talked about this at length throughout this section, but that's because it's important. When it comes to e-mail marketing campaigns, if you don't send anything of value, you will lose subscribers, guaranteed. It's one of the biggest reasons that people opt-out, so avoid being too pushy or sales-focused and always send something that has value.

7. Avoid Spamming

Like we discussed in the previous chapter, if your content looks like spam, it will be treated like spam. Avoid spammy words, links, references, e-mail addresses, and anything that may trigger a spam filter. Spam filters work, but if your e-mail gets through the firewall and still looks like spam, people will move it to their junk folder on their own.

8. Optimize for Mobile

As with everything you do on the Internet, you need to make sure your e-mails are always optimized for mobile devices. More people are using their phones to check e-mail during their down time, with 59% of e-mail opens occurring on a mobile device.[ccxxiv] That's a huge audience. Don't lose their interest with e-mails that need to be scrolled through to read. Keep your design responsive and simple for the best results.

There will always be people that are going to opt-in and then immediately unsubscribe. As long as you work on implementing best practices, adding value to your e-mails, and avoiding overly spammy campaigns, you'll be in good standing.

Chapter 75: Understanding How to Use a Purchased E-mail List and Cold E-mail Outreach

Everything we've talked about so far has been in relation to growing your e-mail opt-in list using natural methods. It will take some time to get a substantial list, but working through the best practices will yield results. However, sometimes you might feel like you need an extra push forward, and purchasing an e-mail list is a potential option. Many of the lists you'll buy are advertised as targeted to your needed demographics, but since the recipients have no relationship with your business or any idea who you are, people don't exactly love receiving unsolicited e-mail. If you decide to use a purchased e-mail list, make sure to take the following precautions to avoid any problems:

✓ **Send From a Different Domain Name**

Avoid using your website's domain name to send e-mails to a purchased list. This could lead to your domain getting flagged, which will cause any future e-mails sent from that domain name to be flagged. Create a unique domain name to use for your purchased list to avoid ruining your reputation.

✓ **Send From a Different Platform**

Make sure you send your e-mails from a platform that allows purchased lists. Different platforms can use algorithms that will immediately flag your business for using the platform in an unacceptable way, which will cause you problems down the road. You can lose essential marketing privileges, so it's just not worth it. Find a platform that you don't regularly use for your opt-in list and use it to send e-mails to your purchased list.

✓ **Scrub Your Lists**

Go through your purchased list and delete any of the e-mail addresses that will bounce back or be undeliverable. You can use a site like *Scrubbly* to do this. This helps reduce your list to only those that will actually receive e-mails, which is better for platform recognition.

✓ **Create Pages**

Direct your purchased list receivers to a specific landing page. This can either be something that offers products or free content—free content always does better. Include a form for them to complete if they're interested, and then you can capture their e-mail responsibly. This helps increase engagement and identify promising prospects from your list.

✓ **Don't Cross Contaminate**

Never cross contaminate your lists. Everything we've discussed involves keeping things separate from your e-mail opt-in list. Cross contamination can quickly ruin all your efforts, so take extra precaution to avoid this at any cost. Whatever you do, never jeopardize your opt-in list. Send everything separately from different sources, IP addresses, e-mails, and be overly cautious in your sending.

As a final note, we want to mention that purchased e-mail lists aren't the best routes to go when focusing on your e-mail marketing efforts. Instead, try to build your own e-mail list naturally using proven opt-in methods and genuine, valuable content. Purchased e-mail lists can be risky and are often flagged for spam, so readers might never even see your content. If you're going to use a purchased e-mail list, make sure you follow the above tips so you don't jeopardize your e-mail opt-in list or cross contaminate any of your marketing efforts.

Marketing Masters Pro Tip: Reading Restaurant Menus Made Us Better at Sending Cold E-mails

This might sound funny, but it's true. Think about when you sit down in a restaurant—you're probably hungry, and you read the menu.

Nowhere on the menu are you going to find the recipe for each dish, the steps of how they cook it, or how many people in the kitchen will touch the dish before it is served.

And in 99% of cases, you also won't find the chef's name, their qualifications, background, or why they should be preparing this dish for you.

Instead, they describe the dish in a way that makes your mouth water. Using adjectives about how it will taste and how exquisite the ingredients are.

They don't sell you on the recipe or how they cook it; they sell you on the end result—the dish itself.

Most marketers screw up cold e-mails because they focus on trying to explain how they do what they do and why they are qualified to do it. They should be focusing on the end result a business owner will get from working with them.

When that steak is placed in front of you, you don't care what temperature it was cooked at, who made it, or how long it was cooked for. You care how it tastes.

Clean up your cold e-mail efforts to focus on the end result and you'll see a dramatically higher response rate.

Part 8: Public Relations (PR)

Creating a good public relations (PR) strategy could be written as its own book and still not even scratch the surface. There are a massive variety of different strategies, tactics, and methods used to help a brand get press exposure.

PR not only helps you reach new audiences, but it can help support your general marketing and SEO strategy as well. News publication links will drive referral traffic, SEO value, and most importantly help build authority in you and your brand.

In this section, we'll delve into the basics of PR, explain how it truly works, and provide some recommendations and strategies around the basics of PR. We'll also cover the digital world of PR, which plays a larger and larger role in the world of PR every single day.

Chapter 76: Understanding Public Relations and How it Works

Public relations (PR) isn't as simple as people think. Many people think it's synonymous with advertising or marketing, but they're far from the same. While there is a strongly connected relationship between marketing and PR, which we'll discuss in Chapter 77, *The Public Relations Society of America (PRSA)* offers a great definition that resonates with us. After thousands of submissions, they've defined public relations as, "a strategic communication process that builds mutually beneficial relationships between organizations and their publics."[ccxxv] This is done through the cultivation of a positive public image over a long period of time.

There's a misconception that all you need to do to be successful is send out some of your content or product launches, hire a PR agency, and wait. In reality, since PR focuses on relationship building, it takes a long time to see results. It's time consuming and takes failures to finally see success.

Public relations include creating a positive image of your brand and your company through good publicity, press releases, speeches, special events, promotions, and more. You need to earn good standing PR, and while every now and then you might get some huge publicity—like being interviewed on *The Today Show* or *Good Morning America*, it isn't going to give you long-term success. You're going to see a surge in business, but then people will move on to the next big thing. To continually get good PR you need to focus on smaller publicity, scattered with larger wins. One guest appearance on a major television station isn't going to bring you ongoing results.

Now, with advertising and marketing, you have full control over what your audience sees, when they see it, and how it's delivered to them. When it comes to public relations and the variety of influencers or consumers available, you lose this control. You have no idea what people will say about your business, or product, which can either help or hurt your company's bottom line. Phineas T. Barnum once said, "There's no such thing as bad publicity."

Unfortunately, this isn't a great motto for businesses to follow today, especially when they're just starting out.

So how exactly do public relations work? The simple answer is it depends.

It depends on your business' goals, your size and influence, and the reach of your network. If you're doing things on your own, you'll need to build, foster, and grow strong relationships with influencers and people connected to the media. You'll foster these relationships and continue to develop valuable content, products, and services and look for opportunities to put your company in the public's eye. PR involves interactions with your audience, relationships with investors and influencers, press conferences, media events, communications, management of any crises, writing press releases, coordinating media contacts, lobbying for article placement, and more.[ccxxvi] It's also important to work on expanding your contact list, promote your company on social media, create and host media-specific events, and make pitches to popular journalists, newspapers, or magazines. As you can see, there are a lot of moving parts to public relations. You need to consistently analyze and anticipate public attitudes about your business and the effects of your business on the community, and then take the necessary action.

It can be a bit overwhelming for businesses, which is why most people end up hiring a professional public relations agency, but it is possible. You'll feel like you're not making any progress, just moving along with small blips on the radar, but with consistent work, it will start to pay off. People will begin to recognize your brand, which will lead to more website traffic and hopefully more conversions.

In addition, public relations offer a slew of benefits for your company. They include the following:[ccxxvii]

✓ **New Investors**

> The better your publicity, the more people will take notice of your company. This includes high-end investors who see

the potential of your business. When people are talking about your company, it's noticeable. It shows investors that you have something that the public wants. This leads to more money for you to invest in growing your business and creating new products or services.

✓ New Clients

When someone reads a magazine or journal that mentions your company's name, they'll be more inclined to use you for their purchases than your competition. PR gives you credibility and increases your brand recognition, which leads to more clients.

✓ More Business

More investors and more clients mean more overall business. They all tend to grow simultaneously from PR, so even if your efforts aren't paying off now, continue to think about the future.

✓ Attract Talented Employees

On the other side of things, public relations can help you attract highly talented employees as your business expands. People will see your company and, if they're in that industry, might consider the benefits of working with you. The more attractive your company is, the more qualified workers you'll have, which leads to more innovative ideas, stronger creativity, and the development of new products or services.

✓ Boost Credibility

One of the main things that PR does is increase your credibility. It doesn't matter who you are, when you're featured in a magazine, newspaper, or online publication, people will see you with a new set of eyes. The more positive attention you have, the more credibility.

✓ **Better SEO**

When your company is mentioned numerous times by reputable businesses or press outlets, you're building natural backlinks. These backlinks help your SEO efforts, which will move you higher up on the search engine results page and further increase the professionalism of your business.

✓ **Create a Positive Image**

A good PR campaign helps you highlight your company in a positive public image. When influencers or prominent businesses back your brand, you'll start seeing benefits both online and offline. Remember, this only works when there is a positive image built—a bad reputation is something to avoid at all costs.

If you want to be successful, you need to have some sort of public relations strategy. During the rest of this section, we'll help you learn how to tackle your PR campaigns on your own, and when you should turn to the professionals for help.

Chapter 77: Utilizing Marketing to Support Public Relations (And Visa-Versa)

As we mentioned in the previous chapter, people often assume that marketing is public relations, and vice versa. We talked about how this was not the case, but they do have a strong, mutually exclusive relationship. In fact, PR and marketing perform stronger when they work together.[ccxxviii] The combination helps to increase the effects of each individually. Any good PR is good marketing, and good marketing will lead to strong PR.

As we've discussed in earlier chapters, marketing works to analyze target audiences, track click through rates, online conversions, and more, while focusing on customer data/actions. The analysis leads to changes that can be made to better focus your company's marketing and advertising efforts, which should lead to more profits and increased brand recognition. On the other hand, PR works with the media, influencers, and press to communicate a specific message to the public. Marketing is a paid effort while PR is commonly referred to as being "earned."

Mashable's Chief Strategy Officer for AirPR, Rebekah Iliff, gives us a strong understanding of the difference. She says, "The highest purpose of marketing is to gather and analyze customer data based on concentrated marketing-related efforts, and then to make conclusive decisions as a result. The highest purpose of PR is to observe and listen to customers, interpret emotional responses and conversations and then create meaningful content or experiences as a result."[ccxxix] The differentiation between the two is clear, but it's also easy to understand how they need each other to succeed.

Some other ways that marketing and PR work together are as follows:[ccxxx]

- ✓ Share common goals for both strategies that will give you stronger results-focused objectives.
- ✓ Facilitate cross-department communications to streamline goals, campaigns, and more.

- ✓ Integrate two campaigns into one to help strengthen blog posts, programs, e-mail campaigns, paid lead generation, and advertising.
- ✓ Receive a more accurate way to monitor and measure your data and results.
- ✓ Share more information between customers, the public, and the media.
- ✓ Build a stronger business with better results from increased collaboration.

Regardless of whether you're with the marketing side of a business or public relations, you'll need to work together to achieve your goals. If you're using marketing strategies to get your brand positive exposure, present yourself well, and answer a need in the market, you'll naturally start to get on the radar for good PR. If you're already doing strongly in PR, chances are you're doing a pretty good job with your marketing.

Chapter 78: Utilizing Digital Publications to Build Recognition

One of the biggest mistakes you can make is not fostering your digital presence to help you build brand recognition. Think about the last time you visited a website. Did they have an area that said, "As Seen In..." followed by a number of highly recognizable brand logos? If so, you likely thought of that company as more credible than before. This is because digital publications help build recognition. It takes a bit of time to do, but there are digital publications available for you to contact, reputable companies that are small or focus on highlighting businesses that they support. Try to get a variety of digital publications to cover your brand, rather than strictly focusing on major talk shows and news outlets. Chances are, you'll get a much more positive response.

This is why it's so important to reach out to a number of these digital publications and build a relationship with them. There are decent amounts of revenue generating opportunities for you, so long as you take the time and effort to build and nurture them. To give you a brief overview, here are some examples of how digital publications can increase your revenue:[ccxxxi]

- ✓ Boost the number of satisfied customers or readers, which leads to customer loyalty and dedication.
- ✓ Increase the accessibility of your content, making it easier for people to read and learn more about your business.
- ✓ Take the opportunity to run paid ads in your digital publications. Just make sure you don't over-do it.
- ✓ Expand your audience through guest writers or bloggers and increase your organic traffic and SEO.
- ✓ Establish yourself as an expert compared to your competition.
- ✓ Increase your online presence as a whole to better engage with and connect to your audience.
- ✓ Grow your e-mail subscribers.
- ✓ Track your metrics from an outside perspective using Google Analytics.
- ✓ Increase your number of social shares.

Sometimes it's as simple as sending an e-mail, and other times it takes years of correspondence. While you can do this yourself, this is an area where a PR specialist could give you help—they already have strong relationships with many digital publications and major media outlets. However, in this chapter we're going to focus on handling this on your own, and discuss PR firms and agencies in more detail in Chapter 81.

With that said, we want to leave you with some good strategies and tactics for getting your foot in the door at digital publications. The main thing to keep in mind is outreach. You need to continue to send e-mails, build relationships, attend events, and network as much as you can. Most of the work that goes into PR is building relationships; don't be afraid to take the time to do this. Send out e-mails introducing yourself and your business and talk about the benefits that your company's content could bring to *their* current readers. Don't be too pushy, but don't be afraid to show digital publication platforms that you bring value to the table. Consider building a list of press contacts and nourishing them throughout the year. Remember, this will take time. It's not a "get rich quick" scheme, and it will take work. Create a list of all your influencers you follow on social media, along with anyone that has publicly praised your product, blog, or company in general. In addition, you can also self- generate press releases and other digital publications—more on that in Chapter 74.

Some digital marketing agencies have these relationships firmly established, and for a fee, can get clients guaranteed in the publications important to your company. This can come in handy if you can't afford an all-out PR agency or an in-house specialist. Whatever route you take, make sure you're consistent.

Always focus your public relation efforts on content that is an extension of your brand, not something that is created merely for the purpose of getting exposure. Be open to new experiences and you might be surprised by what happens.

Marketing Masters Pro Tip: Get Some Early & Big PR Wins

Even if it means paying for a placement or finding some way to grease the wheels to get mentioned in an article, it's important for brands with little credibility and little PR presence to get a few big early wins.

These will not only help build trust and credibility in your brand with your customers, but they will also support your PR efforts. No one wants to be the first big publication to mention a small brand that no one has heard of, but suddenly if your website showcases that you have been featured in a major publication, other publications will feel like they might be missing out on something if they don't cover you.

We've seen this strategy work time and time again. A good friend of ours was trying to get on the TODAY show for seemingly forever. By a chance of luck, he was able to secure a spot on Good Morning America, and following that the TODAY show was literally *begging* him to come on.

While this is an extreme case, if you can secure a few big PR wins by any means necessary early on, it will help your brand and PR strategy dramatically.

Chapter 79: How to Utilize Self-Generated Press Releases to Increase Exposure

One way to increase your public relations is to take advantage of self-generated press releases. A press release is "a written communication that reports specific but brief information about an event, circumstance, or other happening."ccxxxii This information usually revolves around something significant happening that you want to share with your customers and the public. Businesses often send their press releases to different media companies, attempting to be highlighted or publically shared. When you do this, it's not always guaranteed that you'll be put in the spotlight, and when you consistently send press releases that are insignificant, you might squander your relationships. Whenever you write a press release, you should first evaluate whether third parties would find it worthy of promotion. If not, don't send it out.

Now, we don't mean hide it from the world. Instead of sending it to all your influential media partners, you can use self-generated press releases internally to help increase your exposure. Self-generated press releases are simply those that your company writes. They can be written for many reasons, including:

- ✓ Inform the public about an event—include all the major information, time, location, date, and nature of the event
- ✓ Share general news about your company
- ✓ Communicate significant milestones or awards
- ✓ Announce a launch release—whether it is for a new product, website, service, or similar.
- ✓ Feature a popular product that has been upgraded
- ✓ Share information on new hires
- ✓ Establish expertise
- ✓ Help promote your company

The main thing to keep in mind is that press releases are written using a different format and tone than a regular piece of content or blog article. You'll still need a catchy headline, but they are more formulaic by nature.ccxxxiii They should be formal, straight to the point, and relevant to your audience. Tell people why they should care and keep it short.

We recommend doing self-generating press releases often, at least one to two a month. However, if you have more newsworthy information to share, write and publish them more often.

If it's just a minor news update, publish it directly on your website. If it's major news, we recommend using *PR Newswire*. This is one of the largest and most trusted content distribution networks on the Internet, and gives you a more reputable place to share your press releases with the public.[ccxxxiv] Try publishing any press releases in the middle of the week, either early morning or in the evening. Test out what works best for your company and make any changes for future uploads.

As a final note, we want to remind you that for every self-generated press release you write and publish, whether on your website or *PR Newswire*, you need to share it as much as possible. Post it on your website, in your newsletter or e-mail campaign, on all your social media profiles, and anywhere else you are active online. The more you share it, the more exposure you'll receive.

Chapter 80: Properly Highlighting Your PR on Your Website and Social Media

Whether you're using self-generated press releases, have multiple digital publications, or end up landing a segment on *Good Morning America*, you need to take the time to properly highlight all your PR. Doing so will help show your audience that you're serious, and will help establish yourself as an expert to the public. However, you need to make sure you're highlighting things the right way, on both your website and all your social media profiles. Having a strategy in place will help you get the most from your PR and increase the longevity of its effects. Rather than appearing as blips on the media radar, you can create an everlasting "hall of fame" for your business.

Let's walk through some best practices for highlighting your PR.

First, you should create an area on your homepage and any key landing pages where you can highlight your major press exposure. The best way to do this is to have your web designer create an "As seen in/on" section. Include the logos of all the major publications and link back to the article, video, or mention so that your visitors can easily access previous PR moments. This has a huge effect on your credibility, since people will associate you with major media stations, magazines, or trusted websites that they already know and love.

Next, make sure you include a "press" page in your primary navigation bar. This makes it easy to find, access, and promote your PR history to all your visitors, especially journalists who end up on your website. If it takes too long to find, they'll give up and move on to the next company. Whether you label it as "media," "press," "newsroom," or "news"ccxxxv doesn't matter—so long as it's easy to find.

Inside of your press page, you should include separate sub-categories for press releases and places you've been featured in the news. While people may think that press releases are being phased out due to the rise of social media, they still deliver results. As long as they're well written, informative, and provide value, you should continue to generate them. It doesn't matter if they're self-generated or written by journalists and major media outlets, include them on your website in their own sub-section. This process makes them easy to find, reference, and share, and will help you get more from your PR.

Using another sub-section, you should highlight every instance when you've been mentioned in the news. This includes articles that have been written about your company, or one of your products or services, interviews, videos, or segments where you've been a guest on a radio station, TV show, or podcast. The main difference here is that you should focus on third-party references. Doing so helps keep your honorary mentions separate from things that you've announced to the public—new products, advancements, and awards.

You need to saturate this page. Make sure you post every single time your company was referenced, interviewed, or mentioned. You need this section to be impressive to readers, otherwise it tends to have the opposite effect. If you don't currently have a lot of press, consider building your page offline and only launching it once you've gathered a significant amount of PR in the news. Make sure the web design is neat, easy to read, and organized. Only use high quality logos, and make sure all your images are professional.[ccxxxvi] Remember, anytime anyone else publishes something about you or your business, you should publish it on their website. This strategy helps to thank them and grow your collection of impressive news pieces.

After you've optimized your website to highlight all your PR, take the time to regularly share things on your social media. As soon as someone publishes an article mentioning your business, share it on Facebook, Twitter, LinkedIn, and even Instagram. Always link back to the organization that wrote the article to give them credit and show your appreciation. They'll see this and be more likely to feature you again, in an effort to increase their own marketing efforts.

If you haven't had any major things happening, or haven't been referenced by any third party companies in a while, then take advantage of popular social media days like #throwbackthursday (#TBT) or #flashbackfriday. Write a catchy caption, include a picture, and link back to the original content. This process will help you continue to use PR to your advantage, even if it's been a while since your last win.

When things happen in your company, take the time to let people know about them. Properly highlighting your PR on your website, social media, and any other channels is a great way to continually bring positive exposure to your business.

Marketing Masters Pro Tip: Make Your PR Wins Work for You

Press is great. We've helped clients get on *The TODAY Show*, *Good Morning America*, *The New York Times*, *Inc.com*, *BuzzFeed*, *Forbes*, *Entrepreneur*, *FastCompany*, and countless other household publications.

But each and every time, they see a surge in traffic and inquiries, but that quickly fades. We live in a day and age where people are constantly bombarded with information and advertising, and unfortunately that means that big PR mention won't lead to lasting traffic. PR needs consistent practice and attention to achieve long-term results.

But you can make your PR wins work for you. Make sure you add each of your PR mentions to your website and your social media. Schedule "throwback" posts highlighting them. Start an ad campaign with the headline "As Seen In ____".

The most important takeaway is that the PR mention itself isn't necessarily the prize when it comes to marketing—but how you use that going forward will dictate how successful that PR mention can be for your business.

Chapter 81: Knowing When to Hire a PR Agency and What to Expect When You Hire One

Running a successful business takes a lot of work. You need to build a business plan, manage employees, strategize your marketing plans, buy and create advertisements, build a successful website, manage social media profiles, create valuable content, and work toward positive PR. With so much to do, many people decide to hire companies to help with their efforts, especially a PR agency. However, there is a misconception that needs to be addressed before you run off and sign a contract with someone. You need to understand that when you hire a PR agency, that doesn't mean you're going to immediately see your company appearing in major press stories or highlighted in the news.

The reality is that it takes months, sometimes longer, for tangible results to appear. The main benefit of hiring a PR agency is that you'll get access to all their existing relationships, which can help you get in front of notable people. It's important to know when you're ready to hire a PR agency, and what to expect once you do.

When it comes to hiring an agency, it's important to find someone who is connected to your industry. It wouldn't be beneficial to hire a PR firm with connections to health and wellness if you're an industrial company. You want access to a rolodex of relevant contacts and influencers in your industry, and a knowledge of how to communicate with them.

Prior to hiring any kind of outside help, including PR representatives, you need to establish your business goals very clearly. Knowing which direction you're taking your company, what story you want to share, and the kind of culture you want to publicize is integral for the success of positive PR. You should also ensure that you have enough room in your budget to hire a professional PR agency. They can be quite expensive—some cost upward of $144,000 a year[ccxxxvii] or more—and since the results tend to take longer, hiring an agency isn't something you want to do without planning.

Finally, you need to make sure that you and your team are receptive to criticism. You're going to need to listen to a PR agency or specialist when they tell you what part of your story, mission statement, or company culture won't resonate with your target audience. They have an objective viewpoint and will help you create a compelling story, but only if you're receptive to change. You must be willing to make changes and flexible to try new things. It might be scary at first, but PR professionals know what they're doing. If someone in your organization is resistant or hostile when it comes to constructive criticism, it needs to be addressed before you hire a PR firm.

Before doing anything, you need to discuss how the agency or individual plans to measure their success. Gini Dietrich, CEO of *Arment Dietrich,* an integrated marketing communications firm, believes that "the right measurement is all about identifying where you want to move the needle."[ccxxxviii] Make this clear with your future PR agency and ask them specifically how they will be able to show you results. Have certain milestones in place, and discuss how the PR agency will be able to help you reach those milestones. Always be transparent and upfront prior to signing any contract so both parties understand the expectations.

If your future PR agency doesn't have a plan or isn't able to give you an outline of what they plan to do, find a different agency. Outlining your goals and overall focus will make sure that things stay on schedule and you don't waste any money.

Finally, make sure you discuss courses of action if you need to make adjustments when things aren't working. Have a backup plan and make sure you communicate this with the PR agencies you're looking to work with. Make sure you find someone who can create good content, listen to your needs, and bring a creative element to the table. All your expectations need to be laid out on the table if you want a good working relationship.

Marketing Masters Pro Tip: Have the Right, Realistic Expectations

We do basic PR campaigns for clients and have seen tremendous results. With that being said, we are not a specialized PR firm. Oftentimes, we need to hire a specialized PR firm in a specific industry or vertical to help with client goals and projects.

In all honesty, this process is something we dread. Clients have an expectation that because you are hiring a PR firm, you are going to see immediate results and press. While this is a logical thing to think, unfortunately the world of PR doesn't work this way.

Even if you hire the best firm, they probably are going to take months to secure your first major press mention. And even then, it may not be what you hoped for.

In our opinion, hiring an actual PR firm should be reserved for a very specific point in your marketing journey. And you have to go into it with the right expectations and planning to use it for branding more than lead generation. If you go out and hire an expensive PR company with the wrong expectations, you will be disappointed every single time.

Chapter 82: Landing the "Big Fish" in the PR World

We spent some time talking about utilizing smaller digital publications to help build your company's recognition in Chapter 78, but we also want to mention a few things about landing the "Big Fish" in the PR world. Sometimes companies get hyper-focused on one or the other, but the most successful businesses understand the benefits of both. Problematically, the process for getting into larger publications can be a bit more daunting than simple, online digital publications, but the benefits are worth it.

When you land large publications in PR, your reach will grow. Larger publications have larger audiences, and when they publish something that highlights your business, you'll likely get more readers. More readers eventually mean more clients, which translates to more profits. James Clear, creator of *Habits Academy*, grew his e-mail subscription list by 600 valuable contacts from only one piece of republished content.[ccxxxix]

When you land the "Big Fish," you'll grow your network with other businesses and instantly establish a level of credibility that you couldn't get with small publications. Your peers may start to take you more seriously, and after getting your foot in the door, other larger publications may seek you out.

So how can you get your company into these larger publications? Here are a few tried and true tips to implement:

1. **Have Good Content**

    As with everything in the marketing world, having good content on your website is essential to getting where you need to be. Make sure it's well written, valuable, and reflects your company's culture. This way, when writers or publications review your site, they will see the value that you bring to your audience and will be more inclined to feature you.

2. **Create a Unique Pitch**

When you make a pitch to a publication, you need to have something that's unique. Stand out in the crowd. They receive hundreds, possibly thousands, of e-mails asking to be featured, and you need to stand out. Do your research on both the publication and the typical audience that the publication reaches. It might be different than the content you publish on your website, but that's okay. You need to resonate with *their* readers or viewers if you want to even be considered.

3. Reverse Engineer

Think about the publication where you want to be highlighted. Ask yourself what their publishers or editors are interested in. If the publication focuses on "how to" pieces, then pitch some great "how to" pieces. Make sure you pitch content that reflects what's already being published, as larger organizations tend to stick to a theme. Think about *Forbes* and *Buzzfeed* and how different they are. You need to offer something that's relevant for your company that will fit in line with their publications.

4. Ask Your Audience

Put yourself in the shoes of their readers. Ask yourself what they would want to see and then create a pitch that reflects that. You can even directly ask your audience on social media or through a poll if you're struggling to come up with ideas. Make sure you understand their habits, where they get their information, and what their profile is.

5. Build Relationships

One of the easiest ways to get blacklisted from major publications is by cold-contacting their writers and sending them a bad pitch. Instead, you need to work on building relationships and having a great story to tell. This process will take time, but it is much more beneficial than cutting corners and mass-e-mailing hundreds of major publications' writers.

We've seen businesses struggle with their PR, but the most important thing to remember is that you need to be consistent. Growing your brand through PR takes long, hard work, but so long as you stick to your goals and adjust when things aren't working, you'll be on the path to success.

Marketing Masters Pro Tip: You Don't Always Want or Need The "Big Fish"

Let's take this quite literally for a second. If you are out fishing, would you rather catch one, 50-pound fish that takes you a year to catch, or would you rather catch 365, 2-pound fish that you can reliably catch one of every single day of the year?

This is much the same in the PR world. Often times, we have seen clients insist on getting that "big fish," but it isn't necessarily in their best interest. Sure, having a big PR win is great and has value and benefit in your overall marketing and PR strategy, but for most of our clients who are not household names, it makes more sense to target industry publications, local publications, and other specialty press outlets. These mediums will deliver more consistent coverage, and more importantly, will deliver it to the right audience.

Before you spend a ton of money chasing that big fish, step back and you might be surprised at how much easier and more successful it is to focus on a larger quantity of smaller fish.

Part 9: Offline and Traditional Marketing Mediums

All the craze in the early 2000's was: "The Internet is going to kill offline advertising in the next 5 years." And yet, here we are in the 2020's and offline marketing is still alive, well, and buzzing.

If anything, offline marketing has made resurgence in the last few years.

Like anything, marketing and advertising is all about supply and demand. As more money and resources shift to the online world, suddenly the offline world starts to become less expensive which can lead to a better ROI.

In this section, we'll take a brief dive into some of the most common offline tactics we utilize for our clients, and provide some tips in how to make your offline marketing work in combination with your online marketing.

Chapter 83: Different Mediums to Use for Offline Marketing

While most of our focus in this book has revolved around online marketing and tactics, that doesn't mean that offline marketing is dead. In fact, it's a great asset to any marketing strategy. Offline marketing is anything you do that's not directly connected to the Internet. Think television, radio, billboards, magazines, business cards, and similar mediums. Since online marketing began, fewer people are using offline marketing tactics—which almost makes it *more* effective for those who do use it. They end up spending less on ad space and aren't buried in an oversaturated market. Offline marketing gives you a chance to stand out from your competition, because the truth of the matter is, no matter how glued to our phones, tablets, and computers we are, we're still exposed to things offline.

The OOH (Out of the Home Marketing a.k.a., Offline Marketing) advertising market was $7.6 Billion and growing in 2016.[ccxl] This is a decent worth, but it's not nearly as much as the online marketing industry, which was worth $194.6 billion in 2016.[ccxli] With that being said, let's look at a brief overview of some of the most common offline marketing strategies:

✓ **Billboards**

Billboards are perfect for a diverse audience. Since the exposure doesn't discriminate, and thousands of people will see your ad, it gives you strong brand exposure. Be creative and do something that will make a lasting impression in the few seconds that people see it. With the rise of digital billboards, there are even more options—we'll explore these in Chapter 87.

✓ **Direct Mail**

People still love to receive mail. Use this to your advantage and send out targeted, direct mail to help with your lead generation and relationship building. Direct mail is more personal and gives you a chance to form another point of contact.

✓ **Newspapers and Magazines**

Purchasing ad space in print is like online marketing, in a way. You need to design the ad with contact information, enticing imagery, and a strong CTA. Make sure you focus on newspapers and magazines that are relevant to your audience for the biggest ROI.

✓ **Printed Publications**

In addition to purchasing ad space in newspapers and magazines, you can submit guest articles or pitches featured in printed publications like we discussed in the public relations section.

✓ **Radio**

Millions of people drive to work each day and listen to the radio during their commute. It's all about making sure you're on the right station at the right time in the right region. Do your research prior to putting out radio ads. They can be expensive even for short time slots.

✓ **Television**

People still watch TV, so take advantage of a short, 20-second block to provide a powerful message to your audiences. These ads can be increasingly expensive depending on the network, so make sure you spread your efforts out instead of being hyper focused. Think about your local vs. national impact and act accordingly.

✓ **Sponsoring Events**

Event sponsors receive a decent amount of publicity, especially if they're some of the larger ones. This is a great way to get your name on a myriad of merchandise, marketing materials, and more. Plus, people tend to see businesses that sponsor events in a positive light.

✓ Donate Prizes

If there is a large event occurring in your area, consider donating prizes or gift certificates. This is a great way to boost the public's morale about your company, and it gives them a taste of the products or services you offer.

✓ Networking Events

These events increase face-to-face connections in your network, which helps to foster advertising through word of mouth. Attend as many events as you can and talk to a variety of different attendees.

✓ Trade Shows

Purchase a space, set up a booth, and let people come to you. Trade shows are a great way to pass out print materials, network, and build personal relationships all in one place.

✓ Speaking Engagements

People who give strong and meaningful speeches are remembered. Aim for targeted events that are relevant to your industry to gain exposure to an entirely untapped audience, all while building credibility and leadership for your brand.

✓ Cold Calling

While people still seem to hate cold calling, it's an effective offline marketing strategy. It gives you a chance to speak one-on-one with potential customers in a personal setting. Plus, cold calling gives you an instant response and is easy to track for ROI.

✓ **Guerrilla Marketing**

This is anything that is a bit more unconventional in the marketing world. It aims to increase your exposure through things like stickers, business cards, flyers, branded items, and more. We'll talk more about this in Chapter 86.

Regardless of the offline marketing strategies you choose to use, it's important to understand their reach. This way, you won't spend too much money in, say, television and not enough in magazines. It is also critical to remember your targeting options are dramatically lower in offline marketing. Making sure you take the time to research prior to spending your money is crucial, and we'll dive deeper into this topic in the following chapter.

Chapter 84: Understanding the Reach of Offline Marketing

The main difference between online and offline marketing is the ability to track and measure your reach. This is easy to do with online marketing, but offline provides its own set of challenges. You can't get the same metrics or analytics as when you run things digitally, so you need to make sure to do the necessary research prior to spending money on an expensive offline marketing campaign. We see businesses that fail to do *any* research on the actual distribution, reach, or audience when running a new campaign. This isn't a smart way to approach offline marketing and leads to many clients overpaying for services that they could easily have negotiated—more on that in Chapter 89.

Instead, find ways to track your efforts and do research *before* spending money. In this chapter, we want to highlight who you can reach using each of the platforms we discussed in the previous chapter, which include:

✓ **Billboards**

> The reach of billboards is quite vast and diverse. There are people of all ages in cars passing by every day—either as a passenger or the driver. Americans from 30-49 tend to drive the most out of any age group and 71% of Americans said they consciously looked at billboards while driving.[ccxlii]

✓ **Direct Mail**

> Receiving a letter is a personal way to reach your target audience. The age group for direct mail varies, but it was found that 92% of Millennials were influenced to make a purchasing decision because of direct mail.[ccxliii] In addition, for every $167 spent on direct mail in the US, marketers sell $2,095 in goods and services.[ccxliv]

✓ **Newspapers and Magazines**

Print marketing seems to have the highest ROI in offline marketing at 120%.[ccxlv] The important thing to remember when using print marketing is to target your advertisements to your audience and do your research on the publication where you're going to place an ad.

✓ **Radio**

Radio ads reach a lot of people; however, their performance isn't always the greatest. Since people usually hear radio ads while they're driving, they won't take considerable action unless your message is very powerful and resonates with them. Make sure you create something short, yet catchy, and advertise on local stations.

✓ **Television**

While TV isn't dead, it's being pushed out of the spotlight by streaming services like Netflix and Hulu. Since the costs of airing a commercial tends to be higher than any other offline marketing tactic, make sure you understand the viewer ratings and statistics before making any deals.

✓ **Sponsoring Events, Donating Prizes, and Networking**

Both sponsoring events and donating prizes are great to build your brand, but you won't see a big ROI unless you're pairing it with extensive networking. You need to prove your value to your audience while finding an effective way to measure your ROI. This can be difficult unless you hand out coupons, discount codes, or something else specific to your event and prize.

✓ **Trade Shows**

Like events, you need to make an active effort to measure your ROI and do research for prospective trade shows. All businesses have different goals with trade shows, so make sure you clearly define what it is you want to do before buying a booth. Do you want to generate leads, get more media, network, launch a new product or service, or simply increase your brand awareness? Your answer will help you decide whether the cost is worth the result.

✓ **Cold Calling**

This method is a fairly easy offline marketing effort to track and research, since most companies and businesspeople were built on cold calling. Since the cost is close to zero, cold calling and e-mailing should be part of your efforts. Plus, there is a more positive response than you might think. In a survey, 78% of decision makers said that they've attended an event or taken an appointment that came from a cold call or e-mail.[ccxlvi]

✓ **Guerrilla Marketing**

The main reason businesses use guerrilla marketing is to increase brand recognition. In fact, marketing recall impressions are near 100% for guerilla marketing tactics, which is quite impressive when you compare it to the 33% recall for all other traditional offline advertising efforts.[ccxlvii]

In addition to knowing who your offline marketing will reach, make sure you understand the current circulation of magazine ads, newspapers, radio broadcasts, and television commercials. Once you've researched these tactics, it's time to decide which platforms to use based on your target audience, which is our focus in the next chapter.

Chapter 85: Understanding What Offline Marketing to Use Based on Your Target Audience

In an effort to bring together all of the offline platforms available and their respective reach, you need to make sure you understand your target audience. Luckily, by now, you've likely created numerous profiles, researched demographics, and have a good idea of who it is you want to target. Now the question is: where do those people get their information? Do they like to listen to the radio? Watch cable? Read magazines, and if so, which magazines? Do they prefer to pick up a physical copy of the local newspaper every morning to start their day? Once you start to think like your customer and understand how your target markets are accessing information or consuming content,[ccxlviii] it'll be much easier to get higher ROIs in your offline marketing tactics.

You can put up a thousand billboards, or purchase hours of ad time on television stations, you can even buy entire pages in certain publications. But if you don't know where your audience is going, you're throwing your money away. Similarly, you need to ensure your audience trusts the offline medium you are using and it pairs well with your product or service offering.

We get excited to see our business in print, but then we forget to look at who the publication is targeting or who their readers really are.[ccxlix] For instance, if you want to target a group of young adults ages 18-30, you're not going to do well by running an ad in AARP. In addition to targeting the right publication or platform, you need to know whether or not your audience will hear your message on that platform. Witty humor on a billboard tends to catch most people's attention, but whether they appreciate it is another story. Research enough to understand what your audience will and will not find offensive and go from there. Create a strong call to action that's obvious and easy to follow, regardless of the platform you're using.

Another example revolves around television ads. Most of the younger generation have migrated away from cable and now exclusively watch their entertainment on a streaming service. In fact, 61% of young adults rely primarily on online streaming for their "television fix."[ccl] If you want to run a TV ad while the news is playing your target audience will likely be around 60 years old.[ccli]

The type of event you attend will also matter. Do your research, find things that resonate with your audience, and attend the right events.

Everything in offline marketing depends on your research, your specific company's goals, and your target audience. Each company we work with has different needs that are met through a different offline platform; the important thing is knowing yours.

Chapter 86: Understanding Guerilla Marketing and How to Use it

Guerilla Marketing involves going outside the box and making an impression that no other kind of advertising can. It's more unconventional than traditional offline marketing tactics, but it tends to yield very strong results. While many smaller businesses and startups rely heavily on guerilla marketing due to its low cost, guerilla marketing is effective for any company, big or small. It's about creating something newsworthy and unique. Adam Salacuse, Founder and President of *ALT TERRAIN,* says there needs to be a sort of "underground" element to guerilla marketing and that it involves, "brand activation that isn't 100% permitted by the city, event or establishment."[cclii] We are not saying break any laws—please, do not break any laws—we're just saying get outside your comfort zone and be creative enough to captivate your audience. Make them have to look twice *and* create a message that's aligned with your business goals.

The term originates from "guerilla warfare," which is a form of irregular warfare that relates to small tactics used by civilians.[ccliii] Thus, the term guerilla marketing makes sense. It's an irregular form of marketing through small acts of recognition used by businesses. Let's explore some of the top 10 guerilla marketing tactics that we see businesses use today:

1. **Stickers**

   Print out stickers with your logo or create a unique, artistic sticker that includes your logo. Print hundreds and hand them out to everyone, everywhere, for free. Have them at your place of business, hand them out with business cards, and go to shops or other businesses to see if they'll keep some by their register. The more people that have your stickers, the more places you'll end up seeing them. You'll see them in subways, bars, public transportation, construction walls, and more places than you could imagine, which is great for brand recognition.

2. Pop-Up Experiences

Depending on your audience, these can be a great way to increase your company's recognition in a region or neighborhood. The opportunities are endless. Hold a sponsored concert, create a themed bar—with the required permits, of course—or even build a creative showroom for your business' products and services. Be creative, find a space, and hold an exclusive pop-up experience.

3. Outdoor Installations

Use your city or rural area to create outdoor installations instead of expensive marketing campaigns. Recreate manholes into steaming cups of coffee; use a building wall with trees or shrubbery to cleverly display signage, or anything else you can think of. A good example was when the new *IT* movie was being released, and "a number of red balloons appeared attached to drainage grates... accompanied by a stencil chalk note saying, 'It is closer than you think.'"[ccliv] Trailer views skyrocketed.

4. Graffiti, Art, and Posters

Avoid breaking any laws, but talk to your local businesses and see if they would be interested in getting a nice new addition of artful graffiti on one of their outside walls. You can also create legal installments using sidewalk chalk to make a temporary mark on property. Draw something cool, include a hashtag or your website, or simply find a way to resonate with your audience.

An awesome example was when the company *Foursquare* drew a foursquare court on the sidewalk near their business and bought a ball. Thousands of walk-up participants showed up and a long line formed. During this competition, the company handed out t-shirts, buttons, stickers, and explained the game as long as they checked-in to their company on social media.[cclv] The results were incredible.

5. Creative Product Placement

Create marketing materials on unique objects and place them anywhere you can. You can think of traditionally branded pens that you give away, or take an example from the people at *Prison Break*. They used a small file with the return date of the hit TV show and placed it inside a cake. They then sent the cake to a popular media channel that received the message loud and clear, and enjoyed a free cake.

6. Brand Partnerships

If you know a company that you could work with, contact them. There are a ton of ways for brands to partner together to create a memorable and one of a kind guerilla marketing campaign.

7. Unique Direct Mail

Direct mail is a successful offline marketing tactic, but if you want to increase the amount of people that actually read your mail, make it something out of the ordinary. Different things you can send through the mail without packaging include: a box of candy, a flip-flop, a coconut, a potato, a rock, a Frisbee, a box of balloons, anything in a bottle, plastic Easter eggs, and more. Find something inexpensive and relevant to your business, get some stamps, and mail away.

8. Flyers

Flyers are easy to create and dispense, and they have the potential to reach a very large audience. Create something that catches people's attention, then put them up around town, ask businesses to keep a stack at their register, see if bars will put them up, and keep some at your front desk. The key here is brand exposure.

9. Creative Business Cards

Business cards are an essential part of any professional's life. You hand them out whenever you can and make it easy for people to contact you. However, most people just put them in a drawer and, unless they've already built a relationship with you, will never look at them again. You can change that by making them memorable and unique. Focus on standing out from the crowd. Use vibrant colors, odd shapes, or even an object that your contact can use. As long as it's not huge and heavy, give it a try.

10. Free Giveaways

Anything you can give away that bears your company name and logo is a good way to increase your guerilla marketing. Print t-shirts, sunglasses, cups, pens, notebooks, notepads, or *anything* you can think of. As long as the price per unit is fairly cheap, it's a great way for people to see your company name over and over again.

Whatever you decide to implement is up to you, but we want to stress one major thing when it comes to guerilla marketing: do not break the law. It's not worth it, and will cause you more negative publicity than you want. Try something that gets your audience involved and find inspiration from other successful campaigns.

Pro tip: Find a guerilla marketing tactic that relates to your business or your target customer

When we first started our agency, we were desperate to find a cost effective yet innovative way to get clients. We came up with the idea of a sort of digital gorilla marketing approach coupled with an offline follow up.

Specifically, we targeted local businesses online through social media ads then mailed them something unique as a follow up reminder. We mailed a local bakery a spatula with our logo on it. We mailed a local electrician a new mini flashlight. Then followed up these mailings with phone calls.

While this may not be as innovative as some guerilla marketing tactics, it worked and worked well for our industry and target clients. The key is to be different. Do something out of the ordinary to show that your business is unique!

Chapter 87: Merging Offline Marketing with Technology

In recent years, there have been advances in the world of offline marketing. Billboards and signs are becoming increasingly digital, interactive posters are on the rise, and magazines and newspapers publish digital copies of every edition. The technology revolution has changed the way we use offline strategies and is making things easier for everyone. An increase in technology paired with offline marketing strategies has made it much easier to track conversions, determine your ROI, and measure analytics. We've had businesses ask us how they can better integrate online and offline tactics to further their bottom line, so that's what we'll discuss in this chapter. Those include:

✓ **Customized Landing Pages**

One of the easiest ways to combine technology with your offline marketing strategies is to create custom landing pages for each campaign. Put them on your billboards, magazines, business cards, merchandise, subway posters, or anywhere you're using print to market. Include it at the end of a TV ad or mention the URL on your radio segment. The main thing is to create specific landing pages for each different campaign so you can effectively measure the results. Additionally, make sure that the URLs you create are short enough for people to remember so they'll follow through and actually type it into their computers. Since most people are visiting these pages from an offline source, include your phone number for those who may not be comfortable with online interactions. Finally, avoid indexing your landing pages to make sure they stay separate from your online traffic analytics.[cclvi]

✓ **Redirect Domains**

If you have different campaigns in different regions, consider creating domains specifically geared toward those areas and then have them redirect to custom landing pages.[cclvii] This will help you track your efforts for location-specific offline marketing campaigns. Make sure you create a catchy URL that people will remember long after they've seen it. Additionally, you need to make sure that these landing pages are unique and don't include duplicate content from your main website—doing so will only cause you problems with Google's algorithm.

✓ Track Your Communication

Since most offline marketing tactics will result in either a phone call or e-mail, make sure you're tracking both. Track phone lines to better understand where your offline advertising efforts are paying off.[cclviii] You can also track specific e-mail subject lines or unique e-mail addresses that are used in different offline advertisements. Again, just make sure it's short and easy to remember.

✓ Promo Codes

Create specific promotional or discount codes for different offline campaigns. Hundreds of companies already do this in their magazine ads, billboards, and even television commercials. Not only will you be able to track each of your different offline tactics, but also you'll be doing so through people actually making purchases and becoming customers. Keep track of your codes and make sure you don't repeat them on multiple campaigns.

✓ Hashtags

The idea here is somewhat similar to that involving promo codes. You can use custom hashtags on memorable offline advertisements in order to spur public participation. This process allows you to track how many people are talking about you, increasing your online marketing through brand recognition on social media.

After using these tactics to help merging offline marketing with technology, you'll be able to gather enough data to evaluate the success, or failure, of your strategies. Don't neglect your analytics. Since you have the tools to gather the data, pay attention to things that are working and things that aren't so you can make necessary changes to maximize your ROI. Look at your analytics prior to launching a new offline strategy in addition to after its unveiling. This will allow you to see any changes that have occurred that may be attributed to your offline marketing efforts. The more creative your tactics are, the more positive results you'll see. We'll discuss how to break out of your creative shell in Chapter 88.

Chapter 88: Letting Creativity Flow When it comes to Offline Marketing Tactics

Everything we've talked about so far regarding offline marketing is important, but there's one thing that will set you apart from your competition, and that's your creativity. There are thousands of businesses that still use offline marketing tactics, which means people are exposed to millions of advertisements throughout their day. If something doesn't stand out, it gets lost in the crowd. Creativity is one way to make sure that your offline tactics are effective and memorable. We believe it is one of the most important tools for the success of your campaign. Consider the last time you saw a unique ad in a magazine, on a billboard, or even on a subway sign. It's likely you can recall more information from that brief exposure than you can from the number of bland billboards you pass every day on your commute. Creativity is essential to your success. However, sometimes creativity can be difficult to master. To help push you in the right direction, we want to provide a few of our favorite creative offline advertisement campaigns from the past few years.

Offline Interactive Example

The advertising team behind the Olympics knew what they were doing when they launched the interactive element to their 2014 Winter Olympics advertising campaign. To help encourage people to live a more active lifestyle, they took over a train station in Russia and offered free rides in exchange for doing 30 squats.[cclix] This blew up on social media—everyone was talking about it. While the Olympics probably didn't need much help with their advertising, this offline campaign gave them self-generated publicity from participants and bystanders while simultaneously stressing the importance of a healthy lifestyle.

Offline Print Example

With the release of *Deadpool* in 2016, marketers wanted to step up their billboard game. Instead of a traditional movie billboard, they used emojis—a skull, a pile of "poo," and a large L—to turn it into a mini "hidden message" game. The public's reaction was extremely positive, and they used their momentum to release unique commercials promoting the movie. In 2018, when *Deadpool 2* was released, they had one of the most successful marketing campaigns for a movie in years. In addition to releasing a commercial where Ryan Reynolds, as *Deadpool*, apologized to David Beckham for all his previously failed movies, the marketing team went and hijacked famous movies sold at Walmart. They paired together with other 20th Century Fox films, such as *Fight Club*, *Revenge of the Nerds*, *Cast Away*, *Edward Scissorhands*, *X-Men*, and others, printing limited edition movie covers with *Deadpool* in place of the movie's original stars.[cclx] With the purchase of the movie, you also received a $5 off coupon for *Deadpool 2* in theatres. Not only did this increase ticket sales for *Deadpool 2*—also a 20th Century Fox movie—it also increased the sale of classic movies that had seen a slump in profits over the years. This was the first offline marketing tactic of its kind and left a very strong impression on the public.

Guerilla Marketing Example

Reddit, Salt Life, and Life is Good used guerilla marketing to successfully infiltrate the public with their stickers. Reddit's logo, Snoo the Reddit Alien, is a simple sticker that seems to pop up everywhere; while Salt Life and Life is Good stickers are on cars, public transportation systems, and even public buildings. Just the exposure from these stickers causes curiosity, which leads people to their website or prompts a discussion between friends.

More people are using stickers today, but when they started sticker marketing wasn't as widespread. Do something that no one has done before so you can catch the attention of the public and hold on long enough to grow your brand. When it comes to offline marketing, creativity is key. Try holding brainstorming sessions with your team and give some things a try. If it doesn't work, move on to the next idea and keep going forward.

Chapter 89: Negotiating Pricing for Offline Marketing

When you use online marketing, the prices are often set in stone. You can't contact Facebook ads or Google and try negotiating a deal—it simply won't work. However, the world of offline marketing is much different. To purchase billboard, radio, print, or TV advertisements, you'll work with an actual person to go over the parameters. This means that almost 100% of your offline marketing campaigns can be negotiated in price. We see businesses that fail to do this and end up paying up to 50% more than they could have. Instead, if you approach offline marketing the right way, you can end up with more advertising at a lower cost. Usually, businesses can negotiate 20 – 30% off the list price for an offline campaign. If you have a higher volume of ads in your campaign, however, you may be able to negotiate as much as 40-70% off list price. The main thing we are stressing is this: *never* pay full price for offline marketing.

If a company isn't budging on price, ask for more in return for that price. For example, ask for additional impressions: more ads in a publication, extra slots for a radio ad, or copies of a magazine to distribute to your leads and clients and to use in your marketing collateral. Many people avoid doing this mainly because they're uncomfortable, but it's all a part of business and you need to take advantage of it.

Before you go into any meeting, make sure to do your research. Research is an important part of marketing, but it's also essential for a good negotiation. Research the company that you're meeting with, who their customers are, what those customers have paid, how successful their campaigns were, and the reason behind their success. Research that company's competitors. Know what one company offers that another doesn't. Find the leverage you need for your negotiations so you always have something in your back pocket.

Prior to setting anything up, create your budget. Go into every meeting knowing exactly how much you can afford to spend on offline marketing, and when you meet with a salesperson, tell them that your budget is 50% less than what it really is. This gives you some wiggle room and shows that you're willing to compromise. Plus, you might even get a bigger discount than you imagined.

When you head into the meeting, be firm on your budget. Salespeople often have the power to get major discounts from their superiors, so if you work on developing the relationship and being firm with your expectations, there is potential for negotiation. Connect with them on a personal level and communicate openly about your company's goals, philosophy, target audience, and more. Share your strengths, but consider mentioning a few weaknesses as well. Be very clear about your expectations from the company and don't be afraid to ask for a discount.

When you take the time to prepare yourself for a meeting with different publications, you'll set yourself up for successful negotiations. This means that even if you don't have a large marketing budget, you'll still be able to get some exposure. If the marketing company you really want to work with isn't budging on giving you any discount or free added exposure, mention their competitors. It shows that you are educated and that you have options. Don't be afraid to walk away from a company that won't negotiate. There are hundreds of other companies out there. If one doesn't work well with your company before you've even signed a contract, chances are there will be issues down the line.

Marketing Masters Pro tip: Negotiate and sometimes using an agency will save even more!

I remember breaking my back spreading mulch at my house a few springs ago. I went to my local garden center and paid around $90 per yard for some mulch. My friend and client who is a local landscape designer drove by and saw me and said hi. I asked him what he charges for this backbreaking work and it was $80 per yard installed for the same mulch!

Perplexed I asked him how and he explained he buys in bulk and only pays $40 per yard for the materials.

The same goes for offline ads. I had a client relive this same experience with an ad we ran for them for half a decade. One year they decided to go direct to the publication and were confused when the price was higher than our price. This publication not only gives us an agency discount but they also give us free follow up ads when they have an open spot to fill!

The bottom line is that even with an agency markup, sometimes it can save you money to work with a pro. And even if you don't want to, at the very least, directly negotiate your pricing with the publication. It can save you a ton of money on your offline ads.

Part 10: Lead Nurturing and Handling

You spend a massive amount of time, money, and resources generating leads. Yet it always amazes us how many of these businesses massively mess up handling their leads.

Your leads should be treated like gold. This starts with your phone answering and handling and goes all the way to the moment you close them. Even after a lead is closed, in a sense they remain a lead forever; as there is opportunity to up sell, cross sell, and more.

In this section, we will touch on some of the most important lead handling processes and offer tips and suggestions on ways to nurture your leads to maximize your conversion rate.

Chapter 90: The Importance of Properly Managing Your Leads

In the world of business, you will come across a lot of prospective customers, or leads. Whether it's through a personal relationship, an event, online or offline marketing campaigns, your website, or social media, leads should motivate you to work harder and increase their conversion rate. Lead management involves everything from tracking to managing all prospective customers,[cclxi] and is extremely important in the cultivation of profits. For some people, this management comes easily, and for others it can be difficult. As long as you know what you need to do to manage your leads properly, it's easy to integrate into your daily business model. In this chapter, we want to discuss the typical business etiquette that surrounds handling a new lead.

First and foremost, you want to acknowledge them. You can do this by reaching out via a welcome e-mail and thanking them for their interest in your company. Create an automated system so this happens almost instantaneously, and make sure there's a personalized touch in the e-mail. You can also set up a thank you page for people who have signed up for your newsletter, subscribed to your channel, or simply joined your e-mail list. Whatever you do, acknowledge them.

If they've contacted you with a question, comment, or concern, respond as quickly as possible Response time is crucial in lead management and the faster you are, the better. In fact, roughly 35 – 50% of all sales go to the vendor that responds first.[cclxii] Make sure that's you by having a seamless system in place and answering inquiries in a personalized and respectable manner. Don't be afraid to delegate this job to one of your employees so your time is free for business development and the larger picture.

Another tried and true way to manage new leads is to offer them something extra. If they were looking at a product or service, offer them a discount or coupon code. If they signed up for your newsletter, offer them a link to one of your relevant blogs or articles. Show them that you understand their interests and acknowledge them.

After capturing a lead, the next step is nurturing them to become a customer. To do this, you need to know a little bit more about them. Have them fill out a form, but make sure it focuses on relevant information. Depending on your business needs, include different fields to be filled out, but remember: less is more.

Continue to provide your leads with personalized content to further nurture your leads. Do this across several different mediums for the best results, and make sure you're regularly staying in touch. You don't want to lose a lead because of your lack of persistence.

Handling new leads is a delicate process that will be different for each company, depending on their needs and business goals. Remember to keep track of all your efforts and keep an eye on the analytics associated with your actions. When you see things that work, keep doing them. When things aren't working, make some changes and try again. Every lead is different, but if they're properly managed, you'll start to see more conversions.

Chapter 91: The Difference Between Leads and Prospects

Like most businesses, you're probably familiar with the terms "lead" and "prospect," but you might still be confused as to the underlying differences. Knowing which is which is important if you want to classify your future customers properly and increase sales, but it can be tricky for both new and experienced businesses. The primary difference between the two revolves around their current level of engagement with your organization. For things to run seamlessly within your company make sure you take the time to clarify the difference between a prospect and a lead and how you'll treat each accordingly.

A lead is someone you have had contact with either through a form on your website, at a networking event, in an elevator, or wherever. They have expressed interest, but you haven't yet qualified them as someone who fits the shoes of a prospect—someone in your target audience with the money to pay for what you're offering and intent to purchase it. There are different levels and subtypes of leads—some who are more ready to purchase than others. Technically speaking, a "lead is information that indirectly points towards a sale."[cclxiii] Making someone a lead is the first step in converting them into a customer.

Prospects include one of two types of people. The first is any contact who fits into your company's typical buyer persona and qualifies as a potential customer, yet hasn't yet expressed interest.[cclxiv] The others are considered sales-ready leads that have moved down the funnel and are closer to completing your desired outcome.[cclxv] They don't need to have expressed an interest per se; rather it is their personal profile that makes them a prospect.

The difference between the two depends on where they are in the sales funnel. Leads turn into prospects and prospects turn into customers. We'll talk more about this in Chapter 91.

Since they're located in different places in the sales funnel, it's important to treat them accordingly, mainly in terms of communication. Leads are usually contacted through some sort of mass-automated program using specific e-mails, calls to action, and content.[cclxvi] Prospects are contacted on a more individual basis, since they're more likely to turn into customers and are thus more valuable to your organization. The calls to action used for prospects are more action-oriented to continue communication. Their purchase intent should be nurtured until they convert into a paying customer.

This difference is often an area we see business struggle with the most, but so long as you remember the location in the lead funnel and how to communicate with each individually, you'll do fine. Don't waste your time worrying about your labels; just remember that you're working toward conversions by moving your audience down the lead funnel. We'll talk more about this in the next chapter.

Chapter 92: Setting Up and Measuring Your Lead Funnel

Every successful business has one thing in common: they have a powerful lead funnel. A lead funnel is the process in which a lead becomes a prospect and a prospect becomes a customer. It includes all the stages that potential customers move through, from their first exposure to your brand to your post-sale acknowledgement.[cclxvii] Lead funnels are what help you move people through the conversion process. At the top, your funnel will be much wider, as the amount of potential leads and prospects are extremely vast. There are a lot of people that know about your company or your brand, but that doesn't necessarily mean they'll take any action. Working down the funnel, leads get more serious about becoming a customer until the few that trickle out the bottom do so with a product or service in hand and money in your pockets.

There are different stages involved in a successful lead funnel. Your goal is to get high quality leads that will eventually turn into customers. According to a 2012 MarketingSherpa study, Chief Marketing Officers were most focused on achieving or increasing their ROI, optimizing the marketing-sales funnel, getting more insight into their audience, and maximizing the lifetime value of customers. Their biggest hurdle in achieving these goals, according to a study by IDG, was generating high-quality leads.[cclxviii] Without high quality leads that have a higher potential to turn into customers, your efforts are wasted.

Businesses need to take initiative to set up their funnel properly if they want to see results. This is an important step that may need some tweaks over time, but it shouldn't be overlooked.

The stages of a lead funnel include:

1. **Attract**

    Before you can convert your audience into customers, they have to be aware of your company, products, and services. You can use a number of the processes we've discussed in this book to generate company awareness, such as e-mail marketing, SEO best practices, PPC, landing pages, creating free lead magnets or incentives, social media marketing, online and offline marketing strategies, public relations, content marketing, and general advertisements to attract visitors to your website.

The whole purpose of this stage is to make yourself known and to show people what you do. You're trying to generate leads so you can nurture them through the funnel. Use different forms of media to display your products and/or services, create videos, and infuse your website with rich media. Show people why you are better than your competitors and always work on creative techniques that help you stand out from the crowd.

During this stage, you should not attempt to gather anyone's information or come off too sales-driven. Doing so might scare off potential customers or give them the wrong idea bout your company's bottom-line. Work on increasing your website traffic and creating strong brand recognition during this stage.

2. Engage

The next stage involves creating an interest in your company for your audience and getting them engaged. Now that your brand is gaining more recognition, you want to encourage your prospects to learn more about the products and services you offer. Continue to foster the relationship with the people that have learned about your company to keep yourself relevant. Try to demonstrate the problems that your product and/or services can help solve and show your value to the public. Offer them extra videos, whitepapers, polls, and eBooks. Include visually clear calls to action and start collecting e-mail addresses through lead magnets or opt-in forms. This will help you build a solid relationship with your leads.

3. Nurture

If people are moving down your funnel, the next step is the nurture stage. They will start to look at your products and/or services and compare them to your competitors. Price, functionality, convenience, and even design play a part here, so make sure you're marketing efforts are honest and reflective of what you offer. If they show an interest, they might sign up for one of your e-mail lists or give you their e-mail in exchange for one of your popular lead magnets. During this stage, people will also read reviews, ask for recommendations, check for coupons, visit brick-and-mortar stores, and search Google for all available options.[cclxix] During this stage, 70% of buyers will head to Google at least 2-3 times throughout their search to dig deeper into your company and products.[cclxx] This is another reason strong SEO is crucial to your success.

Set up a lead scoring system to further research whether your leads have the potential to become a customer by segmenting your visitors by their persona and interests. Send personalized messages, continue to provide value, and work on becoming their "go-to" company for your industry.

4. Convert

The final stage of the funnel is when it comes time for leads to make a decision. Either they've decided they will benefit from your product and/or service, or they won't. Make sure you've been developing your relationship with them so you can better nudge them in the direction of becoming a customer. The more they trust you as a business, the more likely they'll buy from you rather than your competitors. Offer them something valuable that entices them to take immediate action—such as a coupon, promotional code, or special rate. Provide a stronger lead magnet that leads to sales and help them prioritize their decision.

Most people need to justify their expenses, and the best way to do so is through increased value. Once they've decided to become a customer, don't start neglecting them. Keep the lines of communication open so they will continue to come back to you as the years pass by.

Everything we've gone over in this book can help propel you forward to create a strong lead funnel. Just remember that you need to identify which leads will be worth pursuing, and to communicate with them based on their position in the buying process. Prioritize your time accordingly and you'll help facilitate the evolution of more leads into customers.

Chapter 93: Understanding the Importance of Lead Nurturing

Throughout the lead funnel, there will be periods when you'll need to nurture leads to push them toward making a purchasing decision. Not everyone moves through the process at the same speed, but just because they're not ready to sign up or make a purchase, doesn't mean they won't ever be. In fact, a study showed that 15-20% of people who were not ready to purchase, but were then nurtured, ended up converting into sales.[cclxxi] Therefore it's important to keep your leads warm and well nurtured. According to a recent survey, "nurtured leads in the long run are responsible for about 47% larger purchases compared to leads that were never nurtured."[cclxxii] People recognize when companies and organizations take the time to acknowledge their leads, and it will pay off in the long run. When you stop generating and nurturing leads, your funnel ends up empty, so it's important to integrate this strategy into your daily marketing efforts.

Luckily, building and developing relationships isn't too difficult. The purpose of lead nurturing is to increase the public's trust in your company through different tactics. However, most companies don't have the time to go through and build a relationship with every one of the potentially thousands of leads that they get every day.

Sending personalized e-mails, educating prospects and leads on your company, fostering engagement, and developing content can take a lot of work. That's why these tactics are most successful when they're automated or persistent. It frees up your time and resources and keeps your business in the forefront of their minds. Then you can focus on converting leads that have expressed interest, or high-quality leads, into customers.

Without the right system in place, you could be losing hundreds, or even thousands, of potential sales. "By building specific processes simply to lose fewer leads than normal, organizations can spend less at the top of the waterfall, and more at the middle and bottom where much greater leverage can be gained. In any economy, that's a strategy that should be embraced by both marketing and sales."[cclxxiii] We'll explore how to set up the right system in the next chapter.

Chapter 94: Setting Up a System for Lead Nurturing

As your leads start moving through your funnel, you need to have a system in place to nurture them at every stage of the process. This system runs parallel with your funnel, but there are certain points where they cross. Those are the opportunities where you can nurture your leads by engaging them as much as possible—without being too overbearing. For example, every time a lead signs up, send them a welcome e-mail; every time you have a new or updated product, send an update e-mail, your monthly or weekly newsletter, exclusive content downloads like whitepapers and eBooks. These are all parts of your sales cycle that should be automatic. Although they may fall into place naturally, you need to plan what you will send or how you will reach them at each stage. In most industries, a lead requires 5 – 10 touches before they'll become a customer, so you're going to need to figure out what those will be and how to automate them.

Segment Your Audiences

The first step to setting up your system is to segment your leads. This is to help you understand where they're at in the buying process, what they need from you to convert into customers, and the type of information that will resonate with them best. You can gather data from your leads that visit your website using forms, quizzes, polls, forums, comments, and downloads. Based on the information you receive, you should be able to fit them into one of your customer profiles.

By identifying your leads' different interests, needs, demographics, challenges, location, lifestyles, careers or jobs, and their level in the buying process, you can create customer profiles. Each different group will have its own unique set of content and e-mail marketing campaigns. While it's not realistic for each individual lead, segmenting them will help break apart the whole. A study by *Marketo* found that 23% of e-mail engagement is correlated with how detailed you were in your segmentation.[cclxxiv] Don't be afraid to create detailed lists up front. The more customer profiles you have, the better you can meet the needs of your audience.

Identify Their Place in the Buying Cycle

The next stage is identifying where your leads are in the buying cycle. This will help increase personalization and relevancy. If they've just visited your site, they're working on awareness of your organization, so make sure you're posting high quality content relevant to your business. If they've opted-in to your e-mail list, make sure an automated e-mail is sent with relevant content on your site and/or a free lead magnet. If they continue to visit your site and respond to your e-mails, send them customized content based on their profile that is a little stronger than your original lead magnet—think exclusivity. Do this weekly after initial signs of interest and always practice lead scoring. Lead scoring helps rank your leads based on their potential value to your business.[cclxxv] This helps you understand how much time you should be spending on them based on collected information, their behavior, social media activity, and any relevant segmented information.

If people seem like they're ready to make a purchase—identifiable by people asking you purchasing questions or questions about your products or services—answer e-mails quickly and personally. The timeline you should aim for is within 24 hours, but the faster the better. After they've made a purchase, send them an e-mail thanking them and consider including a promo code or coupon to use on their next purchase. For a more comprehensive overview, let's consider all of the tactics that go into lead nurturing.

Lead Nurturing Tactics[cclxxvi]

✓ **Targeted Content**

Use your segmented lists to provide content that will resonate with each different persona you've created. Create specific content for each of the different personas. It can be difficult at first, but focus on delivering the right content to the right people and you'll be better off than your

311

competitors. Send different types of content, including infographics, videos, blogs, whitepapers, downloadable and printable content, and eBooks. See what works best and make adjustments. Timing also matters, so consider the stage they're in and remember to always respond quickly to any inquiries.

✓ Multi-Channel Nurturing

Most people need a little nudge in the right direction when it comes to making a purchase. You can set up an e-mail drip campaign—or an automated e-mail campaign. This is a specific type of campaign that uses open-rates to continually send automated e-mails based on their perceived level of interest. However, this isn't enough. You need to look beyond e-mail and combine social media, dynamic website content, whitepapers, direct mail, phone calls, marketing automation, paid retargeting, and even direct sales outreaches that include phone calls.[cclxxvii]

✓ Multiple Touches

When you use multiple channels, you'll also be reaching out to them more frequently. "Research from the *Marketing Lead Management Report* indicates that on average, prospects receive ten marketing touches from the time they enter the top of the funnel until they're a closed won customer."[cclxxviii] Work on using each of these points of contact to help deliver high quality content that motivates your leads to convert.

✓ Timely Follow Ups

Like we mentioned before, the time it takes you to respond is crucial. The same holds true for follow-ups. The sooner you follow up with new leads, the better, which is why you may want to consider setting up automated services. For example, if someone signs up for your e-mail list, make sure that as soon as they submit the form, they receive an e-mail.

✓ **Personalized E-mails**

In addition to automated e-mails, make sure you're personalizing them. Anything that's personalized produces stronger results than generic communication. It makes your leads feel important and relevant. You can send triggered e-mail whenever someone downloads your content, engages at a high level, clicks on the links in your e-mail, or visits specific pages on your website.[cclxxix] This helps you reach people you need to at the perfect time in their buying process.

✓ **Lead Scoring**

Lead scoring helps you determine the value of each lead. This is one of the most effective lead nurturing tactics because it gives you specific information as to how much time and effort you should put into each lead. This is easy to implement in your automated CRM platform—a number is assigned to the lead based on their behavior and interaction, and then your pre-set rules will treat them accordingly.

✓ **Sales and Marketing Alignment**

Finally, you need to make sure that your sales and marketing teams are aligned and working toward the same goals. Having them on the same pages increases your conversion rates and lead engagement. Make sure your team communicates clearly and doesn't overwhelm your leads from both sides. Share responsibilities and expectations for how you will move your leads down the sales funnel.

Once you set up a system, you need to monitor your results. See how your leads are reacting to your efforts and experiment with different personas. Every business is different so it's up to you to find out the exact formula that will succeed. All you need to do is avoid a few common mistakes and you'll be on your way. We'll explore some of these historically common mistakes in Chapter 95.

Chapter 95: Avoiding Mistakes Others Have Made

The pitfalls of lead nurturing tend to be repetitive and common. Most businesses make the same exact lead nurturing mistakes, despite all the literature available warning them not to. Most of these failures circle back to not having a strategically planned and comprehensive lead generation and nurturing process. The best way to look at how to avoid dangerous mistakes is to look at the most common mistakes that others have made in the past.

1. **Neglecting your leads:** This is the most common reason that companies lose their leads. According to a *Forbes* study, "only 27% of leads *ever* get contacted. Yet with a combination of awareness, best practices, and technology, companies can contact around 92% of leads."[cclxxx] The neglect often comes from an inability to keep up with or remember them because the proper systems are not in place.

   Companies spend so much time marketing and gathering leads, then they let them sit in their CRMs. If someone shows interest in your company, show some interest back. Inform them about what you offer, ask them questions about their problems, offer solutions, and give them the opportunity to purchase those answers from you. Engage your leads or they will find someone who will.

2. **Being transactional:** Don't be a salesperson or an industry robot. Focus on being a real person and speaking to them in a conversational manner. Avoid constant transactional language, as it will only send red flags. People are constantly being sold to and sometimes it's just too much. Show them that you acknowledge their interest in your company without pushing your products or services.

3. **Bombarding the inbox:** There is such a thing as being *too* nurturing. You don't want to bombard inboxes with

automated e-mails every other day. This is a great way to get a person to unsubscribe from your e-mails, which goes back to what I said about making your e-mails count in terms of content. If you're sending automated e-mails too often, the content will become sub-par or redundant.

4. **Not keeping up with your leads' lives:** In some regard, it's important to know what is going on in your leads' lives. Perhaps they got a promotion and now have way more power to purchase than they had before, but you didn't know because you let their data fester away in your CRM. Some CRMs, like *Contactually*, can be synced with LinkedIn and automatically updated.

5. **Not responding fast enough:** This is extremely common, especially when a CEO lacks proper support or the ability to let go of their inbox and delegate certain tasks to lower level employees. There's really no excuse when it comes to responding by e-mail these days. As for the phone, according to a study done by *Forbes*, it took just shy of two days for a lead to get a response.[cclxxxi] That's unacceptable. One solution here is for the salespeople to use their CRMs to keep up with calls they miss and block off time each day to respond, ideally at the beginning and the end of the day. People simply don't have the attention span to wait two days for you to respond. Another solution is a CRM that also has alerts, automated if possible, so the call can be routed to the next available person.

6. **Relying only on e-mail:** People still like phone calls, especially if they're warranted or directly responding to a leads' inquiry. Social media is another way to address customer issues.

7. **Only calling during office hours:** Most people are at work during office hours and either miss your call, forget to call back, or don't get the message. This is also why you should follow up phone calls with e-mails and call outside of

working hours. The best time to contact leads is between 4pm – 6pm.[cclxxxii] This is another area that will require testing and discretion. You don't want to call during dinner, or too early, but you need to find that sweet spot for each of your different lead personas.

8. **Internal chasms:** You want the different factions of your company to operate harmoniously. If they don't, eventually one will fail. The sales team needs to work with the administrative team in order to get to leads in time, just like both of those teams need to work with the IT team to ensure your automated software is doing its job. Communicate, Coordinate, and make sure everyone understands their roles.

To avoid any complications, make sure you strategize all your lead nurturing and define your process from the beginning. As with everything in the world of marketing: test your efforts, monitor your results, and make any necessary changes.

Part 11: Tying it All Together

While we wish we could share our decades of marketing experience in one book, the reality is at almost 400 pages this book is already one of the longer marketing books most people will read in their entire lives.

By now, we've shared some of the biggest and best tips we've learned about a wide variety of marketing mediums. The foundation of information for digital marketing has been planted, and it's time to tie it all together.

In these final chapters, we'll provide some real world examples of putting together marketing campaigns and the results they can offer. While not each example will utilize every marketing tactic in this book, they will showcase ways to tie together the concepts learned throughout the various sections of this book into a comprehensive, results-orientated marketing campaign.

Chapter 96: Putting Words Into Practice

There is a wealth of information in this book. The key to a successful marketing strategy is not in executing one or two of these aspects correctly. It isn't even in executing all of these aspects correctly. It is in forming a cohesive marketing plan that fits your business, your goals, your needs, and your objectives, and then executing upon that plan day after day.

Like anything in life, there will be ups and downs, good and bad days, things that work and don't work. But just like your journey in life, if you stick at it, are persistent, try to practice and perfect the art and science of marketing, your marketing strategy will succeed and elevate your business to levels you could never have imagined.

The goal of supercharging your marketing and exponentially growing your business is as difficult *and* as simple as following the tips and strategies in this book.

Be unique. Be different. Stand out. The tactics and strategies used in marketing are going to be used by hundreds if not thousands of your competitors. It's critical that you stand out in the crowd if you want to truly grow your business. How you think about your marketing, the creative aspects of it, and how you position your brand are as important as the tactical aspects of carrying out your marketing campaign.

To truly supercharge your marketing and exponentially grow your business, you need to dig deep and think back to the reasons why you are in this business in the first place. You need to harness your inner creativity, think outside the box, and come up with ideas that none of your competitors have.

We find that some of our best marketing ideas come when we are not really looking for them. Some of the biggest and best ideas we have had for any of our businesses have come when taking a shower, getting ready for bed, or working out. These "off" times, when our brains can take a break to go back to their relaxed, naturally creative states, can help us figure out how we can use these tactics and truly stand out from the crowd.

The other equally important aspect is execution. Marketing is not something that can be done in your spare time, when you feel like it, or started and stopped over and over again. To succeed in marketing, you need to live, breath, and sleep it. You need to execute on your plan every waking moment of the day, and ensure that your company, your culture, and your mission are marketing-focused.

In this part, we review some real-world examples of these strategies in action, from the planning stages to the execution stages to the results, and look at how crafting a unique and cohesive marketing campaign can help any business succeed.

We believe it's important to practice what you preach, and this book truly is a representation of what we carry out day in and day out for our clients. These tactics and strategies are exactly what we use at our agency to see massive results for our clients, and we felt there was no other way to conclude the book than to share just a few of our success stories we have seen using these very strategies.

As we offer examples of tactics and strategies as well as real world data, we always put the privacy of our clients' as our highest priority. For this reason, the names of the brands and individuals we worked with will remain anonymous in these case studies.

Marketing Masters Pro Tip: Learn A Thing or Two from Fishing

When I was younger, my dad would often take me fishing. We would often fish in the same spots, year after year, and see countless other fishermen doing the same thing.

I remember stopping at the bait shop on our way out and my dad striking up casual conversations with other fishermen asking what lures they were using and what bait was working best for them.

Once we were out in the boat, we would usually give that bait a try, but only for 15-30 minutes. After that if it didn't work, we would switch.

Almost everyone is fishing for the same fish, in the same lake, using the same bait/lure. This is very similar to almost every business is going after the same customers, in the same industries, using the same tactics.

We all know in real life what happens when you fish for the same fish, in the same spot, with the same bait. So why is it so hard for businesses to realize they are doing the same every day in their business?

Look at the legal niche for example. How many pitches, cold calls, or cold e-mails does it take for a lawyer to simply start ignoring them? The more times a fish sees the same lure, the faster they start to ignore it.

This isn't to say that you won't get lucky once in a while and catch a big fish with this strategy. But, running a business and marketing it is hard enough already, so why make it harder? Why not stand out, fish somewhere new, and target a different species of fish, with an entirely different lure?

Make life easier on yourself and find ways to target a customer no one else is targeting, in a unique niche, and using different creative tactics than any of your competitors.

As simple as this sounds, once we figured out the art and science of setting our business apart from our competitors in our marketing, everything started to fall into place naturally and easily.

Chapter 97: Real World Example – 2,000% Increase in Traffic – 700% Increase in Leads

We started working with a law firm over three years ago to help them completely rebrand, redesign, and redevelop their website, and then engage in on-going marketing. For us, it was a perfect project, as we were able to "touch" every aspect of their business—from brand to photos, from design to videos, from wording to layouts—and we got to do it all the right way.

Prior to working with us, this client worked with several other marketing companies but was never satisfied with the results.

At the start of the campaign, we completely re-branded the firm, including a new logo and color scheme, a completely new, custom built website, and new photography and videos. Upon launching the new site, we immediately engaged in an online marketing campaign consisting of SEO and PPC to attract direct consumer leads and web traffic, e-mail marketing to attract referral business, and PR to help with brand recognition.

We proposed an 18 – 24 month commitment for the marketing campaign, including the following components:

✓ **PPC:** Google Ads campaign to drive immediate traffic and leads. We fully optimized and managed the campaign to ensure our cost per lead and amount of traffic was in line with expectations. We incorporated all of the tactics mentioned in the PPC section of this book to successfully run the campaign and deliver strong results.

✓ **SEO:** We engaged in a full SEO campaign, including all on-site optimization, off-site link building, and content creation, to help establish the brand as an authority and drive massive amounts of traffic and leads. We used all the best practices mentioned in this book, and split our work load about 60/40 between long-tail keywords and competitive ones.

✓ **E-mail:** We built a 10k+ subscriber e-mail list of referring law firms to help the firm gain valuable referral leads and cases, as well as brand and establish themselves as a leader in their market. These e-mails saw a 30+% open rate each time we would send a monthly e-mail blast.

✓ **PR:** We engaged in a PR campaign, including both earned media as well as paid placements, to help with branding efforts and further establish the firm as an authority in their industry.

✓ **Branding:** While these are the techniques we used to drive traffic and leads, the reality is we probably wouldn't have seen such success if it weren't for strong branding. We branded this client as the go-to authority in their space, and backed it up with real world examples and results they have achieved for their clients. While this didn't necessarily impact traffic directly, it certainly impacted our conversion rate in a positive way.

We engaged in all these techniques from day one, and we were fortunate to have a client who understands organic growth doesn't happen overnight, so they stuck at it and remained committed to the campaign for over two years now.

Results really speak for themselves. The first chart below plots the client's organic traffic growth from the start of the campaign to date, which has increased from about 500 visitors per month to over 7,500 visitors per month.

The second chart below plots the client's inbound web lead growth from the start of the campaign to date, which started at about 30 leads per month and more recently has been in the 200+ lead per month range.

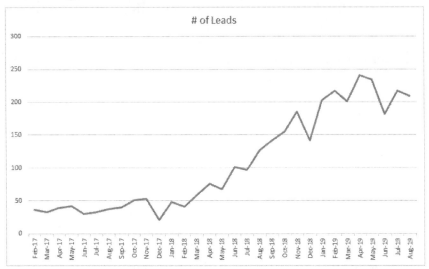

We are still actively working with this client and maintaining rankings for our current keywords, as well as adding a few new terms each month to optimize. We are anticipating that within the next year we will see over 10,000 organic visitors per month and well over 300 inbound leads per month.

This example shows how leveraging everything in this book, holistically, helps create real world success. Had we not properly branded, designed a proper website with conversion optimized pages, taken award winning photographs of the client and their office, and then engaged in a multifaceted online marketing campaign, the results of this campaign would certainly not be as strong as they were.

Key Takeaways

Marketing isn't fast. Quite honestly, it isn't cheap—but neither one of those things matter. What matters is ROI. In the above example, we drove a 2,000+% increase in traffic, a 700+% increase in leads, and while unfortunately we don't have the exact ROI numbers down to the digit, we know through constant communication with our client that they saw a 10x+ ROI on their end.

It's important if you are going to turn to the outside for your marketing needs to find the right partner for you. We will be the first to say we aren't right for every business, but when the right business finds us and we both agree it's a good fit, we can do amazing things together.

This example is a testament to the importance of patience with marketing, especially medium to long-term marketing initiatives. Results won't be felt overnight, but in less than a year we saw an increase in traffic and leads for this client, and in less than two years a dramatic improvement and strong ROI. Both of these were well within the timeline we proposed to our client, and our client is extremely happy with the results.

Chapter 98: Real World Example – 800% Increase in Organic Traffic

Sometimes, we don't have the luxury of doing everything right. In the previous chapter, we saw how powerful these tactics can be when done in unison. However, due to budgets, timelines, and sometimes egos, we don't always get to do everything we would like.

In this example, we started working with a nationwide marketing company that was in desperate need of more inbound leads. Kind of ironic that a marketing company needed help, but their expertise lies in offline marketing rather than online, and as the world becomes more and more digital, they were struggling to find new business.

Prior to working with us, this company did some basic SEO to their website, but never engaged in a full SEO campaign. We proposed to them running an SEO campaign and PPC campaign side by side. This was done because their industry is highly competitive, targeting not only competitive keywords but only working with the best of the best leads that would come in, so we devised a strategy that would drive short-term results and leads through PPC, while keeping our eye on the golden goose of long-term SEO rankings.

At the start of the campaign, this client was seeing about 650 organic visitors per month on average. Our strategy was quite simple and follows the best practices mentioned in the SEO section of this book. It consisted of:

- ✓ **On-site Optimization:** We worked with the client upfront to expand on their service offerings—instead of having one core service page we created nearly 20 sub-service pages so we had pages to work with when optimizing for organic traffic. We also reworked their website and made coding adjustments in their WordPress site to allow us to properly optimize their coding, page load time, mobile experience, title tags, headings, and other SEO factors.

✓ **Content:** We took their current blogging of 2x per month and increased it to 4-6 posts per month. We also engaged in extensive long-tail keyword research so we were blogging about topics that their potential customers were actually searching for on Google.

✓ **Off-site SEO:** Our team began link building, both through link outreach as well as grabbing the lower hanging fruit like business directories and websites. We also took advantage of some of the awards they have won, accreditations they have, and business partnerships to gain links from these high-quality sources.

From there, once the foundation was in place, it became a matter of rinse and repeat. Over time, we built more and more links, created more and more content, and consistently kept their on-site elements up to date.

And like every campaign, the results speak for themselves.

The first chart below plots the number of keywords on pages 1, 2, 3, and beyond on Google. When we started the campaign, there were a few keywords on pages 1 and 2, but most keywords were not ranking at all. Today, we have 61 keywords, which we are tracking on page 1 (and 52 of them are the top 3 results) and 3 keywords on page 2.

And those are just the competitive terms that we are tracking; there are hundreds of other variations and similar terms also ranking on page 1 of Google. In the second chart, we look at organic traffic to the website. It increased from when we started, about 650 organic visitors, to now over 5,500 organic visitors a month and still growing.

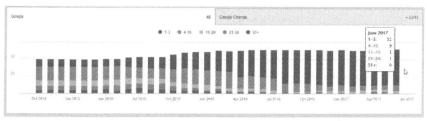

Most importantly, this traffic has resulted in some great leads. This client primarily works with Fortune 500 and Inc 5,000 businesses, and they are generating numerous leads online as a result of our SEO efforts. They have also reported that businesses who they meet offline often search for key terms in their industry and are impressed and given validation when they find our client ranking well for many of their industry terms.

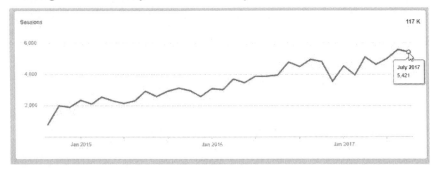

We are still actively working with this client and maintaining rankings for our current keywords, as well as adding new terms each month to optimize. We are anticipating that within the next 12 to 18 months we will yet again double their organic traffic, and they will be receiving around 10,000 organic visitors per month.

Key Takeaways

This particular client was honestly a challenge to work with. They were another marketing company and had an attitude like they knew it all. We quickly showed them that we are the authority in digital marketing, and our results soon followed.

Even though this campaign was just an SEO campaign and we unfortunately didn't have much control over this client's brand, website, or other aspects that impact their marketing, we still were able to find strong results.

This is great example of a campaign that saw some early wins. Since they hadn't done SEO before, we saw results come pretty quickly and steadily rise.

The bottom line is SEO works, and when you target the right keywords and get strong rankings, you will see more traffic and more leads soon follow.

Chapter 99: Real World Campaign Example – 4x Increase in Organic Traffic Over 2 Years

Sometimes bringing old school companies into the 21st century is one of our favorite ways to showcase our marketing expertise. In this example, we started working with a large manufacturing company that has been in business since the 1920s and helped bring them into the 2020s.

When we started with them two years ago, they had a website that was built ten years prior, was not mobile responsive, and didn't really follow any modern best practices. We started by redesigning and redeveloping their website to bring it up to current standards.

Following the launch of their site, we immediately started a combined SEO and PPC campaign with a goal on driving more traffic and leads. Since their old site was doing virtually everything wrong and they had never done SEO before, we saw pretty immediate results.

At the start of the campaign, this client was seeing about 400 organic visitors per month on average. Much like the example in chapter 98, our strategy followed all of our PPC and SEO best practices in this book and consisted of:

✓ **Keyword Research:** This was a challenge for this client, as they are in a very specific niche and most of their keywords have less than 100 searches per month. We had to dig deep to really find the best keywords that had some traffic behind them but also stood a good chance of driving relevant, new leads. We utilized Google Keyword Planner as our primary tool and did exhaustive research to arrive at a list of 35 organic keywords and about 100 paid search keywords.

✓ **On-Site Optimization:** With the new website build, we included pages for all their products, but more importantly categories which were based on our keyword research. We ensured the site was a wealth of information and even included a few calculators and tools as link bait.

- ✓ **Content:** Since our keywords were somewhat limited, we focused on only 2-3 blogs per month on the site, and instead spent some of our time on guest blog posts and content creation for third party sites. This client certainly needed ongoing content creation to be successful, but they also were desperately in need of links and referral traffic, so we included that in our overall content strategy.

- ✓ **Off-site SEO:** When we started, this client had virtually 0 links to their site. We had to start with the basics and make our way into more advanced link building campaigns to not only gain a high quantity of links but also ensure that they were relevant and high quality.

- ✓ **Branding / Messaging:** Unfortunately, there isn't really anything all that different about this company vs. its competitors. Their offering is somewhat of a commodity, and their branding and messaging very plain and corporate. The client insisted that be the case and didn't really want to go outside the box, and while we still saw results, had they let us push the envelope further, we feel we could have really positioned them as the market leader.

With this groundwork in place, it has been about two years since the start of the campaign and we have seen tremendous results along the way. We have maintained this overall structure each month and fortunately, with a very sound plan going into this campaign, haven't had to make many changes along the way.

This has been a great example of having the right strategy from the start, and each and every month executing on that strategy. Traffic growth takes time, and fortunately in this case we saw steady, consistent growth. Clients often want to go from 0 to 100 overnight, and that just isn't a reality. While this client reaped the benefits of slow and consistent growth, it took us well over a year to see truly measurable and impactful results for their business.

The results thus far have been amazing. The first chart below plots our organic keyword movement over the past two years relative to placement. Dark green represents the first 3 spots on page 1 of Google, light green represents the 4-10 spots on page 1 of Google, yellow represents page 2, orange represents pages 3-5, and red anything beyond page 5.

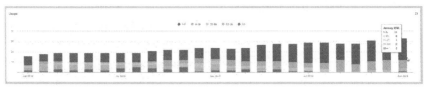

More importantly, this client has seen dramatic traffic growth. While the number of visitors isn't extremely impressive, going from about 450 visitors a month to 2,000 in a two-year period, this 4x increase in traffic is massive considering this client's industry. This particular client is in an industry where there are no high-volume keywords, and the number of transactions can be measured in the dozens not in the thousands. This increase represents a massive gain for this client, and more importantly, they have reported a steady increase in leads and deals closed as a result of this increased traffic.

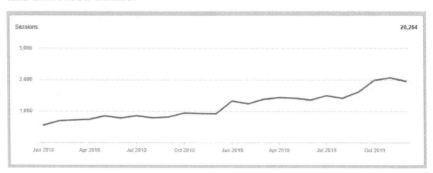

Key Takeaways

Do your research upfront and form a sound plan. If you don't know how, hire someone to help with the experience, even if you plan on carrying out the campaign yourself.

This is a fantastic example of doing proper upfront research, finding those difficult to find keywords, and executing on the strategy.

Don't be afraid to be different. This client wanted to be the same as all their competitors and play it safe, and we still found strong results, but if you go against the grain and stand out in the crowd your marketing results will almost always be amplified.

While the number of visitors per month is low relative to other industries we work in, this 4x increase in organic traffic has resulted in a tremendous ROI for our client and dramatic increase in leads and projects awarded.

Chapter 100: Real World Campaign Example – Doubling Traffic, Tripling Conversion Rates, and Quadrupling Revenue

We love working with e-commerce sites because it's easy for us to measure and gauge results. When you have a 1:1 tracking mechanism for monitoring ROI, it's easy to pivot and adjust on the fly based on performance. In this example, a 100+ year old company made the leap into the e-commerce space with another marketing agency, and while they did a lot of things right, the few things they were doing wrong were causing them to spend more than they should on marketing and lose conversions on their website.

With this particular client, we kept their branding as-is, but we did a facelift to their website to help make it more modern, more usable, and easier to navigate. We also took over their existing SEO and PPC campaigns, as well as assisted with e-mail marketing and remarketing campaigns.

The overall campaign strategy was as follows:

- ✓ **Website Changes:** We re-skinned the website with a new design, made it more mobile friendly, improved the layout to help customers find their product faster, added a predictive, advanced search function, improved their up-sell and cross-sell opportunities for their products, improved their checkout experience, and added a variety of tools, such as A/B testing tools, additional analytics, heatmap software, and cart abandonment e-mails to aid in tracking and improving conversions.

- ✓ **Keyword Research:** Their prior SEO company took the easy way out and picked low competition, low traffic keywords so they could show progress. We picked a mix of some of the highest competition keywords (many with 5-8k searches per month per keyword) and rolled up our sleeves ready to do some real work for this client.

✓ **SEO:** We optimized everything on-site and began an aggressive content creation, content marketing, and link building campaign centered on our keyword set. We started to see results within the first few months.

✓ **PPC:** Amazingly, their prior company was not even tracking sales in their Google Ads. We set up all the proper tracking and quickly realized their PPC campaigns were all running in the red. We totally scrapped their old campaigns and started over, setting up new campaigns with new keywords, utilizing audiences, utilizing Google Shopping more heavily, and adding automation. Within 2 months, we were running in the black, and within 4 months were seeing 2-3x ROI on adspend.

✓ **Conversions**: This was a huge improvement, as we brought their conversion rate from 0.74% to 2.04%. This wasn't easy. It took a combination of things, including, but not limited to:

   ✓ Improving the overall website experience by putting products first, new graphics, new page layouts, and a totally revamped user experience.
   ✓ Incorporating live chat software and chatbots to aid in answering commonly asked questions.
   ✓ Revamping their entire pricing structure to include free shipping and a better return policy, all while helping the client still make as much or more money on their product line.
   ✓ Implementing A/B testing and heatmaps to fix problems during the customer's checkout experience.
   ✓ Leveraging remarketing and audiences to drive better traffic to the site.
   ✓ Focusing on driving relevant traffic through SEO/PPC so that traffic actually converts.

All of these efforts combined are what created success for this client. Over an 18-month time period, we brought them from around 10-11k visitors per month to a high of 24k visitors per month (and an average of around 20-22k visitors per month). We brought their conversion rate from a low of 0.74% to a high of 2.04% (and a new average of right around 1.85%), and most importantly, we brought their revenue from a low of just $16,000 per month to an all-time record high for them of $72,000 per month (and an average of just over $60,000 per month).

With these successes behind us, the client is extremely happy and has increased both our retainer for managing their campaigns as well as doubled their Google Ad budget. Our goal over the next twelve months is to yet again double their traffic, and double to triple their current revenue numbers!

Key Takeaways

Success is never one-dimensional. Had we just tried changing one or two things, we wouldn't have seen such a dramatic improvement in their conversion rate or revenue.

Before you focus on driving more traffic, make sure you are sending that traffic to a properly built website with a proper funnel in place to monetize that traffic. Otherwise, you are throwing money out the window.

We immediately saw returns and improvements on their SEO/PPC, but the largest returns came once we were able to properly dial in their website and the entire shopping experience.

Sometimes these things can take time, but in the end, if you focus on all the right things you will see strong results.

Chapter 101: Real World Campaign Example – 10x Increase in Leads and Establishing A Market Leader

Sometimes the perfect project comes along, and this was exactly that. This particular client was running a successful business, but not fully leveraging the online world to drive leads. At the start of the campaign, we identified that we would need to redo their website, engage in an aggressive PPC campaign, follow up with SEO for long-term gains, and also engage in PR and brand building to help establish them as a market leader. Over the course of the campaign, we achieved all those goals, helping them see a 10x increase in leads and establishing them as the true go-to expert in their market.

The overall campaign strategy was as follows:

- ✓ **Website:** We started by revamping their website, adding over 100 new pages to the site for their services, about their business, and frequently asked questions. We also updated the look and feel of the site, made it fully responsive for mobile users, and coded new landing page templates to utilize in our marketing campaign.

- ✓ **PPC:** This client had an existing PPC campaign but it was terribly managed. They were not utilizing landing pages, were over-bidding on their keywords leading to wasted budget, and were not tracking phone calls or contact forms as conversions. We fixed all that while also restructuring the campaign and adding in new keywords. Over the course of the campaign, we grew their PPC spending from $7,500 per month at the start to $30,000, all while monitoring the conversion rate and ROI at each step to ensure that we were delivering results for our client.

- ✓ **SEO:** This client never really did much with SEO, and we changed that. We engaged in a full SEO campaign, consisting of all the usual elements of on-site optimization, link building, and content creation. We wrote over 250 blog posts for this client over a few year period and saw their organic traffic go from less than 1,000 visitors per month to just shy of 10,000 visitors per month.

✓ **PR:** We engaged in a PR campaign for this client, both in a traditional sense of PR outreach and booking key media placements on some of the largest media outlets in the country, but also launched a campaign to position them as the authority in their space. We built an e-mail list of their peers and industry reporters, issued regular press releases on their successes and business updates, and positioned them with all their messaging as the industry leader. This soon caught on, and our client became the go-to source in their industry.

✓ **Offline Marketing:** We also assisted this client with a variety of offline marketing, including developing a referral program, print advertising, magazine placements, advertorials, and more. We used all the same successes we had online in the offline world for them and tracked it at each step to closely monitor results and ROI.

Overall, after five years of hard work and progress at each step of the journey, we helped this client become an authority and market leader in their space, grew their website traffic dramatically using SEO and PPC, and most importantly helped them increase their leads ten-fold, all the while seeing their business grow from just a few employees to over 70 employees and achieve eight figure revenues.

Key Takeaways

All of these marketing tactics worked together to help this client see massive success. While we don't have an exact ROI metric, we can tell you from conversations with this client that they were investing around $750,000 annually into their marketing and seeing around a 15 times ROI on their marketing spend.

What we love the most out of this case study is the fact that we got to start working with this business at its infancy stages, having just a few employees and low 7 figure revenue. Over the course of a relatively short time period (five years), we helped this business grow to over 70 employees and mid 8 figure revenues.

With a strong focus on ROI and keeping a close eye on all aspects of the campaign, scalability is something that can easily be achieved. Find early success, and scale the things that are working while cutting back those that are not. This will help find long-term ROI, success, and growth in all your marketing efforts.

As you learned in this book, marketing is ever changing. No two businesses are the same and every campaign requires a unique touch. While this book was designed to provide you with 101 tips, tricks, and advice to supercharge your marketing and exponentially grow your business, you may be still looking for more.

If that's the case, we're here to help. Whether you want to just get clarity on a concept in the book or are looking for someone to manage your marketing, that's what we do day in and day out.

Give us a call or drop us an email, and we would love to chat to help you grow.

Brendan Egan
888-788-6880
Brendan@TheMarketingMasters.com

John Shegerian
888-788-6880
John@TheMarketingMasters.com

References

[i] https://www.ama.org/AboutAMA/Pages/Definition-of-Marketing.aspx

[ii] https://capitalandgrowth.org/articles/866/great-products-that-failed-because-of-poor-marketi.html

[iii] https://blog.hubspot.com/marketing/what-is-marketing

[iv] https://www.entrepreneur.com/article/240164

[v] https://www.entrepreneur.com/article/241080

[vi] Ibid.

[vii] Ibid.

[viii] Ibid.

[ix] https://en.oxforddictionaries.com/definition/art

[x] https://en.oxforddictionaries.com/definition/science

[xi] http://www.torok.com/articles/marketing/MarketingArtorScience.html

[xii] Eric T. Wagner, "Five Reasons 8 out of 10 Businesses Fail," *Forbes,* last modified September 12, 2013, https://www.forbes.com/sites/ericwagner/2013/09/12/five-reasons-8-out-of-10-businesses-fail/#673e09776978.

[xiii] Amy Gallo, "A Refresher on Marketing ROI," *Harvard Business Review*, last modified July 25, 2017, https://hbr.org/2017/07/a-refresher-on-marketing-roi.

[xiv] https://neilpatel.com/blog/tracking-online-ad-roi/

[xv] https://blog.marketo.com/2013/03/how-to-measure-the-roi-of-your-marketing-programs.html

[xvi] Ibid.

[xvii] Ibid.

[xviii] Ibid.

[xix] Tom Shapiro, "The ROI of Branding," *Stratabeat*, last modified December 2, 2014, https://stratabeat.com/roi-of-branding/.

[xx] Maria Popova, "Significant Objects: How stories confer value upon the vacant," *Brainpickings,* last modified 8/6/2012, https://www.brainpickings.org/2012/08/06/significant-objects-book/

[xxi] Joshua Glenn and Rob Walker, eds., *Significant Objects*

(Seattle: Fantagraphics Publishing, 2012)

[xxii] Ibid.

[xxiii] Ibid.

[xxiv] Christina O'Connor, "Where Does Brand Building End and Lead Generation Begin?:
Tailoring your tactics for different stages in the funnel," *LinkedIn: Sales and Marketing Solutions EMEA Blog,* last modified January 18, 2016, https://business.linkedin.com/en-uk/marketing-solutions/blog/posts/demand-generation/2016/where-does-brand-building-end-and-lead-generation-begin.

[xxv] https://bluetribe.co/11-steps-to-creating-a-sustainable-business-model-that-works/

[xxvi] Ibid.

[xxvii] Heather Hudson, "Is Failing to Have a Long-Term Business Plan, Planning to Fail?" *Medium,* (n.d.), https://medium.com/the-mission/is-failing-to-have-a-long-term-business-plan-planning-to-fail-b25b65018ab4

[xxviii] Emily Weisberg, "Marketing Goals Examples," *ThriveHive,* last modified May 17, 2016, https://thrivehive.com/marketing-goals-examples/

[xxix] Randi Hicks Rowe, "How Long Should a Medium-Term Marketing Plan Be?" *Chron,* (n.d.), http://smallbusiness.chron.com/long-should-mediumterm-marketing-plan-be-74848.html.

[xxx] Peter Vanden Bos, "How to Set Business Goals," *Inc.,* (n.d.), https://www.inc.com/guides/2010/06/setting-business-goals.html.

[xxxi] Jim Joseph, "Stalk Your Competitors," *Entrepreneur Magazine*, last modified August 7, 2013, http://www.entrepreneurmag.co.za/advice/marketing/marketing-tactics/stalk-your-competitors/

[xxxii] Dave Lavinsky, "Marketing Plan Template: Exactly What To Include," *Forbes*, p. 1–3, last modified September 30, 2013, https://www.forbes.com/sites/davelavinsky/2013/09/30/marketing-plan-template-exactly-what-to-include/#518242f13503.

[xxxiii] Brad Sugars, "8 Tips for Increasing Your Average Sale, *Entrepreneur,* last modified March 27, 2008, https://www.entrepreneur.com/article/191978#.

xxxiv https://www.hubspot.com/marketing-statistics
xxxv Gladwell, Malcolm, 1963-. Outliers : The Story of Success. New York :Little, Brown and Co., 2008. Print.
xxxvi https://www.entrepreneur.com/article/204874
xxxvii No author, "An Illustrated History of Blackhat SEO," *Elite Strategies*, (n.d.), http://www.elite-strategies.com/illustrated-history-blackhat-seo/.
xxxviii https://moz.com/google-algorithm-change
xxxix https://www.wordstream.com/white-hat-seo
xl Moz, "Google Algorithm Change History," last updated March 8, 2017, https://moz.com/google-algorithm-change.

xli Jim Yu, "5 massive SEO and content shifts you need to master right now," *Search Engine Land*, last modified May 17, 2017, http://searchengineland.com/5-massive-seo-content-shifts-need-master-right-now-274647.
xlii https://www.wordstream.com/long-tail-keywords
xliii Ibid.
xliv Marieke van de Rakt, "Blog SEO: befriend the long tail!" last modified on September 16th, 2015, https://yoast.com/befriend-the-long-tail/.

xlv https://www.v9digital.com/blog/2015/01/08/h1-headers-title-tags-seo/
xlvi https://yoast.com/meta-descriptions/
xlvii https://neilpatel.com/blog/seo-friendly-homepage/
xlviii https://www.business2community.com/seo/optimize-homepage-content-seo-01735911#OQdTs6Ue6iXte88a.97
xlix https://neilpatel.com/blog/commandments-of-internal-linking/
l https://backlinko.com/google-ranking-factors
li https://neilpatel.com/blog/the-ultimate-guide-to-writing-blog-posts-that-rank-in-googles-top-10/
lii https://www.seoblog.com/2014/09/google-rewards-sites-regularly-post-great-content/
liii https://www.hubspot.com/marketing-statistics
liv https://neilpatel.com/blog/the-ultimate-guide-to-writing-blog-posts-that-rank-in-googles-top-10/
lv https://moz.com/beginners-guide-to-seo/measuring-and-tracking-

success

[lvi] Ibid.

[lvii] Ibid.

[lviii] Ibid.

[lix] Ibid.

[lx] https://www.forbes.com/sites/forbeslacouncil/2018/01/11/seven-things-you-should-know-about-digital-advertising-this-year/#2f40ae5a424e

[lxi] Ibid.

[lxii] https://www.adskills.com/library/7-types-of-online-advertising

[lxiii] Google Adwords Management: Paid Traffic AdWords Agency, "What is PPC?" *Paid Traffic*, last modified 2017, https://www.paidtraffic.io/what-is-ppc/.

[lxiv] Jordan Beyma, "What are Google Responsive Ads?" originally posted in *Google Adwords*, last modified September 29, 2016, retrieved from http://www.cpcstrategy.com/blog/2016/09/google-responsive-ads/

[lxv] Guide, "A Pay-per-click and paid advertising: advantages and disadvantages of display advertising," *NI Business Info*, no date, https://www.nibusinessinfo.co.uk/content/advantages-and-disadvantages-display-advertising

[lxvi] Google Adwords Management: Paid Traffic AdWords Agency, "What is PPC?" *Paid Traffic*, last modified 2017, https://www.paidtraffic.io/what-is-ppc/.

[lxvii] https://blog.marketo.com/2015/11/join-the-big-league-7-reason-to-go-digital-with-your-advertising.html

[lxviii] Joseph Kerschbaum, "5 Critical Factors for Optimized Mobile PPC Targeting," *Search Engine Watch*, last modified January 22, 2014, https://searchenginewatch.com/sew/how-to/2324303/5-critical-factors-for-optimized-mobile-ppc-targeting.

[lxix] https://radiumone.com/battle-static-ad-vs-dynamic-ad-wins/

[lxx] Ibid.

[lxxi] https://support.google.com/google-ads/answer/2471185?hl=en

[lxxii] Ibid.

[lxxiii] https://radiumone.com/battle-static-ad-vs-dynamic-ad-wins/

[lxxiv] https://support.google.com/google-ads/answer/2497836?hl=en

lxxv https://www.wordstream.com/keyword-match-types

lxxvi https://support.google.com/google-ads/answer/2497836?hl=en

lxxvii Ibid.

lxxviii https://blog.tryadhawk.com/google-adwords/adwords-ad-extensions/#manual-ad-extensions-in-adwords

lxxix Ibid.

lxxx Ibid.

lxxxi Ibid.

lxxxii Ibid.

lxxxiii Ibid.

lxxxiv Ibid.

lxxxv Ibid.

lxxxvi Ibid.

lxxxvii https://www.wordstream.com/google-remarketing

lxxxviii Ibid.

lxxxix Ibid.

xc Ibid.

xci Hannapin Marketing, "Ultimate Guide To Adwords Remarketing," *PPC Hero, http://www.ppchero.com/ultimate-guide-to-adwords-remarketing/*

xcii https://support.google.com/google-ads/answer/6168766?hl=en.

xciii Ibid.

xciv Ibid.

xcv Ibid.

xcvi https://www.ppchero.com/ultimate-guide-to-adwords-remarketing/

xcvii Ibid.

xcviii https://support.google.com/google-ads/answer/2497940?co=ADWORDS.IsAWNCustomer%3Dfalse&hl=en

xcix https://searchengineland.com/10-common-mistakes-setting-audiences-adwords-229858

c Ibid.

ci Ibid.

cii https://support.google.com/google-ads/answer/2497940?co=ADWORDS.IsAWNCustomer%3Dtrue&hl=en&oco=0

ciii https://support.google.com/google-ads/answer/6095821?co=ADWORDS.IsAWNCustomer%3Dtrue&hl=en&oco=0

civ https://neilpatel.com/blog/track-conversions-with-google-analytics/

cv Ibid.

cvi Ibid.

cvii Ibid.

cviii Ibid.

cix https://www.dreamgrow.com/21-social-media-marketing-statistics/

cx Ibid.

cxi Evan Asano, "How Much Time Do People Spend on Social Media?" *Social Media Today*, last modified January 4, 2017, https://www.socialmediatoday.com/marketing/how-much-time-do-people-spend-social-media-infographic.

cxii https://zephoria.com/top-15-valuable-facebook-statistics/

cxiii https://www.bigmouthmarketing.co/which-social-media-platforms-should-my-business-be-on/?cn-reloaded=1

cxiv https://www.nytimes.com/guides/business/social-media-for-career-and-business

cxv https://business.linkedin.com/

cxvi https://www.nytimes.com/guides/business/social-media-for-career-and-business

cxvii https://www.dreamgrow.com/21-social-media-marketing-statistics/

cxviii Ibhttps://www.nytimes.com/guides/business/social-media-for-career-and-businessid.

cxix https://adespresso.com/guides/facebook-ads-beginner/facebook-ads-types/?utm_source=shopify&utm_medium=referral&utm_campaign=Shopify_Facebook_Ads_Guide/

cxx Ibid.

cxxi Ibid.

cxxii Ibid.

cxxiii Ibid.

cxxiv Ibid.

cxxv http://www.seerinteractive.com/blog/types-linkedin-ads/

cxxvi Ibid.

cxxvii Ibid.

cxxviiiIbid.

cxxix Ibid.

cxxx Ibid.

cxxxi https://blog.hootsuite.com/instagram-ads-guide/

cxxxii https://blog.hootsuite.com/twitter-ads/

cxxxiii Ibid.

cxxxiv Ibid.

cxxxv Ibid.

cxxxvi https://blog.hootsuite.com/how-to-create-a-social-media-marketing-plan/

cxxxvii Ibid.

cxxxviiihttps://www.forbes.com/sites/forbescommunicationscouncil/2017/11/14/what-is-influencer-marketing-and-how-can-marketers-use-it-effectively/#1f2a01f623d1

cxxxix Ibid.

cxl *Entrepreneur*, "Retailer Vera Bradley launches a "girly" campaign," no date, https://www.entrepreneur.com/slideshow/272286#

cxli Jayson DeMers, "5 Fatal Mistakes That Will Kill Your Social Media Marketing Campaign," Forbes, last modified October 8, 2015, https://www.forbes.com/sites/jaysondemers/2015/10/08/5-fatal-mistakes-that-will-kill-your-social-media-marketing-campaign/#58872cbe31eb

cxlii Ibid.

cxliii https://kwsmdigital.com/minding-your-manners-5-tips-to-improve-your-social-media-etiquette/

cxliv Mandy Kilinskis, "7 Ways I Accidentally Got More Twitter Followers (and 7 Ways You Can on Purpose!" *Buffer*, last modified August 26, 2016, https://blog.bufferapp.com/7-ways-i-accidentally-got-twitter-followers-and-7-ways-you-can-on-purpose..

cxlv https://blog.hootsuite.com/how-to-create-a-social-media-content-calendar/

[cxlvi] Jose Angelo Gallegos, "What is User Generated Content (and Why You Should Be Using it)," *Tint*, last modified August 23, 2016, https://www.tintup.com/blog/user-generated-content-definition/.

[cxlvii] bazaarvoice, "Bazaarvoice and the Center for Generational Kinetics Release New Study on How Millennials Shop," last modified Jan 30, 2012, no author, http://investors.bazaarvoice.com/releasedetail.cfm?releaseid=649677.

[cxlviii] Ibid.

[cxlix] eMarketer, "Millennials' Social Media Posts Influence Peers to Buy New Products
Nearly seven in 10 millennial social users are at least somewhat influenced to purchase based on friends' posts," last modified February 4, 2014, https://www.emarketer.com/Article/Millennials-Social-Media-Posts-Influence-Peers-Buy-New-Products/1010576.

[cl] https://blog.hootsuite.com/social-media-monitoring-tools/

[cli] Sprout Social, "Shunning Your Customers on Social?" last updated Q2, 2016 https://sproutsocial.com/insights/data/q2-2016/.

[clii] https://hootsuite.com/platform/analytics#

[cliii] https://www.socialmediaexaminer.com/5-ways-to-analyze-social-media-marketing-performance/

[cliv] Ibid.

[clv] Ibid.

[clvi] Ibid.

[clvii] Ibid.

[clviii] Double Click Creative Solutions Help, https://support.google.com/richmedia/answer/2417545?hl=en

[clix] Ibid.

[clx] No author, "Consumers Get Engaged with Rich Media," *eMarketer* October 23, 2014, https://www.emarketer.com/Article/Consumers-Engaged-with-Rich-Media/1011282

[clxi] No author, "Consumers Get Engaged with Rich Media," *eMarketer* October 23, 2014, https://www.emarketer.com/Article/Consumers-Engaged-with-Rich-Media/1011282

clxii No author, "Rich Media: Its Evolution and How It Amplifies Your Message," February 1, 2017, https://www.workfront.com/blog/rich-media-its-evolution-and-how-it-amplifies-your-message

clxiii Ibid.

clxiv Ibid.

clxv Ibid.

clxvi https://blog.bannerflow.com/7-reasons-start-building-html5-rich-media-ads/

clxvii Matt Bowman, "Video Marketing: The Future Of Content Marketing," Last modified February 3, 2017, https://www.forbes.com/sites/forbesagencycouncil/2017/02/03/video-marketing-the-future-of-content-marketing/#28e041fa6b53

clxviii Matt Bowman, "Video Marketing: The Future Of Content Marketing," Last modified February 3, 2017, https://www.forbes.com/sites/forbesagencycouncil/2017/02/03/video-marketing-the-future-of-content-marketing/#28e041fa6b53

clxix https://www.entrepreneur.com/article/233521.

clxx https://www.socialmediaexaminer.com/rich-media-share-on-google-plus/

clxxi No author, "Rich Media: Its Evolution and How It Amplifies Your Message," February 1, 2017, https://resources.workfront.com/project-management-blog/rich-media-its-evolution-and-how-it-amplifies-your-message

clxxii https://support.google.com/richmedia/answer/2417545?hl=en&ref_topic=2417434

clxxiii https://www.digitaland.tv/blog/rich-media-ads-marketers-care/

clxxiv https://support.google.com/richmedia/answer/2417545?hl=en&ref_topic=2417434

clxxv Stephen Diorio, "How Marketers Are Driving Growth Through Personalized Content," no date, https://www.forbes.com/sites/forbesinsights/2016/02/11/how-marketers-are-driving-growth-through-personalized-content/#30277fa070f9

clxxvi No author, "Top 5 Benefits of Dynamic Creative Campaigns,"

Sojern, https://www.sojern.com/blog/top-benefits-dynamic-creative/

clxxvii Double Click, "Rich media creative types," *Google*, https://support.google.com/richmedia/answer/2417545?hl=en

clxxviii Ibid.

clxxix Mobile Ads, "The What, Why and How of Social Rich Media for Mobile Marketing," last modified December 5, 2015, https://www.mobileads.com/blog/the-what-why-and-how-of-social-rich-media-for-mobile-marketing/

clxxx https://www.clickz.com/what-is-rich-media-in-a-social-mobile-world/30908/

clxxxi https://www.mobileads.com/blog/the-what-why-and-how-of-social-rich-media-for-mobile-marketing/

clxxxii Digital Advertising Blog, "6 Innovating Rich Media Ads To Inspire Your Next Campaign," no date, https://www.digitaland.tv/blog/6-innovating-rich-media-ads-inspire-next-campaign/

clxxxiii Mobile Ads, "Mobile Rich Media Ads: 16 Examples that will impress your audience (Part 1)," last modified December 29, 2015, https://www.mobileads.com/blog/mobile-rich-media-ads-examples-impress-audience-part-1/

clxxxiv Ibid.

clxxxv Jennifer Mueller, "How Often Should You Update or Rebuild Your Website?" *Zift Solutions*, last modified February 11, 2016, http://ziftsolutions.com/blog/2016/02/update-your-website/.

clxxxvi Christina Hawkins, "How Often Should We Redesign Our Website?" *Global Spex*, last modified May 23, 2016, https://globalspex.com/how-often-redesign-website/.

clxxxvii Beat Köck, "10 Website Performance Indicators You Should Monitor," *Paessler*, last modified August 18, 2017, https://blog.paessler.com/10-website-performance-indicators-you-should-monitor.

clxxxviii John Hagel, "The power of platforms," *Deloitte Insights,* last modified April 15, 2015, https://dupress.deloitte.com/dup-us-en/focus/business-trends/2015/platform-strategy-new-level-business-trends.html.

clxxxix Ibid.

cxc Ibid.

cxci https://mashable.com/2012/02/09/website-must-haves/#doTT74Acv8qD

cxcii https://www.forbes.com/sites/denispinsky/2018/02/12/website-design-standards/#54770b84f54f

cxciii https://mailchimp.com/help/single-opt-in-vs-double-opt-in/

cxciv https://blog.hubspot.com/blog/tabid/6307/bid/32892/why-purchasing-e-mail-lists-is-always-a-bad-idea.aspx

cxcv https://optinmonster.com/features/exit-intent/

cxcvi Ibid.

cxcvii Ibid.

cxcviii Pam Neely, "13 Best Practices for a Killer E-mail Opt-in Form," *Pinpointe,* no date, https://www.pinpointe.com/blog/best-practices-for-killer-e-mail-opt-in-forms

cxcix https://optinmonster.com/30-content-upgrade-ideas-to-grow-your-e-mail-list/

cc https://blog.hubspot.com/marketing/what-is-a-whitepaper-examples-for-business

cci https://www.shortstack.com/blog/creative-ways-to-grow-your-e-mail-list/

ccii Dean Levitt, "5 Reasons Why You Need An E-mail Newsletter," *American Express: Open Forum,* last modified September 3, 2013, https://www.americanexpress.com/us/small-business/openforum/articles/5-reasons-why-you-need-an-e-mail-newsletter/

cciii Ibid.

cciv Debra Jason, M.A., "4 Reasons Why Newsletters Should Be In Your Marketing Toolbox," *LinkedIn,* last modified May 19, 2015, https://www.linkedin.com/pulse/4-reasons-why-newsletters-should-your-marketing-toolbox-debra-jason

ccv https://fulcrumtech.net/resources/10-winning-e-mail-newsletter-best-practices/

ccvi Jesse + Becky, "7 Reasons You Should Start a Newsletter and How to Make People See It," *Idealust,* http://idealustlife.com/7-reasons-why-you-should-start-a-newsletter/

[ccvii] https://blog.hubspot.com/marketing/guide-creating-e-mail-newsletters-ht

[ccviii] Matt Bowman, "Video Marketing: The Future Of Content Marketing," *Forbes*, last modified February 3, 2017, https://www.forbes.com/sites/forbesagencycouncil/2017/02/03/video-marketing-the-future-of-content-marketing/#4daa11256b53

[ccix] Lucia Moses, "What's the Best Time of Day to Send an E-mail?" *Ad Week*, last modified March 27, 2013, http://www.adweek.com/digital/whats-best-time-day-send-e-mail-148113/

[ccx] Ibid.

[ccxi] Susanne Colwyn, "Triggered E-mail Campaigns," *Smart Insights,* last modified on December 13, 2013, https://www.smartinsights.com/e-mail-marketing/behavioural-e-mail-marketing/triggered-e-mail-campaigns-infographic/

[ccxii] https://neilpatel.com/blog/avoid-the-spam-folder/

[ccxiii] Ibid.

[ccxiv] MailChimp, "Common Rookie Mistakes for E-mail Marketers," no date, *Mail Chimp Resources*, https://mailchimp.com/resources/guides/common-rookie-mistakes-e-mail-marketers/

[ccxv] No author, "A 101 Guide To E-mail Marketing," *When I Work Blog*, last modified Nov. 4, 2014, https://wheniwork.com/blog/e-mail-marketing-guide/

[ccxvi] Kim Courvoisier, "70 E-mail Marketing Stats Every Marketer Should Know" (see above)

[ccxvii] https://neilpatel.com/blog/avoid-the-spam-folder/

[ccxviii] Sujan Patel, "10 Ways to Improve the Open Rates of Your Marketing E-mails," last modified March 2, 2015, https://www.entrepreneur.com/article/242799#

[ccxix] Sujan Patel, "10 Ways to Improve the Open Rates of Your Marketing E-mails," last modified March 2, 2015, https://www.entrepreneur.com/article/242799#

[ccxx] Ed Hallen, "How to Use E-mail List Segmentation to Drive Sales for eCommerce," Klaviyo, last modified May 12, 2014, https://www.klaviyo.com/blog/list-segmentation-how-to

[ccxxi] Erica Swallow, "Top Reasons Why Consumers Unsubscribe

Via E-Mail, Facebook & Twitter," *Mashable*, last modified
February 8, 2011, http://mashable.com/2011/02/08/why-
consumers-unsubscribe/#Js_tP7dDy5qI

ccxxii https://fulcrumtech.net/resources/increase-conversion-rates-e-
mail-list-segmentation/

ccxxiii https://fulcrumtech.net/resources/increase-conversion-rates-e-
mail-list-segmentation/

ccxxiv https://www.e-mailmonday.com/mobile-e-mail-usage-
statistics/

ccxxv http://prdefinition.prsa.org/

ccxxvi Al Lautenslager, "Why You Need PR," *Entrepreneur,* last
modified November 17, 2003,
https://www.entrepreneur.com/article/65672#

ccxxvii https://www.huffingtonpost.com/zach-cutler/5-top-benefits-
your-compa_b_2349144.html

ccxxviii https://glean.info/pr-marketing-work-better-together/

ccxxix https://mashable.com/2014/09/25/marketing-pr-art-
science/#XR44GTubUgq2

ccxxx https://glean.info/pr-marketing-work-better-together/

ccxxxi https://www.3dissue.com/10-ways-digital-publications-can-
help-you-generate-revenue/

ccxxxii https://www.thebalancesmb.com/what-is-a-press-release-
3515529

ccxxxiii https://www.forbes.com/sites/robertwynne/2016/06/13/how-
to-write-a-press-release/#b3eff603b932

ccxxxiv
https://account.prnewswire.com/OnlineMembershipFormStep1/

ccxxxv https://sonuspr.com/8-tips-for-a-better-website-press-page/

ccxxxvi Ibid.

ccxxxvii Kevin Leu, "5 reasons you'll regret hiring a PR firm for your
startup — and what you should do instead," last modified May 3,
2013, https://venturebeat.com/2013/05/03/how-to-hire-a-pr-firm-
dont-do-it/

ccxxxviii https://www.inc.com/rebekah-iliff/10-things-you-should-
know-before-hiring-a-pr-agency.html

ccxxxix https://sumo.com/stories/traffic-from-republishing

ccxl Larry Myler, "Offline In The Digital Age: Why Traditional

Advertising Isn't Dead," *Forbes*, last modified October 28, 2016, https://www.forbes.com/sites/larrymyler/2016/10/28/offline-in-the-digital-age-why-traditional-advertising-isnt-dead/#f69fbb71f96b

[ccxli] https://www.statista.com/statistics/237974/online-advertising-spending-worldwide/

[ccxlii] http://imagine-express.com/billboard-advertising-effective/

[ccxliii] Ibid.

[ccxliv] http://www.printisbig.com/

[ccxlv] James Trotter, "Online vs. Offline Marketing: An Infographic," *Social Media Explorer,* last modified March 9, 2017, https://www.digitaldoughnut.com/articles/2017/january/online-and-offline-marketing-which-channels-to-use

[ccxlvi] James Trotter

[ccxlvii] James Trotter

[ccxlviii] Larry Myler, "Offline In The Digital Age: Why Traditional Advertising Isn't Dead," *Forbes*, last modified October 28, 2016, https://www.forbes.com/sites/larrymyler/2016/10/28/offline-in-the-digital-age-why-traditional-advertising-isnt-dead/#f69fbb71f96b

[ccxlix] https://www.enthusem.com/blog/6-basic-principles-for-the-ultimate-offline-marketing-plan

[ccl] http://www.pewresearch.org/fact-tank/2017/09/13/about-6-in-10-young-adults-in-u-s-primarily-use-online-streaming-to-watch-tv/

[ccli] https://www.adweek.com/tvnewser/heres-the-median-age-of-the-typical-cable-news-viewer/355379

[cclii] Brought to you by *Business Insider,* "How to Pull Off a Guerrilla Marketing Campaign," last modified April 19, 2010,

Entrepreneur, https://www.entrepreneur.com/article/206202

[ccliii] http://www.creativeguerrillamarketing.com/what-is-guerrilla-marketing/

[ccliv] https://medium.com/initium/10-creative-guerilla-marketing-tactics-to-boost-your-brand-company-or-cause-8dc02e43f02d

[cclv] Melissa Tsang, "Guerrilla Marketing Tactics – 18 Top Case Studies and Examples (Updated!)," last modified 7 months ago, *Referral Candy Blog*, https://www.referralcandy.com/blog/guerrilla-marketing-tactics/

cclvi https://thrivehive.com/ways-track-offline-advertising/

cclvii https://neilpatel.com/blog/offline-marketing-tracking/

cclviii https://thrivehive.com/ways-track-offline-advertising/

cclix https://blog.bizzabo.com/offline-marketing-examples

cclx https://www.fastcompany.com/40574210/deadpool-hijacked-the-dvd-covers-of-16-movies-sold-at-wal-mart

cclxi https://technologyadvice.com/blog/sales/what-is-lead-management/

cclxii https://www.fronetics.com/50-of-sales-go-to-the-vendor-that-responds-first/

cclxiii https://www.hipb2b.com/blog/lead-prospect-whats-difference

cclxiv https://www.hipb2b.com/blog/lead-prospect-whats-difference

cclxv https://www.hipb2b.com/blog/lead-prospect-whats-difference

cclxvi https://www.hipb2b.com/blog/lead-prospect-whats-difference

cclxvii https://www.singlegrain.com/blog-posts/content-marketing/how-to-create-marketing-funnel/

cclxviii Marketing Sherpa, "Marketing Sherpa Lead Generation Benchmark Study," *MarketingSherpa*, fielded January, 2012.

cclxix https://www.singlegrain.com/blog-posts/content-marketing/how-to-create-marketing-funnel/

cclxx http://www.pardot.com/buyer-journey/

cclxxi https://www.impactbnd.com/blog/what-is-lead-nurturing

cclxxii No author, "What is Internet lead nurturing and how to do it right," *Paperless Proposal*, no date, https://www.paperlessproposal.com/what-is-internet-lead-nurturing-and-how-to-do-it-right/

cclxxiii Ibid.

cclxxiv Phillip Chen, "How to Effectively Segment Your Database for Lead Nurturing," no date, https://blog.marketo.com/2013/10/how-to-effectively-segment-your-database-for-lead-nurturing.html

cclxxv https://www.hellobar.com/blog/lead-nurturing/

cclxxvi https://blog.hubspot.com/marketing/7-effective-lead-nurturing-tactics

cclxxvii https://blog.hubspot.com/marketing/7-effective-lead-nurturing-tactics

cclxxviii https://blog.hubspot.com/marketing/7-effective-lead-nurturing-tactics

[cclxxix] https://blog.hubspot.com/marketing/7-effective-lead-nurturing-tactics

[cclxxx] Ken Krogue, "Why Companies Waste 71% Of Internet Leads," *Forbes*, last modified July 12, 2012, https://www.forbes.com/sites/kenkrogue/2012/07/12/the-black-hole-that-executives-dont-know-about/#aa17d5738e3a

[cclxxxi] Ibid.

[cclxxxii] Ibid.

Made in the USA
San Bernardino, CA
08 June 2020